CHRISTOPHER HIRST is a freelance writer who lives in south London and North Yorkshire. He wrote the witty 'Weasel' column in the *Independent* for over a decade and a drinks column called '101 Cocktails That Shook The World'. A contributor on food matters to the *Independent*, *Daily Telegraph* and *Intelligent Life*, he was nominated Glenfiddich Food Writer of the Year in 2005 and runner-up in 2007.

'This is far more than a mere cookbook. It's a beautifully written love letter; the story of a romance that blossomed at the stove. Impossible to put down, elegantly erudite and often belly-shakingly funny, this is one of the best books on food, cooking, and dare I say it, love, that I've read for years.'   TOM PARKER BOWLES

'Christopher understands that the way to a woman's heart is through her stomach. That is NOT aiming too high. Proof that many a true word is spoken ingest.'

KATHY LETTE

'I have always been charmed and hilariously delighted by Christopher Hirst's musings on cookery and kitchens. *Love Bites* is brilliant.'   SIMON HOPKINSON

'I hugely approve of Mr Hirst.'   JONATHAN MEADES

LOVE BITES

LOVE BITES

MARITAL SKIRMISHES IN THE KITCHEN

CHRISTOPHER HIRST

FOURTH ESTATE · London

First published in Great Britain by
Fourth Estate
A division of HarperCollins*Publishers*
77–85 Fulham Palace Road, London W6 8JB
www.4thestate.co.uk

Copyright © Christopher Hirst 2010

1 3 5 7 9 8 6 4 2

A catalogue record for this book is available from the British Library

ISBN 978-0-00-725550-4

The author and publishers would like to thank Waitrose Ltd for its
permission to reproduce the recipe for Christmas cake on page 243 and
Fergus Henderson for his permission to reproduce the recipe for seed cake
on page 247, which is taken from *Beyond Nose to Tail* (Bloomsbury, 2007)

Typeset in Adobe Garamond by Birdy Book Design

Printed in Great Britain by Clays Ltd, St Ives plc

Mixed Sources
Product group from well-managed
forests and other controlled sources
www.fsc.org Cert no. SW-COC-001806
© 1996 Forest Stewardship Council

To Mrs H, whose real name is Alison

Contents

A CULINARY COURTSHIP

GIVEN OUR COMMON INTEREST, it was appropriate that Mrs H (as she then wasn't) and I met in a kitchen. It was at a party in south London, Darling Road to be precise, in 1982. When one thing happily led to another, food emerged as a joint passion. The first meal I ever made for Mrs H was a giant pile of smoked salmon sandwiches. I noticed that they went down well. This was promising. I doubt if a longstanding relationship would have resulted if she had turned out to be one of those females whose main nutritional intake is a breath of air.

The first meal she ever made for me was a Mongolian hot pot. This takes the form of a great plate of raw titbits – slivers of chicken breast, pork and steak, along with prawns, sliced scallops, broccoli florets, mangetouts – that you cook piecemeal in a large pot of stock over a methylated spirit burner. When you've simmered a piece, you eat it. Mongolian hot pot is an ideal dish for a couple in the exploratory stages of courtship. Because you use chopsticks to fish out the various items, there is plenty of scope for intimacy. You might steer your companion towards a succulent piece of steak, while she hands over a juicy prawn. There might be a certain amount of light-hearted competition for a scallop. The culinary foreplay is prolonged but not so heavy on the stomach as to preclude subsequent activity.

The meal was a revelation. My passion for food began when I became passionate about Mrs H. After living in an all-male flat, where food was fuel rather than feast, I was astonished by the flair and generosity of her cooking and also the remarkable amount she spent on ingredients. Not that I was entirely indifferent to food when we met. I don't suppose many men would have proposed the Royal Smithfield Show as a destination for a first date. Somewhat to my surprise, Mrs H expressed keenness to attend this agricultural jamboree. The first thing we saw inside Earls Court was several lamb carcasses suspended over an enclosure containing their living siblings. Mrs H did not seem too alarmed by this vivid depiction of before and after. We bought a pair of pork chops at the show, which she grilled for supper. They were excellent.

Nibble by nibble, our relationship blossomed. We did a certain amount of the restaurant work that courting couples are supposed to go in for. Not that we had many candlelit dinners for two. Economy was a greater priority than romantic surroundings. Restaurants don't come much cheaper or less romantic than Jimmy's, the Greek joint staffed by famously cheerless waiters in Frith Street, Soho, while Poon's on Lisle Street came a close second. Though far from ideal for a tête-à-tête – you ate at shared tables covered by greasy oilcloths – Mrs H was impressed by the robust generosity (she says 'greediness') of my ordering: roast duck, sweet and sour crispy won-tons, oyster and belly pork casserole ...

Mostly, we dined at home. Since I spent almost all of my twenties in the pub, I missed out on the prawn cocktail era. Mrs H introduced me to a few delights of that distant time – snails in garlic butter (I was impressed that she owned snail tongs), kidneys in mustard sauce, chocolate mousse and cheese fondue. I'm still fond of her fondue, made in a large Le Creuset pan, though we restrict our intake of this dish, which is of doubtful value for the arteries unless you have spent the day climbing an alp or two, to once or twice a year. In her turn, Mrs H had missed out on certain areas of gastronomy that I regard as essential. I brought pork pie, rhubarb tart and shellfish to her attention. This did not, however, prevent her from refining my technique for moules marinière. 'You don't need great big chunks of onion. Could you chop it finer?'

Through Mrs H, I discovered the difference between proper paella and the Vesta variety. I also enjoyed the revelation that curry could be a pleasure, where you tasted the ingredients, rather than a form of trial by ordeal. She acquainted me with homemade pâté and salads that did not involve floppy lettuce. She even maintains that I didn't like broccoli before we met. I find this hard to believe. I've always been a big fan. 'You haven't! YOU HAVE NOT! And, it's only in the last couple of years that you've eaten curly kale and spring greens.' Well, she may be right on the last point, though I can now see the point of such vegetation. Mrs H also recalls my eruption when she tried serving flowers in a salad, which was fashionable some years ago. 'You objected very strongly and described it as "poncing it up".'

I gained an additional impetus towards culinary matters when I began writing a weekly column called 'The Weasel' in the *Independent*. Though its contents could be anything of a vaguely humorous nature, food and drink began to make a regular appearance. As with any habit, it started innocuously enough. You happen to write a piece about eating muskrat (dark, tough, springy meat not unlike Brillo pad) at a restaurant called Virus in Ghent. Soon after, you find yourself eating betel nut near Euston station, aphrodisiac jam in Paris, illicit ormers in Guernsey ...

This new direction for the column bemused some executives on the paper. Objections to the high gustatory content were passed from above ('Can't he write about anything else?'), but I found it difficult to comprehend such griping. After all, what could be more interesting or amusing than food? Indeed, what else is there? Maybe I did ease up on the nosh from time to time, but this only produced an even greater flow of food pieces when I turned the tap back on: setting fire to the kitchen when trying to crisp Ryvita under the grill (they curled and touched the electric element); blowing up the fusebox when I tried to put a fuse on the fridge; making frumenty, the alcoholic porridge that prompted Michael Henchard to sell his wife and child in *The Mayor of Casterbridge* ('Well, I'm not sold on it,' said Mrs H).

Perhaps the real theme, which steadily emerged in

column after column, was the difference between men and women in the kitchen. Or, at any rate, the difference between Mrs H and me in the kitchen. Though I came to spend much time cooking in the kitchen – more, possibly than Mrs H – it remains her bailiwick. Never having been taught the essential rules of the kitchen, such as tidying up and putting the right thing in the right place, I came in for a certain amount of brusque character analysis. Recently, when I foolishly asked Mrs H to refresh my mind concerning my shortcomings in this milieu, it prompted a Niagara-like flow that proved hard to turn off.

Woman on men (i.e. her on me)

Men want a huge amount of praise for anything they do.

Whatever they do, men always create a vast amount of washing-up, but they never think of washing up as they go along.

Men are reluctant to follow recipes in the same way that they are reluctant to ask for directions when they are lost.

Men plunge into cooking without sorting out the ingredients and utensils they will need. Then they can't find what they want. When things are found for them, they never put them away.

Men tend to over-season. They think that if a little is good then a lot will be even better. This particularly applies to salt and Tabasco.

Men give up easily – e.g., if they get a pain in their arm when whisking cakes.

Men disappear if they have to do some work, but they are quite handy for reaching things from high shelves.

Men are not keen on washing burnt pans. (This is simply not true. I'm always washing up pans that Mrs H has managed to fuse food on to.)

Men always want to pinch a bit of a dish that is in the process of being made. They are very keen on eating between meals.

Men fill the dishwasher any old how so it seems packed even though there aren't many items in there.

Following these lacerating comments, it struck me that Mrs H might appreciate a few words of mild correction. Hence:

Man on women (i.e. me on her)

Women are very, very, very bossy.

Women tend to be excessively pedantic about recipes and timings.

Women are very keen on vegetables, even when old and fibrous. They have an inexplicable fondness for purple-sprouting broccoli that is too woody to eat.

Women take a lot of luring into eating oysters. When you finally manage to do this, they can often be sick and look at you reproachfully.

Women are very difficult to get out of kitchen shops. Their favourite reading tends to be the Lakeland catalogue. They spend money like water in such places. I'd never spend £18.99 on a jelly strainer set, though Mrs H says, 'It's worth its weight in gold.'

Women always remember to put on a pinny when cooking. Despite the consequent stains and splotches on my clothes, I would never wear such an emasculating garment.

Women are obsessed with cleanliness to the extent that it imperils our natural resistance to bugs and germs.

When clearing cupboards, women have a tendency to chuck out perfectly good foodstuffs that are only a year or two past their sell-by date.

Women are very willing to eat lobsters and most forms of fish, but show a marked reluctance to kill, gut or scale these creatures.

Women constantly complain that they have not received an equal share of food. They are particularly assiduous in checking the level in their wine glass. 'It's not fair!'

So why did we decide to test our relationship further by cooking the stuff in this book? Lots of food books will give you the recipes, but this one tells you what it was like to make these dishes, and where irritations and cock-ups occurred. We tried a variety of methods and recipes for items ranging from pasta to raspberry jam, pizza to pancakes. While avoiding outré ingredients (OK – we did a hamburger with wagyu beef) and complicated techniques, we aimed to produce versions that were, if not exactly perfect, pretty damn good and capable of being reproduced on the domestic range. From Lady Shaftesbury's hot cheese dip (page 56) to Fergus Henderson's seed cake (page 247), I'd recommend that anyone even vaguely interested in cooking should have a bash. There are, however, some exceptions. Heston Blumenthal's Black Forest gateau is definitely not easy to do. Rocket science is a doddle by comparison. I would never have dreamed of making the damn thing if the features editor of a newspaper had not commissioned me to do so. For sanity's sake, I earnestly entreat you not to try it. Mrs H would say the same about geoduck clams and similar maritime oddities I treated her to in Chapter 11.

Most chapters involve the tutorage of Mrs H. I suppose I could have gone to other authorities for instruction but this would have caused problems. Having experienced several cookery schools over the years, I've come to the conclusion that I'm not very good at being taught things in the kitchen. I claim this is because I'm too much of an anarchist to take orders. 'Actually,' says Mrs H, 'you don't listen when people tell you things.' Well, yes, I do seem to have some kind of mental block when people try to teach me practical skills. (After four years of learning woodwork at school, my sole production was a test-tube rack with three wonky holes.) Having lived with me for twenty-odd years, Mrs H was able to put up with this minor foible. Even so, several dishes were seasoned with salty language and peppery outbursts. But our flare-ups, both verbal and actual, were quickly extinguished. Mostly, it was a rewarding, or at least filling, adventure. Some couples climb Kilimanjaro: we made a pork pie.

1

Cracking the egg

Battle of the boil

HAVING MOVED MY TOOTHBRUSH into Mrs H's house, I found myself eating very well, though a surprising deficiency in her abilities emerged early in the day. After I'd cooked the breakfast egg for perhaps a dozen times on the trot, it occurred to me that Mrs H didn't do boiled eggs.

'Of course I can boil an egg,' she insisted.

'But have you ever done a soft-boiled egg?'

Her resistance crumpled like a toast soldier encountering a ten-minute egg.

'Well, rarely.'

'When did you last do one?'

'Can't remember. My father was always in charge of egg boiling. I followed my mother's example.'

'You mean you both just sat there and waited for them to arrive?'

'Yes. Like chicks in a nest with our beaks open.'

'Just like you do with me?'

'Yes.'

Of course, it was no great hardship to plug this unexpected gap in Mrs H's culinary repertoire. It gave me a *raison d'être* of sorts. But her lack of enthusiasm for this little dish was mystifying. In my view, the breakfast egg is 0-shaped bliss. I formed this opinion at an early age. While other boys invested their spending money on footballs or Ian Allan train-spotting books, I bought a humorous egg-cup etched with the injunction, 'Get cracking!'

Mrs H's take-it-or-leave-it approach to the soft-boiled egg did not prevent her pointing out my occasional failures with some vigour. I concede that it is not a good start to the day when you crack open your egg and find a yolk surrounded by a mainly liquid white. Still, I generally press on and eat the sad swirl. Not so Mrs H. 'I think that's the worst egg you've ever done for me,' she said once, pushing away her untouched breakfast. She was so disturbed that it was several days before she could contemplate another boiled egg.

In order to improve my technique, I began to explore the unexpectedly vexed business of boiling eggs. Though the war between the Big Endians and the Little Endians about the best way to tackle an egg was a Swiftian satire, this stalwart of the breakfast table sparked a vigorous conflict in 1998. The cause of combustion was Delia Smith's advice in her BBC programme *How to Cook*. Her method involves making a pinprick in the big end to prevent cracking, then simmering for 'exactly one minute'. You then remove the pan from the heat and leave the egg in the water, resetting the timer for five or six minutes, depending on whether you want a white that is 'wobbly' or 'completely set'. This advice was described as 'insulting' by fellow telly chef Gary Rhodes. 'I really don't believe the majority of people cannot boil an egg,' he huffed. Obviously, he hadn't met Mrs H.

In 2005, there was a further kerfuffle when Loyd Grossman tested the boiled egg techniques of five chefs for *Waitrose Food Illustrated*. Giorgio Locatelli's method involved constantly stirring the egg in boiling water for six minutes. The resulting centrifuge, he claimed, should keep the yolk exactly in the middle of the boiled egg. Antonio Carluccio insisted that the egg should be boiled for three minutes and then left to stand in the water for thirty seconds. But it was the procedure advocated by Michel Roux of the Waterside Inn at Bray that caused feathers to fly. In his book *Eggs*, he recommends that an egg should be placed in a small pan, covered generously with cold water and set over a medium heat. 'As soon as the water comes to the boil, count up to sixty seconds for a medium egg,' Roux explained to me. 'It requires neither a watch nor an egg timer and it is infallible.' Grossman reported disaster when he attempted this method: 'It was so close to raw that I didn't want to eat it.' I met Roux a few months after this criticism and he was still incandescent about Grossman's comments.

In order to achieve an impartial view, I tried the Roux method using an egg at room temperature. The result was a lightly boiled egg. To achieve a medium set, I had to count for another thirty seconds. Obviously, the time varies depending on the temperature of the egg before it goes into the water and the size of the egg. My main objection to the method is that counting up to sixty or, worse still, ninety is excessively demanding for some of us at breakfast time.

I attempted several methods that claimed to produce the perfect boiled egg, though I drew the line at St Delia's suggestion of simmering for the time it takes to sing three verses of 'Onward Christian Soldiers'. Eventually, I evolved a technique that eschews any form of timer, whether human or mechanical. It involves putting two eggs into simmering water, looking at the digital clock on the oven and adding another four minutes to whatever time is displayed. When this period clicks up, I add a few more seconds for luck, making (I hope) four and a half minutes in all. I then whip out the egg. It works, more or less. The result is usually a nicely set white and liquid but slightly thickened yolk. Mrs H's customary response is 'Very nice'. This is satisfactory, though on her scale of responses it is not as ecstatic as her top accolade, 'Yum'.

Occasionally, for inexplicable reasons, this method produces an underdone egg and accompanying complaints from Mrs H, but I still prefer human approximation to mechanical certainty. 'An egg is always an adventure,' said Oscar Wilde. 'The next one may be different.' In that spirit, I stick to guesswork even if it means a variable outcome at the breakfast table. That's me, living for kicks.

If Mrs H wanted a certain outcome in her boiled egg, she could, of course, break the habit of a lifetime and start doing them herself. Instead, she continues sitting there with beak open. Had she ever considered attempting the break-fast simmer in our two decades together?

'Nope. See what you can get away with if you keep quiet.'

The scramble for success

The boot was on the other foot when it came to scrambled eggs. My inadequacy was brought home when I made some for Mrs H. 'This is fine,' she said, 'as long as you like scrambled eggs that are pale, hard and rubbery.' I scrutinised my effort, which leaked a watery residue that made the underlying toast go soggy.

'It's not all that bad,' I protested, risking a nibble.

'Hmm,' considered Mrs H. 'Perhaps I've had worse scrambled eggs in hotels.' Recalling my encounters with terrible hotel scrambles – friable, evil-smelling, desiccated – I realised that this was not saying very much.

'Chuck it in the bin and buy some more eggs,' said Mrs H.

Swallowing my pride, which was easier than my eggs, I reassessed my scrambling technique. At some point in the past, I'd conceived the idea that speed was of the essence with scrambled eggs. Plenty of heat and plenty of spoon-whirling guaranteed success. Occasionally, I would examine the chewy results of my speed-scramble and ponder, 'This can't be right.'

Mrs H put me right: 'You need four eggs, plenty of butter and plenty of patience.' Of all the culinary lessons imparted by Mrs H in this book, the one that has taken root most effectively, at least in her opinion, is how to do scrambled eggs. 'You've learned to do them very well,' she said, rather like an old master dispatching a talented apprentice into the wide world. 'I like your scrambled eggs as much as mine.' Since then, scrambled eggs have become my default snack. Nothing as simple to cook tastes quite so good.

For two people, five lightly beaten and seasoned eggs are added to a pan that is just warm enough to melt a walnut-sized lump of butter. Cooking at low heat is of the essence. Unlike boiled eggs, poached eggs and soufflés, scrambled eggs demand the near-constant involvement of the cook. They should also be consumed immediately. (That's why the hotel breakfast scramble is usually hopeless.) Nothing seems to happen for ages while you keep stirring. Then, just when you have given up all hope, curds begin to form on the bottom of the pan. These have to be gently broken by the rotating spoon. When the eggs are heading towards setting but still liquid, you add another teaspoon of butter (a splat of cream also works well) and stir again, remove from the heat and serve. The final result should be a slurry, not a set.

If you're trying to do anything else at the same time, especially the manifold demands of the full English breakfast, disaster is likely. But with unceasing attention and quite a lot of butter, you can produce a dish that is luxurious in both taste and texture. It is one of the few items where the amateur can achieve three-star finesse – or nearly. I must admit that Michel Roux's formulation incorporating crab and asparagus tips, which I sampled once at his reataurant in Bray, has the edge on my version. 'There are two schools of scrambled egg,' explained Roux. 'My brother Albert does his for hours in a bain-marie. I do mine over very low gas using a diffuser. His are still half-cooked when mine are finished. Less than three eggs in scrambled egg and you get nothing. Five or six are best.'

My decision not to use a diffuser was assisted by my inability to find the damn thing in our kitchen cupboard. Not that the lowest possible heat is always regarded as a *sine qua non*. In a heretical deviation, Roux's nephew Michel Roux Jr, who is chef at Le Gavroche in Mayfair, dispenses with both diffuser and tiny flame. He recommends 'a medium to high heat' in his recipe for 'the perfect creamy scrambled eggs'. It goes to show that there is no golden rule for a great scramble.

My in-depth research into scrambled eggs was curbed by Mrs H's concern for my arteries. I would have tried Ian Fleming's recipe – his obsession with scrambled eggs is indicated by their repeated appearance as James Bond's breakfast – but requiring six ounces of butter and twelve eggs, it is as potentially lethal as Bond's Walther PPK. Along similar lines, the scrambled egg recipe from the surrealist Francis Picabia in *The Alice B. Toklas Cookbook* calls for eight eggs and half a pound of butter. 'Not a speck less,' insists Toklas, 'rather more if you can bring yourself to it.' Since the result is described as having 'a suave consistency that perhaps only gourmets will appreciate', Mrs H's prohibition was not too painful.

I had better luck with 'Portuguese-style scrambled eggs', one of the variations proposed by Michel Roux. Currently the Sunday breakfast *de choix* at Hirst HQ, it is a good dish to make if you happen to have some meat stock in reserve. (Years ago, I saw a tip in a newspaper about storing concentrated stock in plastic ice-cube bags in the freezer. Aside from being a bit fiddly to achieve – you tend to end up with a lot of stock on the floor – and the tendency of the frozen cubes to get lost in the freezer, it's a fine idea.) The scrambled eggs are served in a soup plate topped with a sprig of grilled cherry tomatoes and fringed by a narrow moat of warm stock. Serve with buttered toast. Mrs H's response is most satisfactory. 'Simply fantastic. It's the very best sort of brasserie food. Just the thing to revive an ailing spirit. Perfect for a late breakfast on a Sunday.'

A dish called scrambled eggs Clamart, which incorporates a sprinkling of fresh peas, sliced mangetouts and sweated lettuce, elicited a similar reaction from Mrs H. 'Yum,' she said, bestowing top gastronomic marks. 'Sweet and crunchy. A perfect spring lunch.' The only drawback is that it is a bit of a faff to do. You cook the peas and mangetouts separately, refresh in cold water, then reheat for twenty seconds before adding to the scrambled eggs with the sweated lettuce. In order not to break the unremitting attention required during the scrambling phase, this requires some deft before-and-after work. By the end, the lettuce isn't the only thing that is sweated.

I came across a robust hybrid in *The Perfect Egg and Other Secrets* by the designer Aldo Buzzi (oddly, the book does not contain much about eggs). Scrambled eggs Frankfurt-style is described as 'more Olympian,

Goethe-esque' than the standard scrambled egg. This is pretty heady stuff at breakfast time, but I gave it a bash. You are directed to use one egg per person and one for the pan. They are whisked with a teaspoonful of water for each egg. Buzzi directs the reader to cook the eggs in 'well-browned butter' over a very low heat. A frying pan seemed to be the best utensil for this, since you have to 'use a spatula to gently move the part that is setting while you make the still liquid part run on to the hottest part of the pan'. Turn off the heat when the eggs have achieved a very light set. The result is a cross between an omelette and scrambled eggs, though lighter and more liquid and glistening than either of them. I followed Buzzi's suggestion of blending in 'well-cooked pepper and tomatoes, in which case what you'll have is a sort of Basque piperade'.

Mrs H was quite taken with it, though her praise came with reservation. 'The tomatoes are nice and fresh, the peppers quite peppery. You've managed to capture the omelette-style scramble. Certainly worth bearing in mind for future, except ...'

'Yes?'

'It might be better for supper than at seven thirty in the morning.'

Poacher's pockets

After two decades of making poached eggs for Mrs H, I came to a sudden realisation. She can't poach for toffee. I mean real poaching with eggs in a pan rather than using an egg poacher. She admits it herself. 'My poached eggs are always rotten compared to yours. Don't know why. One of the great mysteries of life.'

This is an unfortunate culinary omission considering the many admirable applications of the poached egg, a dish that provides its own sauce in a sachet. Hence the word 'poach', from the French *poche* (pocket). What could be nicer or simpler than poached eggs on buttered toast? They're also splendid in a warm salad and in eggs Benedict, which happens to be one of Mrs H's specialities. This is when the egg poacher makes an appearance.

Though some of us might look on this as cheating, it was a method advocated by Mrs Beeton. 'To poach an egg to perfection is rather a difficult operation,' she wrote. 'So for inexperienced cooks, a tin egg-poacher may be purchased, which greatly facilitates this manner of dressing eggs.' People in ancient Rome must have felt the same. A drawing of cooking equipment from Pompeii includes two utensils that look very much like egg poachers (one for four eggs, another for twenty-eight).

My objections to using the poacher involve danger (you are likely to scald your fingers when you remove the little pans from the saucepan), taste (the white of the steamed or buttered egg lacks the pleasing texture of a naturally poached white) and aesthetics. The perfectly round steamed egg is industrial in appearance. It is the kind of egg you get on an Egg McMuffin.

When I imparted my critique to Mrs H, she responded with a delicate yawn. She also pointed out that she never got scalded by the egg poacher because she has the gumption to turn off the gas before removing the egg, unlike others she could mention. However, she agreed that my orthodox version of the poached egg had the edge. Moreover, she expressed willingness to learn.

This reversal of our usual relationship in the kitchen did not prove to be a very happy experience, though we managed the first step of boiling a pan of water without dispute or mishap.

'Get up a good boil,' I pontificated, 'then reduce the heat to a gentle simmer – no bubbles – and break an egg into a cup so we can gently introduce it into the water.'

'What sort of cup?'

'Just a cup.'

'But what kind?'

'What do you mean what kind? A cup from Buckingham Palace! Just get any old cup. Why are you so concerned about cups?'

What she was meaning, it turned out, was the size of cup. When I snatched down a half-pint mug, Mrs H rejected it and used a ramekin to introduce her egg into the water.

'Aren't you supposed to stir the water round so it forms a funnel for the egg?'

'My funnels never last long enough. Just pour your egg in.'

After doing this, she peered sadly into the pan. 'My egg is like a rolling blanket of fog. I told you it would spread.'

'Never mind. Just get it out after four minutes.'

'What with?'

'I usually use the large slotted spoon.'

'Where's that?'

'In the place where we keep slotted spoons!'

'It's not there.'

'Grr!'

Eventually the slotted spoon emerged from its hidey-hole and Mrs H hauled out her dripping creation. 'My poached egg isn't anything like yours,' she groaned. 'Look at that yolk. Completely hard. Mind you, I had a hopeless instructor. You shouted at me.'

'When did I shout?'

'Buckingham Palace! Slotted spoon!' She drew a small figure with black fringe, toothbrush moustache and upraised arm in my notebook. 'How do you think you rated as a teacher?' she continued. 'I'll tell you how many marks you got out of ten.' Mrs H made an O with her forefinger and thumb and squinted at me through the hole.

I felt it was time to return to her poached egg.

'It's quite nice but a bit, er ...'

'Watery and all over the place, you mean. I've done them before and they've consistently spread. I can't get them into a nice little lump like you.'

Then I did a poached egg.

'See – that's perfect,' said Mrs H when I got it out. 'It's all nice and round. You can just tell the yolk is going to be perfect. How annoying.'

'I think I might have given you some elderly eggs.'

'You might blame the eggs, but I say rotten maker, rotten teacher.'

Still, I might have been even more demanding as a tutor. Considering the beautiful simplicity of a poached egg, it is remarkable how much complexity some experts have managed to bring to the topic. Culinary titan Joel Robuchon says you should boil your eggs in their shells 'for exactly thirty seconds' before chilling them in iced water and starting an orthodox poach. This is supposed to 'firm up the surface edge of the white a bit', but in my view it indicates a chef who has had a battalion of sous-chefs doing his poaching for him for years.

Michel Roux recommends that you fish your egg out of the pan after one and a half minutes and 'press the outside edge to see if it is properly cooked'. The picture in his book resembles someone pressing home a point by prodding the waistcoat of a rotund gent. 'Now, see here, Carruthers ...' If the egg is not sufficiently poached, you put it back in the water. Roux does not say if you have to do more waistcoat-prodding to the egg after its second appearance, though I presume so. Some recipes say that a three-minute boil is sufficient, though I'd advocate four minutes if you stick to a bubble-free simmer. A slotted spoon helps no end when it comes to extracting the egg. Scooping out your egg with an ordinary spoon means waterlogged toast. Some authorities suggest that you should rest the egg on a towel to dry off, rather like a holidaymaker on the beach.

Many recipes suggest a dollop of vinegar in the poaching water to help keep the egg together, but Mrs H doesn't like the resulting vinegar tinge and she could be right. Anyway, a really fresh egg doesn't need any assistance in coagulation.

Culinary scientist Harold McGee dispenses with vinegar since it 'produces shreds and an irregular film over the egg surface'. His solution is to pour off the thin white that causes poached egg untidiness before simmering, but I wouldn't bother. Michel Roux advocates post-poaching tidying. 'Trim the edges with a small knife to make a neat shape. This will also cut off the excess white that inevitably spreads during cooking.' Trimming poached eggs strikes me as cheffiness. As Mrs H will confirm, I am not a great devotee of neatness.

Mrs H's recipe for cheat's eggs Benedict

Our lovely friend Carolyn Hart was so knocked out with this dish, which I served at my birthday brunch party, that she included the recipe in her book called *Cooks' Books*. Because I cooked for around thirty people, it involved the use of an egg poacher (you can handily whack out four servings at a time) and fresh ready-made hollandaise sauce from the supermarket. If the muffins are pre-toasted and kept warm (ditto the bacon), you can rapidly serve quite a crowd, although the quantities given below are per person. I heat the hollandaise in a double boiler at the gentlest simmer whilst poaching the eggs. A child still at the age of pliability is useful for handing round the eggs Benedict to your guests while you try to fend off greedy whatnots demanding seconds. A pitcher or two of Bloody Marys aids the party spirit.

1 toasted muffin
2 grilled rashers of good-quality back bacon (your choice of
   smoked or unsmoked)
1 poached egg
1 generous dollop of gently heated hollandaise sauce

After variously toasting, grilling, gently heating and
poaching the four ingredients, assemble the cheat's eggs
Benedict in this order on top of each other: muffin, bacon,
poached egg, dollop of hollandaise. Don't forget to save
some for yourself.

SEEKING GLORY

DESPITE HAVING SCORED some notable successes in the breakfast area, I began to experience a twinge of dissatisfaction. A boiled egg is fine in its way, but it does not generate the ovations and rave reviews that male cooks crave. It is not enough for our dishes to be nutritious, tasty and satisfying. They should also produce a storm of applause, amazement, even adulation. 'Bravo! Bellissimo! Wunderbar!' Extreme examples of this phenomenon are commonplace in the higher echelons of the gastronomic world. It always strikes me as curious that when, at the end of a banquet, the chef appears from the kitchen, he is greeted with a round of applause. Where else, outside the theatre, does anyone get such acclamation for doing his everyday job? Do we clap a road-layer when he completes a particularly fine bit of motorway? Or the refuse collector when he empties our bins with aplomb?

There was another less egocentric reason for expanding my culinary repertoire. Three years into our relationship, I went freelance and began working from home. Mrs H continued working on the other side of London. On her return journey, she would often call in Reggie Perrin-style, 'Only just reached Victoria. Points failure at Acton. Have pipe and slippers waiting.' It was obviously unfair to expect her to start bashing away in the kitchen when she staggered through the door at 8.30 p.m. My gallantry was given additional impetus by the hunger pangs I began to feel three hours earlier.

Starting with salads, I moved on to pasta, stews and casseroles (all remain gastronomic mainstays at Hirst HQ). Eventually, the day came when I graduated from hob to oven. Like a small, super-heated theatre in the corner of the room, its productions are more likely to elicit acclaim than something scooped from a saucepan. Mrs H was certainly impressed by my efforts. 'I'd come home completely drenched to find the house full of delicious smells and you with a spoon in your mouth having a tasting session. Even though bits of mashing potato were often flying through the air, it was very welcome.'

Mrs H was referring to my slightly feverish construction of fish pie. 'I remember that it always contained large quantities of cockles. A bit odd but rather delicious.' She was also fond of my robust version of coq au vin: 'Your great glug of brandy made it very sustaining. I had to go to bed immediately afterwards.' Pheasant casserole in a Calvados and cream sauce was even more satisfying. 'After a single bowl, I felt as if I might go pop!'

All good stuff that provided much in the way of the requisite congratulation, acclamation, etc. The response to my next production was more ambivalent. While not exactly a flop, it received a mixed review. 'I remember coming home and there was this Desperate Dan-style thing on the kitchen table,' Mrs H recalls. 'It was a vast pie with a patchwork lid. You stood behind it covered in flour and exuding pride from every pore.'

Well, yes, maybe I did generate a hint of righteous self-satisfaction at my first substantial baking achievement. 'It was certainly substantial,' says Mrs H. 'I don't think I've ever seen a bigger pie. In some parts the pastry was very thick, in other parts it was so thin that it disappeared. Still, it tasted OK if you ignored the very doughy bits. My problem was with the inside. I don't like sweet pies and I particularly don't like them filled with rhubarb.'

This is a mystery to me. How can anyone not like rhubarb pie? 'Quite easily,' says Mrs H. 'Rhubarb is quite nice tasting but it collapses into a pink, stringy mush in a pie.'

Her antipathy is supported by one of Britain's greatest food writers. 'Nanny food,' Jane Grigson seethed in her *Fruit Book*. 'Governess food. School-meal food.' In case we haven't got the message, she went on: 'I haven't got over disliking rhubarb, and disliking it still more for being often not so young and a little stringy … Only young pink rhubarb is worth eating.'

Though expounded by two of my favourite authorities, Mrs G and Mrs H, I strongly disagree with this view. We almost always used mature stalks in the most memorable dessert of my childhood. Though somewhat bulkier than Proust's madeleine, a rhubarb pie has the same effect on me. Its combination of bittersweet, tooth-etching filling and juice-infused pastry instantly whisks me back to the West Riding of Yorkshire *circa* 1962. I grew up near the legendary Rhubarb Triangle between Leeds, Wakefield and Morley. Or is it Bradford? Opinions vary about the location of this locale, almost as mysterious as its Bermudan counterpart, but we certainly had several rhubarb plants in the garden of our house in Cleckheaton. In consequence, I ate a lot of rhubarb as a child – almost always in pie form, very occasionally stewed, never under the crunchy awning of a crumble.

If Mrs H was a non-starter in the Rhubarb Pie Appreciation League, I found a more willing recipient in the form of Mrs H's mother. If she was surprised when her daughter's live-in boyfriend started serving her rhubarb pie on a regular basis, she did not express it to me. Admittedly, my Proustian pud did not whisk her back to a Yorkshire childhood, but this was scarcely surprising since she came from Surbiton, Surrey.

2

Rhubarbing

IN HIS BOOK *Rhubarb: The Wondrous Drug*, Clifford Foust, Professor of History at the University of Maryland, explains 'the several advantages' of my home turf of West Yorkshire as the perfect *terroir* for rhubarb. It had 'a climate northerly enough for a lengthy autumn dormancy period' and 'high rainfall for maximum plant development'. The 'smoky and polluted atmosphere' helped 'induce early and full dormancy ... for early forcing' and 'urban sludge' provided plentiful fertiliser. No wonder I have rhubarb juice in my veins.

Perhaps the first dish I ever made for myself was chunks of raw rhubarb dipped in sugar. Half a century ago in the West Riding of Yorkshire, we would have been mystified by Jane Grigson's insistence on 'only pink young rhubarb'. This is a 'forced' winter crop grown in large, dark sheds. It tastes great, but why limit yourself to this etiolated stuff when outdoor rhubarb continues to delight the palate throughout summer? Unless you use telegraph-pole-sized rhubarb, you need not fear stringiness. And what if there is a suggestion of the fibrous? Is that going to kill you?

The pie I made as a treat for Mrs H's mother was equipped with a pastry floor, walls and roof, because that's the kind of pie my mother made. I still feel short-changed if I receive a pie, whether sweet or savoury, where the pastry consists only of a lid. Unlike my mother, I cheated by using ready-made pastry, shortcrust because that's what I grew up with, though puff, which Mrs H prefers, is also OK. Either way, a highlight of the pie is the sweetened pink rhubarb juice soaking into the pie floor. You don't get that with rhubarb crumble.

After rolling out the pastry, I used the majority of it to line a large dish. I chopped the rhubarb stalks into cubes and put them into the pie. I then added sugar (a 5:3 ratio of rhubarb to sugar is about right) and installed the roof. As Mrs H points out, it usually required a certain amount of patching. After sealing the joints by pinching, I brushed it with milk and slashed three holes for steam-release as I'd seen my mother do hundreds of times. Emerging from the oven, the pastry patchwork had, I thought, a fine manly vigour. Lumps of rhubarb were visible through the three crevasses.

'Just a small slice for me,' said Mrs H's mum.

While she nibbled, I enlightened her about the mysterious story of rhubarb. For exoticism, its etymology beats everything else in the larder. The 'rhu' bit derives from Rha, the Greek name for the River Volga, where the plant was transported, while 'barb' comes from the Latin *barbarus* (meaning 'foreign', 'strange' and, ironically, 'uncultivated'). This, in turn, came from a Greek onomatopoeic coinage because barbarian speech sounded like 'Ba, ba, ba'. The 'rhubarbing' of film extras is an unconscious return to the plant's distant origins. It was possibly first cultivated in Mongolia by the Tartar tribes of the Gobi Desert. We don't know if anyone told Genghis Khan that rhubarb was nanny food.

'Fancy that,' said Mrs H's mum. 'It was lovely, but I won't have another slice, thank you.'

At our next meeting, I produced another monumental construction. 'I've made you a rhubarb pie,' I announced, a trifle superfluously, as I cut her a chunk.

'Oh, lovely.'

'Did you know that we all come from rhubarb?'

'Really, dear?'

The Zoroastrians, I explained, believed that 'the human race was born of the rhubarb plant'. I gleaned this insight from *The Legendary Cuisine of Of Persia* by Margaret Shaida, who notes that *reevâs*, the Persian name for the plant, comes from a word meaning 'shining light'. The association came about because 'from ancient times, rhubarb has been considered good for cleansing the blood and purifying the system'. Until the eighteenth century, rhubarb was mainly used as a laxative in Britain. Only the root was consumed, with Chinese rhubarb being particularly prized for its cathartic properties. A great rarity by the time it reached here, it cost four times as much as opium in medieval times. I once saw some Chinese rhubarb root in the Fernet-Branca factory in Milan. It took the form of large powdery, purple-brown lumps. Along with forty other wonderfully weird ingredients (white agaric, cinchona, aloes, zedoary, myrrh), it is used to enhance the bitterness of this acerbic potion.

The plant's stalk only became used for culinary purposes with the arrival of Siberian rhubarb in the eighteenth century. Hybrids developed in the nineteenth century combined with the declining price of sugar to make rhubarb a favourite dessert of the Victorians. (You certainly need sugar in rhubarb pie. It's the oxalic acid in rhubarb that makes it such an interesting food.) The types known as Victoria and Royal Albert were developed by Joseph Myatt, evidently an ardent monarchist, in his market gardens in Deptford and Camberwell (the latter is now a park called Myatt's Fields), while the imaginatively named Champagne came from a rival grower called Hawkes in nearby Lewisham. The three heroes of *Three Men in a Boat* (1889) dine off rhubarb pie before setting out on their great adventure. The laxative property of rhubarb continued to be utilised even when the stalks became a foodstuff. In America, rhubarb was known as 'a broom for the system'.

'How interesting,' said Mrs H's mother. 'Actually, I don't know if I'll be able to finish this piece.'

I had no doubt what Mrs H's mum expected the next time she paid a visit. 'Guess what I've made!' I said. Hewing a wedge for her, I returned to our favourite topic. 'Do you know how many cookbooks have been devoted to rhubarb?' The answer is over 300, mostly produced during the 'Rhubarb Craze' that swept Britain and America in the early years of the twentieth century. But for those of us from the

Rhubarb Triangle there is one supreme rhubarb dish. Sadly, my dear mother-in-law is no longer around to enjoy my rhubarb pie. At least, I thought she enjoyed it, though her daughter cast doubt on this.

'It was funny that you always made rhubarb pie when my mother came round.'

'What do you mean, "funny"?'

'You never saw her face when you produced your pies.'

'She enjoyed them!'

'She was too polite to say she wasn't very fond of rhubarb.'

In subsequent years, Mrs H has continued this weird familial objection to rhubarb pie, but she grudgingly agreed to indulge my passion by making some other recipes that involve rhubarb. By way of encouragement, I obtained a volume called *Rhubarb – More Than Just Pies*, published by the University of Alberta Press. They grow a lot of rhubarb in Alberta.

Her preliminary report on rhubarb and ginger mousse was optimistic. 'You simmer sliced rhubarb and orange zest with powdered ginger till the fruit is soft,' she explained. 'Then you add gelatine. When it's half set, you beat egg whites to peaks and fold in to create the mousse. It's got a nice orange and ginger taste that complements the rhubarb. It looks lovely.'

'Should it have separated like this?' I asked after peering into the fridge at four glass beakers containing a murky orange jelly topped by a gnarled-looking mousse of greyish hue.

'It hadn't separated when it went in,' said Mrs H, resentfully. It didn't taste impossibly bad. Just odd. The mousse had a curious texture, like fibre-reinforced resin. It might have been an early experiment in making plastic. It was edible, just about, but not mousse as we know it. The jelly part was tasty but very hard indeed. 'Maybe I used too much gelatine,' groaned Mrs H. 'I used a new kind of gelatine that gives directions for making a litre and I only wanted a pint. I sat there for ages trying to work it out and I think I got it wrong.'

'Do you want to give it another go?'

'No.'

Mrs H thought she might have better luck with savoury rhubarb dishes. Currently, the use of rhubarb as a savoury is very fashionable in trendy restaurants, where, of course, the chefs stick to the wimpy, pink stuff. 'Rhubarb-carrot relish sounds nice,' she said, poring through *Rhubarb – More Than Just Pies*. But it wasn't. Considering the tastiness of the two main ingredients, which were boiled separately in salty water, puréed, then mixed together with butter, the determined blandness of the rhubarb-carrot relish was a disappointment. Maybe they like things bland in Alberta.

'It is slightly reminiscent of aubergine dip,' I said encouragingly. Helped along with Tabasco, it became somewhat more toothsome, but Mrs H would not be consoled. 'Into the bin,' she said.

The nadir of her rhubarb experimentation came with rhubarb relish, consisting of diced rhubarb along with the usual suspects – brown sugar, vinegar, chopped onion and spices. The instructions could barely be simpler: 'Combine all ingredients in a large saucepan and boil until thickened.' So what could go wrong?

'The postman,' said Mrs H.

'The postman?'

'Yes. I did the relish and I was just putting it into jars when the postman rang at the door with lots of parcels for you. While he was giving them to me, a woman came up and said she wanted him to take a letter because the postbox had been sealed. He said he wasn't supposed to take it …'

'What's this got to do with rhubarb?' I asked, feeling we were straying from the point somewhat.

'Hang on! A long discussion followed about where there was an open postbox. The woman said, "I don't know where that is," and the postman reluctantly accepted the letter. Eventually, I brought the parcels back into the house and thought "Oh, hell." I knew something had gone very wrong when I couldn't lift my bailing jug from the bottom of the pan. Look, there it is, stuck fast.'

Yes, there it was. I pulled at the jug. It was like trying to lift the Chrysler Building from the Manhattan bedrock. With the assistance of a kettle of boiling water, I managed to pry the jug from the world's toughest relish. I turned to Mrs H expecting grateful thanks, but all I got was a glum look. Her mouth turned down at both ends like a banana. She pointed at the jars of 'relish' that she had filled before her jar got stuck. The contents were akin to bitumen. It was a sort of rhubarb toffee and might even have been chewable if I'd been able to get any out, but I didn't want to risk my fillings on it.

A few days later, Mrs H returned to the fray. She amended the relish recipe with more onion, more rhubarb and a spoonful of ground allspice, but her major refinement concerned the cooking technique. 'Instead of "boil until thickened", I brought it to the boil then turned it down to a very low simmer and reduced the mixture. Every time I smelled it, I gave it a stir.'

'So how long did that take?'

'I put it on at 8:30 a.m. and finished it at 3:15 p.m.'

The result of the seven-hour simmer was a sticky, brown goo. Sweet-sour but wonderfully rounded, it was excellent. The chunks of rhubarb radiated a profound flavour that tinged on the palate for ages. Maybe it would improve with maturing, but a vintage version of Mrs H's rhubarb relish is unlikely because it is so addictive. Particularly when consumed with pork pie, the contents of a jar can magically disappear in a matter of minutes.

Her next effort concerned a rhubarb sauce intended for pork chops. Made with red wine, vinegar and chicken stock, it looked slightly dubious to me. Fruit with meat (apple with pork, cherries with duck, etc.) is one of my blind spots. I know I should like it, but I feel instinctively drawn to the mustard pot. 'I don't think I'll bother with the sauce,' I announced.

Mrs H took a mouthful of the combination and asserted, 'Well – ner, ner, ner – it goes quite well with the pork.'

After risking a taste, I had to admit that it did. The

sharpness of the sauce, which the wine had made ruby-red, was a perfect foil for the pork chop. Even when the chop had vanished, the sauce was pretty good. Mrs H scribbled in my notebook: 'Mr H said he didn't want any rhubarb on his pork chops, thank you, but he ended up nicking a great spoonful from the serving bowl.'

Even better was her rendition of Persian khoresh, a stew with rhubarb and shoulder of lamb. You may recall that the Persians regarded rhubarb as a holy vegetable, and going by the taste of this they were not far out. 'It's been simmering on top of the stove for about seven hours,' said Mrs H. 'The rhubarb only goes in for the last quarter of an hour.' Each forkful delivered contrasting flavours – the sweetness of the lamb, the tartness of the rhubarb, sweetness again with caramelised onions – which were magically complementary. 'Mmm, this is nice,' I gushed.

After this triumph, I felt it was time for me to have a go at a savoury rhubarb dish. I tried a Gary Rhodes recipe for steamed oysters with rhubarb. Though I am possibly the world's greatest oyster lover, certainly one of the greediest, I was a little hesitant about this weird combination. But Rhodes points out that a sauce of chopped shallots in red wine vinegar (known as mignonette) is a traditional accompaniment to oysters, so he came up with rhubarb softened in red wine vinegar with a touch of sugar as a partner to steamed, buttery oysters.

Inevitably, he calls for '3–4 sticks of forced rhubarb', but I used thin sticks of the ordinary kind. The recipe is a bit fiddly for my liking. Even with shortcuts, I found myself cussing when it came to putting a teensy-weeny pile of rhubarb in each empty shell and placing a steamed, buttery oyster on top of each pile. 'Bloody fiddly, cheffy nonsense.' (I give you an expurgated version.) But, yes, I admit it, the sweetness of the oysters and the sourness of the rhubarb worked remarkably well together.

My final bash at rhubarb came from Robin Lane Fox, biographer of Alexander the Great, who presumably knew a thing or two about rhubarb. According to him (Fox, not Alexander), rhubarb stewed with 'masses of caster sugar', then mixed with the grated rind and juice of an orange and left overnight, is not only 'the supreme recipe' but 'the true king of all English puddings'. It has a very good acidy flavour, but maybe it's more of a delicious accompaniment to stuff like blancmange or yogurt than a pudding as such.

'Mmm. It's very refreshing,' said Mrs H. 'A bit like eating those Haliborange tablets I had as a child.' This was a new one on me, since I had a Haliborange-free childhood, but it was evidently high praise. 'Lovely.'

She also astonished me by reminiscing about another rhubarb dish. 'I rather miss those days when you were always pulling huge, patched pies from the oven.' Mrs H wanted her own Proustian moment.

Mrs H's recipe for lamb khoresh with rhubarb

We make this dish for friends for informal suppers or lunches and it always produces lots of oooh's and ahh's and satisfied slurping noises. Shoulder of lamb has more fat than other cuts but compensates with its sweet flavour. The fat is eventually skimmed off anyway. The herbs complement the lamb in an entirely satisfactory way and the tang of the rhubarb gets the tastebuds going. We usually serve this with a generous quantity of nutty basmati rice, to mop up the juices, and a green salad. Depending on the size of the lamb shoulder and the appetites of the guests, the ingredients below should serve six to eight people.

1.4 kg boned shoulder of lamb
2 large Spanish-type onions
4 tablespoons butter
a generous pinch of saffron
625ml beef stock
4 tablespoons lemon juice
salt and pepper to season
2 bunches of fresh flat-leaf parsley
6–8 sprigs of fresh mint
450g rhubarb, cut into 2.5cm pieces

The khoresh has different cooking times for different stages.
I like to think that you are building up the flavours.

Deal with the meat first by chopping the shoulder of
lamb into 5cm chunks. Trim off any bits you don't want,
but remember you need the fat to flavour the meat.

Next chop up the onions and sauté them gently with two
tablespoons of the butter in a large flameproof casserole until
they are transparent. Once cooked, remove from the pan
and set aside. Now turn the heat up a little more and quickly
seal the lamb pieces in the casserole, using the pan drippings
from the onions to fry and brown the meat. Lower the heat
again, then add the saffron strands to the meat and stir well.
Now reintroduce the onions to the pan. Add the beef stock
and lemon juice. Season with salt and pepper. Bring
everything to the boil, then turn the heat down, cover the
pan and simmer the khoresh gently for about 1 hour.

While you wait, chop the parsley and mint. Set aside
some of the herb mixture for garnish, then sauté the rest of
the leaves briefly with the remaining butter and add to the
casserole for another 30 minutes.

Add the chopped rhubarb to the casserole for the last 15
minutes. Test the meat for doneness and check the
seasoning. The final element of flavour is added when you
concentrate the sauce. Use a slotted spoon to remove the
meat mix to a serving dish. Keep it warm. Skim the fat from
the top of the remaining pan juices and boil the liquid hard
until it is reduced by one third. Pour the thickened juices
over the meat, and garnish with the saved mint and parsley.
Serve with basmati rice and salad.

Mrs H's recipe for savoury rhubarb sauce

Based on a recipe from *Rhubarb: More Than Just Pies*, this was a revelation. Although we served it with pork, I cannot see why it could not accompany other meats. This recipe should be sufficient for four. The pork was grilled and marinated in olive oil and the juice and zest of an orange. We had a fresh spinach and asparagus salad for veg.

4 rhubarb stalks
250ml red wine
125ml red wine vinegar
180ml chicken stock

Chop the rhubarb into smallish pieces and transfer to a saucepan. Mix in the red wine and vinegar and let everything marinate for 30 minutes. Add the chicken stock to the pan and bring everything to a slow boil. Stir the sauce now and again to prevent it sticking. Cook for around 20–30 minutes, by which time the rhubarb should fall apart and the liquid be reduced enough to coat the back of a wooden spoon. Keep the sauce warm until it is ready for use. Spoon it over the meat and wait for the taste explosion.

THE FIRST ERUPTION

THE PUB STEADILY BEGAN to lose its allure, as I stayed in for Mrs H's casseroles and soufflés. During summer, she toiled away over the hibachi, a primitive but effective form of barbecue. As a form of recompense, I attempted a fashionable dish of that time. Mrs H has often recalled it over the years. It was the moment she realised what she had got herself into. Always keen on soups, I decided to attempt French onion soup, regarded as excitingly bohemian twenty-odd years ago. Desiring to bring a whiff of the old Les Halles to the suburbs of south London, I peeled a mass of onions, sliced them into fine discs and started gently frying them in Mrs H's biggest pot. Nothing too unusual there, surely? Except Mrs H came downstairs, poked her head round the kitchen door and asked, 'What on earth are you doing?'

'Making French onion soup.'

'But it's four in the morning.'

'Couldn't sleep.'

'So you decided to make some soup.'

'I was trying to be quiet. Didn't want to wake you.'

'Well, you have.'

'I never knew you could be woken by a smell.'

Afterwards I restricted my soup-making to more social hours.

The main thrust of my culinary proposals concerned the foods of northern England. I was particularly pleased when she showed enthusiasm for pork pie, a delicacy that continues to hold great appeal for me. I had less success in persuading her to enjoy another northern treat. 'No! I am not eating that. It looks revolting.' It was the first sighting of an eruption that became more familiar in subsequent years. Who would have thought that a plate of chopped honeycomb would have prompted such antagonism?

Maybe I should explain that the honeycomb in question was honeycomb tripe. In retrospect, I've come round to her view. Over-bleached and tasteless, English tripe is rubbish, but Italian tripe from veal calves is sensational and French tripe is pretty good. Persisting in my campaign to convert Mrs H, I secured a tin of *tripes à la mode de Caen* (cooked with carrots, onion and leek). While she was otherwise engaged, I opened it, emptied the contents into a saucepan and secreted the telltale tin.

'A bit curious,' she said warily as she tasted a spoonful. Moments later, my ploy ended in disaster. 'Argh! What have you made me eat?'

'It's just a tin of French stew.'

'I've just found a hairy bit.'

'It can't be hairy. There aren't any hairs in tripe.'

'TRIPE!'

It took several minutes for the plaster to stop falling from the ceiling. Even now, Mrs H insists that she found a hairy bit in the French tripe.

I realised that I would have to change tack pretty rapidly if my toothbrush were to retain its position in Mrs H's bathroom. Luckily, I had a sure-fire weapon in my culinary armoury. There was a certain savoury that Mrs H received with such enthusiasm that it would not be overstating the case to describe her reaction as ecstatic. It occurred to me that it would do our relationship no harm if I were to try every known variation of this dish. The path to Mrs H's heart was paved with Welsh rabbit.

3

Rabbiting on

'IT'S MY IDEA OF HEAVEN.' Mrs H's rapturous reception
of my cheese on toast could prompt a new direction for
theology, though I must admit that my productions in this
department are occasionally satanically singed. 'I can't make
it at all,' she admits. 'I know it involves Worcestershire
sauce and there's a lot of washing-up afterwards, but I don't
know your secret method on account of lolling in bed like
Lady Muck while you make it.'

Where better to eat toast covered by a blanket of molten
cheese than when one is covered by a duvet? It is one of
those rare situations where dish mirrors diner. (I can't think
of many others. You rarely eat soup in the swimming pool.)
I don't want to give the idea that our decadent indulgence
of cheese on toast in bed is a frequent occurrence. We only
eat it on Sunday mornings and then maybe once a month.
Moreover, this sybaritic breakfast is not without drawbacks.
Toast crumbs can be a problem. 'But I'm a very neat eater,'
insists Mrs H. 'I have to make the bed afterwards to de-
crumb your half.' It is also a very rich dish. You can only
take a certain amount on board. I once held a dinner party

consisting solely of different kinds of cheese on toast. Everyone turned greenish around the fourth course.

For some reason, this dish tends to fall into the male sphere of gastronomic activities. It could be something to do with a manly partiality for savouries. Something cheesy on toast forms a traditional finale to the meal in gents' clubs and chophouses. Very nice it is too, if you happen to have sufficient space. Maybe I'm in charge of cheese on toast because I happen to be more intuitively brilliant about the ingredients and their proportions. Maybe it's because I allow an extra minute or two under the grill so the seething cheese attains dark, speckled perfection. However, it has occurred to me that Mrs H might just have ceded authority so she can stay in bed while I am grating and grilling in the kitchen. This was not the cause of our dispute when I asked Mrs H if she would like some Welsh rabbit.

'Yes,' she replied. 'But it's not rabbit. It's rarebit.'

'Rarebit is a pointless, annoying bit of eighteenth century gentrification. It just sounds better than rabbit.'

'Well, what does a rabbit have to do with cheese on toast?'

'Well, what the hell is a rarebit, anyway?'

'Nobody calls it Welsh rabbit. Everyone calls it Welsh rarebit.'

'Well, everyone is wrong.'

The more I consider Mrs H's explanation for not doing this dish of disputed nomenclature, the more I think it is baloney. After all, Welsh rabbit is scarcely Blumenthalesque in its complexity (though I'm sure Heston could invent an impossibly complicated version if he put his mind to it). My own formula goes along the following lines. Grate up a quantity of mature Cheddar – though, as we shall see, many other cheeses also work well – and put the result in a bowl, add the yolk of an egg, a few splats of Worcestershire sauce, a generous teaspoon of smooth Dijon mustard and stir well. Lightly toast a few slices of good bread, preferably sourdough. Spread the cheese mixture on the toast. Shove under a hot grill until the topping begins a lava-like bubbling and emits a concentrated aroma of cheesy savouriness. Is any culinary smell more alluring? The point to aim for – and this requires constant vigilance – is when the cheesy mix has melted and gained a dark-brown mottling but the toast has not carbonised too radically round its edge.

'Yum,' said Mrs H as she munched the combination of cheesiness and ooziness and crunchiness and almost-burntness. 'When you come down to it, there's nothing better than Welsh rarebit.'

'Rabbit.'

'I'll do anything for a bit of cheese on toast, as long as it's not too strenuous.'

Crumbs! No wonder I decided to explore every feasible variation of the dish in order to keep the fire of love burning. Or at least lightly toasted.

There turned out to be no shortage of possibilities. A traditional nibble for rich and poor alike, cheese on toast is the great British snack. The French may have their croque monsieur and the Swiss their raclette, but it was toasted cheese that Ben Gunn lusted for during his three years on

Treasure Island. 'But, mate,' the castaway informed Jim Hawkins. 'My heart is sore for Christian diet. You mightn't happen to have a piece of cheese about you, now? No? Well, many's the long night I've dreamed of cheese – toasted, mostly.' Welsh rabbit remains a distinctly British speciality.

A classic formulation appears in Jane Grigson's book *English Food*. Compared to my shortcut version, her 'Welsh rabbit' (note correct name) is a bit complicated. It involves gently warming grated cheese (she suggests Lancashire, Cheddar or Double Gloucester) in a small pan with milk or beer until it melts into 'a thick cream', then adding butter, English mustard and salt and pepper to taste. The result is then heated 'until it is very hot but below boiling point'. You pour it over two slices of toast in a heatproof serving dish. Grigson warns: 'The cheese will overflow the edges of the toast.' The toast is grilled until 'the cheese bubbles and becomes brown in appetising-looking splashes.'

Though this dish shows distinct signs of being a meal rather than a snack – for aforementioned reasons, the view at Hirst HQ is that Welsh rabbit should be something you can eat with your fingers – it came from an authority of such eminence that I gave it a whirl. I decided to do Cheddar with beer. It was a strange sensation to open a bottle of beer at breakfast time (though I dare say one could get used to it). The resulting slurry, tipped over two slices of sourdough toast in a cast-iron pan, didn't do much browning under the grill and the toast became distinctly wilty under the cheese mix. The dish also involved a slight singeing of the fingers and quite a bit more washing-up than my version.

But Grigson's rabbit went down a storm with Mrs H. 'Mmm. I could eat it all day long.' Even the wilting toast escaped censure. 'I quite like the toast soft rather than crunchy. It makes you concentrate on the cheese more.' Maybe due to the beer or the mature Cheddar, Grigson's Welsh rabbit had a profound depth of flavour, addictive yet satisfying. 'Of course, I prefer your eggy version,' Mrs H added diplomatically, 'but this is a real treat.' Milk will probably also work well in the dish. (A friend of mine had a Lancashire grandfather whose favourite meal was grilled cheese with milk. His method was to put milk and bits of cheese on a tin plate, toast it under the grill and mop up the result with bread.)

Keen to keep up the fusillade of cheesy *billets d'amour*, I tried the version advocated by several professional cooks, which involves making the topping first and allowing it to set. Melt a knob of butter in a saucepan, stir in a small quantity of flour, a pinch of mustard powder, a hint of cayenne and a few splats of Worcestershire sauce, then add a good splash of Guinness and half a pound of good grated cheese. When it's turned creamy, turn out the cheesy mixture into a container and leave to set in the fridge. This is then spread on toast and grilled. Cheese-on-toast purists may complain that the protracted nature of this style of Welsh rabbit lacks spontaneity. You have to think ahead. However, it is very quick to make when you have the topping in the fridge, which explains its appeal for chefs.

Most significantly, its intense flavour transported Mrs H to a transcendental plateau of pleasure. 'Coo!'

I turned to the subcontinent for my next variation. Colonel Arthur Robert Kenney-Herbert of the Madras Cavalry was, I'm sorry to say, a rarebit man. In *Culinary Jottings for Madras* (1885), he observes: 'For a really good Welsh rarebit, you should have a sound fresh cheese, not over-strong.' But his other ingredients do not eschew piquancy. You are instructed to mix two ounces grated cheese with one ounce of butter, two egg yolks, a dessert-spoon of English mustard, salt, and a pinch of something called 'Nepaul pepper' (apparently it was along the lines of cayenne, though not quite as strong) until thoroughly smooth. I used Double Gloucester and substituted a tiny amount of cayenne for the mysterious Nepaul stuff. The bright yellow result is spread on toast that has been buttered *on both sides* (the Col's italics) and baked in a buttered pie dish in a really hot oven for ten minutes.

With its brown and gold topping, the result looked tempting. 'It's quite mustardy,' said Mrs H after taking her first nibble. 'In fact, it's very mustardy. Phew!' While not exactly unpalatable, it was an astonishingly robust, take-no-prisoners Victorian snack, somehow both rich and austere. Mrs H quite liked it, but I found the overdose of English mustard slightly queasy-making.

'The Colonel must have liked his food very hot,' said Mrs H. 'It's OK but I don't agree with him that it is a really good Welsh rarebit.'

'Rabbit.'

'Well, he says rarebit.'

Cheesed off with this bickering, I decided to sort out the moniker once and for all. Jane Grigson said that it has to be 'rabbits, not rarebits or rare bits, which are both false etymological refinement'. The *OED* dates Welsh rabbit to 1725, with rarebit appearing sixty years later. In the forthright view of Fowler's *Modern English Usage*, 'Welsh rabbit is amusing and right. Rarebit is stupid and wrong.' According to Peter Graham's *Classic Cheese Cookery*, the 'Welsh' part may have stemmed from that nation's traditional fondness for cheese, which is alluded to in *The Merry Wives of Windsor* (the jealous Frank Ford declares: 'I would rather trust ... the Welshman with my cheese ... than my wife with herself'), but it was probably also a joke against the Welsh. In the unremittingly carnivorous eighteenth century, Welsh rabbit was a substitute for the real thing, ersatz, a bit of a con. If the expression was originally pejorative, the Welsh have had the last laugh. Two other national variants in Hannah Glasse's *The Art of Cookery Made Plain and Easy* (1747), Scotch rabbit (pretty much plain cheese on toast) and English rabbit, have both failed to stay the course.

I decided to make English rabbit as the next volley in my campaign to retain the heart of Mrs H. Hannah Glasse's recipe seems to derive from the medieval dish of sops, which is bits of bread soaked in wine. (In *Richard III*, one of the murderers of the Duke of Clarence says, 'Let's make a sop of him,' before that gruesome business involving a butt of malmsey.) You pour a glass of red wine over a slice of brown toast 'and let it soak the wine up; then cut some cheese very thin, and lay it very thick over the bread, and put it in a tin oven before the fire, and it will be toasted and brown'd presently. Serve it away hot.' Made with Lancashire and Chianti, the snack, not quite as soggy as you might expect, proved to be a mystery mouthful for Mrs H. 'I don't know what the underneath is. Tell me. Tell me.' I cruelly refused to say. Like most females, Mrs H cannot bear the withholding of information. 'Tell me. Tell me! TELL ME!'

Eventually she twigged without me spilling the beans. 'Is it something to do with wine?' The dish caused a diversion of opinion. I thought it was an interesting combination of flavours, slightly like fondue, that delivered a nice, boozy aftertaste. Mrs H was unpersuaded. 'Five out of ten. There's a slight bitterness there that doesn't entirely appeal. It's middling.'

I then tried the Scotch rabbit recipe in Peter Graham's *Classic Cheese Cookery*. This is entirely different from Hannah Glasse's but it does have the merit of being authentically Scotch. It appeared in *The Cook and Housewife's Manual* (1826) by Margaret Dods, the nom-de-plume of Christian Isabel Johnstone, a Peebles pub landlady. Using a cast-iron saucepan over a gentle heat, you stir together five ounces of Stilton (or Gouda) with four tablespoons of stout (Graham recommends Mackeson but I used Guinness), one teaspoon of ready-made English mustard and a lot of black pepper. When transformed into a smooth cream, pour into ramekins and brown under a hot grill. Eat with hot buttered toast. 'Quite nice,' Mrs H hesitated. 'A bit like dunking a biscuit in tea. It's rather drippy. The Stilton is a bit odd.' This was not quite the reaction that I was aiming for. She ate it all though.

Pushing my luck, I then made her another rarity from Graham's book called Irish rarebit. He admits that this dish, which appeared in a First World War cookbook, has no obvious association with Ireland. 'Perhaps the other nationalities had been used up,' he suggests. A combination of grated Cheddar, fried sweet onions, chopped gherkins, fresh herbs and a reduction of 'best vinegar' (I used red wine vinegar) is cooked first in a frying pan and then grilled on toast. Unfortunately, it did not prove to be the food of love. Mrs H was alarmed by the smell ('Poo!') and dismayed by the taste. 'What *are* we eating?' This highly assertive dish was marginally better cold, when its acetic aggression had calmed down. Since cold, vinegary cheese on toast is not renowned as an aphrodisiac, I broadened my research.

The more you look into cheese on toast, the more possibilities you find. Food historian Dorothy Hartley suggested: 'For a rich rabbit, fry the bread in bacon fat.' I didn't put that oily treat in front of Mrs H, but an anchovy-enhanced version from Patricia Michelson's book *The Cheese Room* went down well. Entitled 'A Sort of Welsh Rarebit', the recipe specifies fillets from salted whole anchovies. These are excellent but somewhat hard to locate. I found standard anchovy fillets worked fine. You make anchovy butter, by mashing four anchovy fillets into two ounces of butter. Use it to butter some slices of toast. Pile thin slices of cheese (Michelson suggests Caerphilly) into a dome on the toast, splat on some Worcestershire sauce and grill until the cheese melts and turns gold. 'Rather nice,' said Mrs H. 'Subtle, not too salty. Quite a revelation. I was expecting it to be a bit harsh but it's not strong at all. Very impressive.'

She was even more impressed by a dipping version of cheese on toast. Lady Shaftesbury's toasted cheese, which appears in Jane Grigson's *English Food*, comes from the recipe book of the wife of the Victorian social reformer Anthony Ashley Cooper, 7th Earl of Shaftesbury. However, the dish is not all that grand. 'By the standards of the aristocracy they were poor.' Intended to feed six, Lady Shaftesbury's snack requires rather small quantities: two ounces of butter, seven ounces of grated Cheddar, six tablespoons of cream, two egg yolks, salt and pepper. Impossibly titchy, I thought, but the combination of dairy products is very rich. You don't want much. (A food blogger who ate rather a lot of it reported nightmares.) The ingredients are mixed together in a saucepan and stirred over a low heat until dissolved into a thick cream. You then pour this into six small ovenproof dishes or ramekins and brown under the grill. Serve with toast fingers. Mrs H's reaction: 'Marvellous. Like an individual fondue. Hurray for Lady Shaftesbury!' This was everything I could have hoped for, though I would have preferred 'Hurray for Christopher.'

A CHILLY MOMENT

MY INVASION OF HER KITCHEN was a mixed blessing for Mrs H. Though she saw the advantage when she woke up to scrambled eggs and toast on Sunday mornings, there were a few minor drawbacks arising from my culinary activities. 'There's always a mountain of washing-up to be done after you've done any cooking,' she pointed out. 'And there are breadcrumbs everywhere and bits of kitchen roll. You put infinitesimal bits of cheese and butter back in the fridge and empty chutney jars back in the cupboard.'

I did, however, come in handy for replacing large casseroles on high shelves. It also became evident that my services were required when the lid of Mrs H's elderly chest freezer was forced open by a build-up of pack ice. In my fine manly way, I demolished the ice wall with a wooden steak mallet. There were some comments about the small pools of water that resulted from ricocheting chunks, but I deemed it a job well done.

With surprising speed, the pack ice returned. One day when Mrs H was out at work, I decided that a more radical defrosting of the freezer was required. What was the use of having a man about the place unless he made himself useful? Besides, the cleaving of great lumps of ice from the walls of the freezer was vaguely satisfying. Now I realise that you're not supposed to use a sharp metal object for defrosting freezers, but when did you hear of a snowplough with a wooden blade or an icebreaker with a plastic bow? This was serious, industrial-strength ice, the sort that did for the *Titanic*. After bending several of Mrs H's utensils in the attempt, I found the most effective method of de-icing involved a hammer and chisel.

After dislodging a few berg-sized lumps, I gave a particularly hefty whack and the chisel clunked against the metal wall of the freezer. Worse still, there was the slight but unmistakable hiss of escaping gas. Despite my chilly location, I found myself perspiring freely. I discovered a quarter-inch gash in the side of the freezer. I put my finger over the hole like the Dutch boy and the dyke, and the hissing stopped. Though effective, I recognise that this provided only a temporary solution. In the long term, keeping my hand in the freezer would be a distinct hindrance to my social life. In the short term, my finger was beginning to turn numb. Leaving the ozone-munching chlorofluorocarbons to escape heavenwards, I dashed to the iron-monger's for something to block the hole.

A tube of gunk called 'Chemical Metal' seemed the best bet. Though it made the inside of the freezer smell like a petrochemical plant, the hissing stopped. (It later occurred to me that chewing gum might have sufficed.) I closed the lid and hoped for the best. Peering at the crime scene on the following day, the signs were not good. The ice that had caused the problem in the first place had turned to slush and the long-frozen contents of the freezer were turning distinctly soggy. 'Did ...' I remarked over breakfast as casually as possible, 'I mention that I had a bit of an accident yesterday?'

The court of inquiry was uncomfortable and protracted. 'You used a hammer and *chisel*?' For a while, it looked as if my budding hobby of gastronomy was at an end. Peace was eventually restored when I bought a new freezer, my first-ever purchase of white goods. I managed not to destroy this freezer, but I had a slight mishap with a new fridge that we bought soon afterwards. It was all to do with attaching a plug. Yes, it came with a plug attached, but this would not fit where it had to go. So I cut it off, put the flex in the required location and attached a new plug. At least that's what I wanted to do, but the job got more and more complicated. As one thing led to another, I spent the entire day getting ever more embroiled with Mrs H's domestic electrical system. At a late stage in proceedings, when my mind might not have been entirely focused on the job, I found two stray wires that appeared to have no function. I twisted them together, jammed them into the corner of a plug and turned the electricity back on. The result was a blue flash and a massive bang from the fusebox. The resulting loss of electricity involved quite a bit of explaining to Mrs H when she came home. Unfortunately, I didn't have an explanation. Still don't, as a matter of fact. When I took the fragments of ceramic fuse plug that resulted from my mental aberration to an electrical suppliers, the man behind the counter scratched his head and said, 'Never seen anything like this before.'

Unfortunately, another mishap soon followed. Returning home after taking refreshment one night, I decided to restore the tissues by frying up a few links of sausages (Mrs H had gone to bed). Afterwards, I kindly washed up the cast-iron frying pan. This, as it turned out, was not a good idea. 'You've washed up my pan?' exploded Mrs H the following morning.

'Yes. It was dirty.'

'It's my special crêpe pan. You should never, ever wash it up. Just wipe it with a paper towel.'

'What? Even after frying sausages?'

'Sausages? You fried sausages in it?'

Despite my insistence that its admirable qualities would return after a protracted period of non-washing, the crêpe pan never again found favour with Mrs H. She may have had a point. The output of the post-washed pan never had the mottled élan of the pre-washed pan. This unfortunate business had the effect of putting me off pancakes. Making them, I mean. On Shrove Tuesdays, I still sat there like a great red pillar-box receiving consignments of this slender foodstuff, but their manufacture did not appeal. Pondering my lack of pancake proficiency recently, I came to realise that this was a serious omission in my repertoire. I surprised Mrs H with a sudden announcement that I was going to make pancakes. Lots of pancakes.

4

Crêpe souls

'YOU WANT TO MAKE LOTS OF PANCAKES?' Mrs H
repeated in a disbelieving tone. 'Er, why?'

Maybe pancakes aren't the most exciting of foods,
though some are better than others. A crêpe stall rarely fails
to attract my custom, and I am particularly partial to the
galette, a Breton speciality made from buckwheat flour.
Though pancakes were lifted by the invention of baking
powder in the nineteenth century, they remain a primitive
dish. As Alan Davidson points out in *The Oxford Companion to Food*, 'The griddle method of cooking is older
than oven baking and pancakes are an ancient form.' There
is a primal satisfaction about food that is cooked in an
instant and consumed an instant after that. This is particularly so with drop scones or Scotch pancakes, eulogised
by Davidson ('this excellent pancake'). Where better to start
my pancake adventures?

My first renditions of drop scones were a bit too primitive and ancient, but eventually they stopped tasting like
shoe soles. Whipped off the pan after a few seconds on each
side, there is a delicious contrast between the lightly tanned

exterior and the soft, sweet, creamy inside. Davidson insists that these delicacies are 'best eaten warm with butter or jam or both', but in my view the main thing you need with a freshly made drop scone is more drop scones. Especially when a sprinkling of dried fruit is added to the mix, they can be a seriously addictive snack. A frequent treat of my Yorkshire childhood, these sultana-gemmed nibbles have lost none of their appeal.

The main problem with drop scones is when do you have them? Not quite right for breakfast, lunch or dinner, they are perfect for that forgotten delight, the high tea. The only time I've had high tea in recent years was at a Scottish castle, where Scotch pancakes formed part of a massive late afternoon spread. I didn't tackle dinner with my customary gusto. Still, judging by Mrs H's coolness towards these tasty splats ('I haven't cooked them since school and I don't particularly want to start now'), I doubt if I will face this problem very frequently.

The difficulty about time of consumption also applies to the conventional pancake. Once or twice I've eaten them for breakfast in America in the form of a big stack dripping with maple syrup. This oozy construction is so substantial – it resembles the Capitol Records Tower in Hollywood – that you feel like going back to bed immediately afterwards. Pancakes are better eaten later in the day, especially if that day is Shrove Tuesday. While the Latin world enjoys the unfettered orgy of Mardi Gras, the British tuck into pancakes in an atmosphere hazy with particulates. Though I've tried any number of ways with pancakes, I always come back to the traditional partnership of lemon juice and sugar. The lemon counteracts the sweetness of the pancake, while the sugar neutralises the acidity of the lemon. There is also a distinctive combination of sensations: hot pancake, cold lemon juice and the crunch of partially dissolved sugar.

As I remarked, it is customarily Mrs H who stands at the stove on Shrove Tuesday. Wreathed in smoke, she bears a passing resemblance to St Joan. 'I never get to eat one because I'm always making them,' moans this modern martyr. 'I hear noises from the table like a cuckoo: "Feed me. Feed me." By the time I get to eat mine, you've finished and you say "Can I have a bit of yours?" No, I don't like making them. My clothes always smell of oil afterwards. Pancakes are all right but I wouldn't want to do them more than once a year.'

I embarked on my first-ever pancake by making batter, which you have to let stand for an hour or so. Even this most instantaneous of foods demands a degree of forward planning. I used a non-stick frying pan, but the technique came from *The Art of Cookery Made Plain and Easy* by Hannah Glasse (1747): 'Pour in a ladleful of batter, moving the pan round that the batter be all over the pan ... when you think that side is enough, toss it; if you can't, turn it cleverly.' I turned cleverly enough for my pancakes to earn Mrs H's damning-by-faint-praise: 'Quite nice.' The lemon-and-sugar pancake starts light, but ends up as a substantial dessert. The first one disappears as if by magic. Then you take a second and probably a third onboard and begin to feel well ballasted. With this treat as the dessert, it is unwise to have a large quantity of savoury pancakes as the main course. Maybe you shouldn't have savoury pancakes at any time. It is a dish that lies heavy on the plate and heavy in the stomach. Yorkshire puddings without ambition.

'Thank goodness we've got that over with,' Mrs H said after my exploration of the British pancake. 'Crêpes are much better than those doughy things.' Who is going to argue with that? Ever since we had some holidays in Brittany, when I ate them once a day, sometimes twice, I've had a hankering for the crêpe (from the Old French *crespe*, meaning curled) and the buckwheat galette (imaginatively derived from *galet*, a worn pebble good for skimming). The problem with making them at home is that, until recently, we did not have a large enough pan. Though fine for an English pancake, our non-stick frying pan produces only a mini-crêpe. A professional electric crêpe maker, as used on crêpe stalls, costs around £250, which seemed a little excessive to bring back memories of St Malo. The solution materialised when we were mooching round a Le Creuset shop in York. In one corner, I came across a pile of cast-iron crêpe pans. Measuring twenty-six centimetres in diameter, with a lip running round the edge, it had a pleasing heft in the hand and radiated homespun Gallic wholesomeness. From the instant I got it on the hob, I felt sure that my crêpes were going to be the stuff of legend.

Confident that I'd mastered the pancake, I thought that it would not take long to get the knack of the crêpe. In order to learn the rudiments, I took an informal lesson by hanging around a crêpe stall in a French market that visited our corner of London. First, *le patron* lightly lubricated the surface of his electric crêpe-maker with what looked like a large candle. In the centre of the hot plate, he deposited a dollop of crêpe mix and deftly distributed this over the surface of the plate with a T-shaped wooden utensil. It looked like a small version of the wooden rake used by croupiers to rake in roulette chips. When the bottom of the crêpe was cooked, he flipped it over with a spatula and then let the other side cook for a minute or less. Finally, he drizzled an infinitesimal quantity of Grand Marnier (my choice of topping) over the crêpe, folded it twice and handed the fat, multi-layered cone over to me. £3, *s'il vous plait*. Obviously, it was a doddle. As Ken Albala remarks in his book *Pancake: A Global History*, 'Pancakes ... are utterly indulgent and completely predictable.'

Unwrapping my Le Creuset crêpe pan from its shrink-wrap, I was assisted by a hole in the plastic. The reason for this hole was because the T-shaped spreading utensil had been removed. Mrs H recalled that the same applied to all the crêpe pans on sale in York. Le Creuset supplied a wooden spatula with the pan, but the company apparently thought that inclusion of a T-shaped utensil would prompt mystified inquiries from UK customers. That it should have been included was evident from the instruction booklet. This directed purchasers: 'Use the *râteau* in a circular motion to spread out the batter.' Aha! So the T-shaped utensil was a *râteau* (a word omitted from my big Oxford-Hachette French/English dictionary). At this point, I should have badgered Le Creuset for a *râteau*, but I thought it would be easy enough to find one in London. This turned out to be a misapprehension. The nearest I got was a shrugging excuse: 'We had some once ...' Eventually, on a day-trip to Calais, I bought a *râteau à crêpe* at the Carrefour *hypermarché* for one euro.

At last I was able to use the griddle. Under Mrs H's direction, I proved the pan by slowly heating it, pouring a small puddle of sunflower oil in the centre and wiping round with a kitchen towel until only a sheen remained. 'It seals the pan a bit like a non-stick surface,' explained Mrs H. 'You need to do this if you haven't used the pan for a while. And NEVER wash it up.' Having made my batter an hour or so earlier, I was now ready to tackle my first crêpe. After heating the griddle to the right temperature (water dripped on the pan should evaporate immediately), I was faced with the task of lubrication for crêpe purposes. Here, the booklet indicated another difference in the treatment of French and English customers. In the English text, we are told to 'lightly oil the surface of the pan between each crêpe (half an apple placed on the end of a fork and dipped in the oil is a good way of doing this)' but French readers were told to utilise '*une demi-pomme de terre piquée au bout d'une fourchette*'. A spud seemed to have the greater authenticity for this peasant dish.

After smearing a light coating of sunflower oil on to the griddle with my half-potato-on-a-fork, I poured in a small amount of batter and plied the *râteau* like the bloke in the market. Instant disaster. The mix started cooking and proved impossible to spread. My attempt to use the *râteau* 'in a circular motion' only shifted a tiny bit of the mix. When the first side seemed to be done, I edged the wooden spatula under and flipped it over. The result was a crepe of a disturbingly alien shape, burnt in some areas, under-cooked in the middle. 'The first one is always rotten,' sympathised Mrs H. 'You don't know how much mixture to put in.' The second crêpe was equally bad, while my third one looked like a highly inept English pancake. So much for pancakes being 'completely predictable'.

The Le Creuset booklet suggested that expertise did not come immediately with crêpes: 'Once you have mastered the traditional crêpe recipe, you can experiment with different ingredients'. Kate Whiteman's cookbook *Brittany Gastronomique* is more explicit about the tricky craft of the crêpe: '[The batter] is spread outwards in a circular motion using a wood rake. This requires a flexible wrist and a light hand and is definitely not as easy as it looks.' Lacking both flexibility of wrist and lightness of hand, it would obviously take me years of daily crêpe-making to wield the *râteau* with the proficiency of the market man. Mrs H pointed out another deficiency in my approach. 'Your batter needs to be a lot thinner,' said Mrs H, 'It's too floury at present, so your crêpes are too thick.'

Thinning it down helped with the spreading, but the resulting crêpe was *too thin*, more like a crisp than a pancake. Though thinness is of the essence with crêpes, I realised that I was not putting enough batter in. Obviously, the lip on the griddle was intended to contain the batter. I also discovered that a paper towel dipped in sunflower oil was better for lightly oiling the pan than any vegetable on a fork. When I finally managed to make an acceptable crêpe with my seventh batch, I felt battered but triumphant. Though it would never be mistaken for a professional rendition, it was pretty much circular and, better still, pretty much edible.

There are no end of crêpe possibilities, both sweet and savoury, but I stuck to the topping I'd enjoyed in the market: Grand Marnier, but more of it. My generously doused version won an ovation from Mrs H. We also tried a smear of Nutella as advocated in Nigella Lawson's *Nigella Express*. This was acceptable in a highly sweet, nutty sort of way, but prodigiously high in calories. Check the ingredients of Nutella and you'll find that it contains a large percentage of vegetable oil. Nigella's suggested accompaniment of whipped cream infused with Fra Angelico (a hazelnut liqueur) does little to reduce the calorific content.

There is one significant exception to my keep-it-simple rule for crêpes. This is the late nineteenth or early twentieth century invention known as crêpes Suzette. It is one of the few instances that a member of the pancake family soars in social esteem (blinis with caviar is another). According to *Larousse Gastronomique*, Henri Charpentier, a French cook working for John D. Rockefeller in the US, claimed to have invented the dish in the Café de Paris, Monte Carlo, in 1896 'as a compliment to the Prince of Wales and his companion, whose first name was Suzette'. In his autobiography, the chef said that the Prince gave him 'a jewelled ring, a Panama hat and a cane' for his creation.

'One taste,' Charpentier insisted, 'would reform a cannibal into a civilised gentleman.'

While Suzette sounds the right sort of name for a 'companion' of the Prince of Wales in Monte Carlo, Larousse says the story is baloney. 'In actual fact, at that date Charpentier was not old enough to be the head waiter serving the prince.' (He would have been sixteen.) John Ayto's *A-Z of Food and Drink* puts us right. The first reference to crêpes Suzette in print was by Escoffier in 1907. His 'Suzette pancakes' was an unflamed dish, as it remains in the recipe offered by Larousse. The encyclopedia notes a bit sniffily that Charpentier 'introduced the fashion for flamed crêpes Suzette to America'.

Though the pancake-loving Suzette remains a mystery, the dedication was no small honour. The tangy orange sauce marries happily with the blandness of the crêpes and, at least, in the Anglo-Saxon version, the flaming brandy provides a dramatic dénouement to a meal. You don't often see the billowing alcoholic explosion from restaurant dessert trolleys these days, but my version of crêpes Suzette – which tested my newfound prowess as a crêpe-maker twelve times over – went down a storm when I did it for some friends. You make the crêpes in advance, roll them up like English pancakes and warm them in the oven before performing the *coup de théâtre* with the flaming brandy. 'Oooh, it's lovely,' said Mrs H. 'Can we start having it instead of pancakes on Pancake Day?' I preened like the dubious Charpentier.

For a savoury pancake, I prefer a galette, which is made

from buckwheat flour. Its flavour is so assertive that many books, including Larousse, suggest a half-and-half mix with wheat flour. The darkness of the flour explains the French name *sarrasin* (Saracen). Over 12,000 tons per year are imported into Brittany for galettes. The batter is pale grey (it looks a bit like mushroom soup) and smells rather nutty. Recipes used to be egg-free, but most modern versions are less austere. Spurning tradition, the galette recipe in *Larousse* includes '5–6 beaten eggs', but I based my recipe on the one in *Brittany Gastronomique*, which requires a single egg for 250g of flour. The ancient Breton mixing technique is described: 'You should beat the batter energetically for at less 15 minutes, slapping it from side to side of the mixing bowl.' I used a hand-held electric whisk for five minutes, which felt quite long enough. The resulting galette was striking in appearance, like a map of dark-brown islands on a light brown sea, edged with lacy filigree. The folding of the galette is different from the crêpe. First, you put a dollop of the savoury filling – two favourites are chopped asparagus in a cheese sauce and shellfish in a cream sauce – in the middle of the galette. Then you fold over an arc of the galette on four sides – about five centimetres left and right, then five centimetres top and bottom – so the result is a squared envelope with the filling visible through a little window.

As with the crêpe, it took me a while to get the knack of galettes, which are thicker and moister. In a less-than-appetising comparison, one Breton writer said galettes are macramé while crêpes are Valenciennes lace. Eventually

I steered a middle course between the soggy dishcloth galette and the so-brittle-it-cracks galette. I even managed to do the fried-egg galette. After cooking one side, you flip it over and break an egg in the middle. The intention is that this cooks through the pancake. When both galette and egg are just about cooked, you fold over the four edges so the yolk appears in the little window. This is all easier said than done. When the galette is cooked, the egg tends to be underdone. When the egg is cooked, the galette is heading for burnt. Still, my effort scored highly with my severest judge. 'Mmm, this is really good,' said Mrs H, when I presented her with a galette filled with an egg and grated Gruyère. 'Lots of potential here. It could be breakfast, lunch or light supper. Do you fancy doing another?'

Somewhat less demanding in construction is the galette with sausage, sold at crêpe stalls in Breton markets. The pancake is simply wrapped round a hot meaty sausage. Mrs H is a big fan. This delicacy is known as the *galette robiquette* after La Robiquette, a district of Rennes noted for the excellence of its bangers. There are a number of rules for the consumption. La Sauvegarde de la Galette Saucisse Bretonne (Society for the Preservation of the Breton Sausage Galette) demands that the sausage should weigh at least 125g, be consumed without mustard, accompanied only by cider and cost no more than two euros. However, local taste is questioned by Kate Whiteman, who advises readers to make sure the galette is hot off the press: 'The Bretons are partial to sizzling hot sausages wrapped in a cold soggy galette.' I haven't tried the cold soggy version, but

I once made the mistake of accepting the offer of a double wrapping of galettes round my sausage. I managed to chomp my way through it but the after-effect is a little hard to describe. Have you ever eaten a blanket?

Mrs H on pancakes, crêpes and galettes

To make any pancake, crêpe or galette, you need to think ahead a bit. At least an hour is required to let the batter mix stand or rest in order to release the starch in the flour to swell and soften. A well-stood batter makes a lighter pancake or crêpe. So make an early start if you have a meal at a certain time in mind. You can make pancakes by hand – using a wooden spoon to beat the mix – but for those who don't want to develop uneven biceps an electric hand-mixer is the gadget you need. A proper crêpe pan (a frying sized pan with a shallow rim) is ideal for batter products as you can flip and turn with greater ease. But you can't beat a decent non-stick pan that is heated to the right temperature.

N.B. I always look upon the first pancake as a bit of a practice run. Sometimes in your haste and response to the clamours from the table to 'get a move on' you find you haven't let the pan heat up properly or the pan hasn't quite become non-stick. The first pancake will also tell you if your batter is too thick or too thin. Add a little extra milk if the batter is too thick. Once you get going, pancakes take no time at all to cook – perhaps 1–2 minutes for the first side and about a minute for the second. Give the batter mix a stir before cooking each pancake – the mix can settle.

Mrs H's recipe for Shrove Tuesday pancakes

This is a standard recipe for the sort of pancake you only have to make once a year – when the price of lemons goes up. A mix with 125g of flour should make about eight pancakes. Alter the ingredients if your table greedily demands more. Because you set up a sort of production line, making this sort of pancake is a smelly business however little fat you try to use for frying – so don't wear your best clothes and keep the windows open.

125g plain flour
a pinch of salt
1 large egg, beaten
300ml milk
a little oil for frying
caster sugar and lemon juice to serve

Begin by sifting the flour and salt into a bowl and make a well in the centre (or as I saw once in an American recipe, 'sink a shaft'). Add the egg and mix in. Next gradually add the milk, drawing the flour in from the sides. Continue whisking until a smooth creamy batter is formed. Let the batter stand for at least 30 minutes. After heating the pan and adding a tiny amount of oil, pour in enough batter to coat the base of the pan. Cook the first side until you see that the centre is drying and the sides crisping. Flip or toss and cook the second side. After turning out on to a plate, sprinkle caster sugar and lemon juice on the pancake and roll up in a sausage shape. Add more sugar and lemon if the diner starts grizzling that you haven't added enough.

Mrs H's recipe for basic crêpes

This crêpe recipe differs from the English pancake because you add melted butter to the mix. Depending on the size of your pan, you should make eight to twelve pancakes.

150g plain flour
3 large eggs
300ml milk
large pinch of salt
55g butter, melted, plus extra for cooking the crêpes

Start by sifting the flour into a large bowl and make a hollow in the centre to hold the liquids. In a smaller bowl, beat the eggs and combine the milk, salt and melted butter. Add this mix to the eggs. Gradually pour the liquid milk/butter/egg mix into the flour well, stirring vigorously to incorporate all the flour – but not so wildly that you swoosh the flour up and over the top of the bowl. Beat until a smooth mixture is achieved – no lumps. The use of an electric hand-held mixer will save time and temper. A thinnish batter is what you want to aim for. Now put the batter mix aside for around an hour to rest. Why not rest yourself as well, since things will get pretty active once you start cooking? Or you can use this time to prepare any filling for the crêpes. When you are ready to cook, heat a frying pan or crêpe pan slowly until it is really hot. Lubricate the pan with the addition of a little hot butter or light oil, then add a ladleful of batter and rotate it in the pan so it spreads evenly. Cook over a medium heat until you notice the edges crisping up and curling slightly. Turn or toss and cook the other side until golden. Turn the crêpe out on to a plate. Add a filling of your choice. Roll the crêpe up or fold over, and deliver to the person with the hungry look on their face.

Mrs H's recipe for buckwheat galettes

Based on the recipe in *Brittany Gastonomique* by Kate Whiteman, this works well. The most difficult part is finding somewhere that sells buckwheat flour. (Hooray for Waitrose.) A light and lacy look to each galette is what you should aim for. I usually get about six to eight galettes per batch with the quantities given. Note, though, that the batter needs a very long resting time. Kate Whiteman suggests overnight, but the mix will separate too much if you let it hang around your kitchen all day too. Cook each galette until the base is a golden brown before flipping. Galettes stack well – which means that the cook can sit down to eat with everyone else. If you make a pile, use non-stick baking parchment to separate the galettes and keep them gently warm in the oven. But not too long or you could end up with a pile of Frisbees.

250g buckwheat flour
1 large egg, beaten
1 teaspoon salt
100ml milk
200ml water
unsalted butter or light oil for cooking the galettes

All batter mixes start in the same way – sift the flour into a
mixing bowl. Make a well in the centre, then add the beaten
egg and salt, drawing in the flour. Next mix the milk and
water and add the liquid a little at a time until the batter is
smooth and creamy. You may find that you have to whisk
away for a while – it usually takes around 7–8 minutes by
hand. As I said before, an electric whisk is invaluable. Then
you let the batter rest for at least 2 hours. Before you start
cooking the galette, give the batter mix a good stir. Heat a
frying pan or crêpe pan slowly until hot. Add a little butter
or light oil to lubricate the pan, then pour a ladleful of
batter into the pan, swirling as you do so the batter covers
the pan evenly. Cook until you spot the edges turning
brown, then flip or toss the galette to the other side. Cook
this side until golden. Add any fillings – savoury or sweet –
and fold in the edges to make a square.

TASTE FOR TRAVEL

DURING A SUNDAY NIGHT STROLL along the seafront of a town on the heel of Italy, we spotted a crowd of young people buying hamburgers from a van with a charcoal grill. It seemed a strangely popular draw. 'Fancy a burger?' I asked Mrs H, though we were planning a more extended meal.

'All right.'

Shoving my way into the throng, I came back with a couple of the inexplicably appealing snacks. 'You're in for a surprise,' I told Mrs H. But before she could take a bite, a tentacle dangled out of her bun. They contained the best octopus I've ever had. A decade on, my mouth waters at the memory of this tender cephalopod surprise.

From our first holiday together on the Greek island of Serifos, where I heroically dived for sea urchins (too gritty to eat), Mrs H became aware that for me foreign food is a major reason for foreign travel. One of the most perplexing things I've ever seen was a stall in a southern French market that catered for the expat market. Its stencilled signs advertised such necessities of Anglo-Saxon cuisine as 'BISTO',

'OXO' and, bizarrely, 'FISH SHOP FISH'. 'CHEDDAR' was also available for those who failed to appreciate the nation's unequalled cheeseboard. The dusty stock seemed precisely calculated to confirm French prejudice about the barbarian appetites of their neighbours across La Manche.

Not all *rosbifs* are so gastronomically insular. I am still racked by regret that the lack of a kitchen during a stay in Barcelona prevented my purchase of the snails that were doing their best to escape from a stall in the splendid Boqueria market on Las Ramblas. We ate snails braised in red wine in a restaurant, but their excellence only served to heighten the pain of my loss. Back home, a way of salvaging something from this missed opportunity occurred to me. 'There are plenty in our garden. Why don't we use those?'

'I think not.' Mrs H shot me a look in a manner that suggested negotiation was not on the cards.

In the course of our travels, a substantial quantity of food makes its way into my luggage, which is inevitably decked with 'HEAVY' stickers when it appears on the airport carousel. I've brought back foie gras from Strasbourg, nutmeg from Grenada (I wish I'd managed some conch), ham from North Carolina, salted anchovies from Collioure and an impressive quantity of tinned sardines from Quiberon in Brittany. 'Quite a good buy,' admitted Mrs H. She was also pleased – if somewhat surprised – by the dozen pots of lox and cream cheese, baked salmon and other fishy salads I acquired in Zabar's, the big, rackety deli on New York's Upper West Side. She was less keen on the plastic bag of saffron I snapped up for a bargain price in the

Old City market in Jerusalem. 'Do we really need a lifetime's supply of turmeric?' Nor did she express fondness for the large lump of *bacalhau* (salt cod) that I brought back from Lisbon. 'It was fantastically smelly and fell out of the cupboard so I threw it away.'

'I wish I'd still got that.'

'Then you should have done something with it. You've still got some tins of that fishy stuff you brought back from Nîmes.' Mrs H is referring to *brandade de morue*, a Provençal dip made with salt cod. I found a shop in Nîmes that sold nothing else. (Raymond at 34 rue Nationale is mentioned in Elizabeth David's *French Provincial Cooking*.) Of course, it would have been unforgivable not to make a heavy investment.

Recalling the fate of the *bacalhau*, I brought back two large tentacles of salted octopus on my next visit to Lisbon. Keen to try this souvenir, I left one soaking in the sink when I went out for the evening. Unfortunately, I forgot to warn Mrs H about its presence. 'I nearly shot through the ceiling,' she told me later. 'I thought it was a dead eel. Not the sort of thing a girl wants to come home to on a dark night.' She was placated somewhat when I barbecued the tentacle. It was delicious in a salty sort of way.

Mrs H has even looked askance at foods that she has requested. Before I went to Mexico she put in an order for dried chilli peppers, which I bought in bulk. In fact, the quantity proved a bit daunting. They are still sitting in a big cool box. This is because someone gave us a warning that the peppers might contain insects we would never get rid of if they escaped into the house. So the lid of the cool box remains tight shut, though I intend to use them one day, possibly in the world's largest chilli con carne. 'Have you thrown them away yet?' Mrs H inquires from time to time.

'I didn't lug them all the way back from Mexico City just to throw them away.'

Equally dismaying was her reaction to the gift I brought back from New Orleans. Though she initially looked pleased at the large, foil-wrapped parcel I pulled from my bag, delight turned to perplexity when she discovered that it contained a vast, circular sandwich. Around a foot in diameter, it was somewhat squashed by its journey of 4,637 miles. 'It's called a muffuletta. There's olive salad in there and salami and mortadella and provolone and ...'

'You've brought me back a squashed sandwich from New Orleans?'

'Yes. It's from this fantastic shop called the Central Grocery on Decatur Street. They wrapped it twice when I said where it was going. It's supposed to be one of the great sandwiches of the world.'

'How lovely.' It turned out to be rather nice in a soggy way, though Mrs H was unimpressed.

There is another American delicacy that I prize above all others. Displaying considerable strength of character, I have never brought it back across the Atlantic. Particularly in America's heartland, where restaurant meals tend to be as mundane as they are vast, it has often been a lifesaver. I have consumed this glory of stateside cuisine from Providence,

Rhode Island, to Carmel, California, and it has rarely failed to satisfy. The dish in question looks pretty similar to the snack we had in Apulia, but in America you don't get octopus in a bun. You get hamburger. I might not have been able to bring American burgers back across the Atlantic, but there was no reason why I couldn't make my own version.

5

Burger king

EATING ONE OR MORE HAMBURGERS a day for two weeks produces some strange effects. I don't mean the alarming physical deterioration recorded in Morgan Spurlock's documentary *Super Size Me*, about consuming Big Macs for thirty days on the trot (he put on 11.1 kilos). It is possible to be spared such ballooning by downsizing the portions and skipping the fries, though you are never actually going to lose weight by eating burgers (the fattiness of the meat is the key to their juiciness). As a consequence of our diet, an outside observer would have seen a household behaving in a bizarrely eccentric fashion. We took to keeping the mincer in the refrigerator. (Yes, the *mincer*, not just the mince.) We grilled food containing ice-cubes. We acquired a slab of beef costing £174.95 per kilo.

We were simply trying to make the best possible hamburger. I'd been making them on and off for years. 'You used to make little round ones like squashed meatballs, then they got bigger over the years,' says Mrs H, who has a better memory for these things than me. The results were only so-so, often on the dry side. I'd eaten far better burgers in the

States and felt an urge to reproduce these paragons of the genre. As a result of our investigations, I am now able to answer a number of significant questions.

Are the best burgers made from steak? No. Do you need to mince your own beef? Usually. Should you press on the hamburger to get singe marks while grilling? No. Was it a mistake to compress our research on this topic into two weeks? Yes.

The reason for this untimely haste is that a magazine accepted my proposal for an article about making the best hamburger. The only drawback about this sponsorship was the deadline, which caused our normally (fairly) balanced diet to go radically haywire. We ate as many hamburgers in a fortnight as we would normally do in five years.

For us, hamburgers are a rare (in both senses) treat. Somehow, they're all the better for being an occasional indulgence. Though I relish a good burger, I can't see the point of most products sold as such. I suspect that I am not alone in being baffled by the success of the Big Mac and everything else sold by the big hamburger chains. I doubt if I've had more than three or four such transient nibbles in my entire life. (They are not a memorable experience.) At its best, the American burger is incomparably superior. A plump disc of minced beef briefly grilled, it has a gently charred crust and a rare, juicy interior. This quintessence of beefiness is more satisfying than many steaks you are liable to encounter.

Mrs H shared my desire to achieve excellence in the hamburger. At least she joined in my intense experimentation.

Later, I discovered that she was not so ardent. 'They're OK,' she said, while waggling her hands in an I-can-take-it-or-leave-it fashion. 'I like the smell, but if I were to have anything minced it would be spicy lamb meatballs with mint and yogurt.' And there was me thinking she had been enjoying them all along. It was like rhubarb and her mum all over again.

In order to assist our experimentation, I acquired an extensive library of burgerology. 'You bored me stupid for weeks with interesting facts on the topic,' Mrs H recalls. 'Did I know that a recipe for Hamburg sausages appeared in Hannah Glasse's cookbook of 1758? Or that Wimpy was originally a character in Popeye? Or that White Castle, the first American hamburger chain, still sells hamburgers from little castles? Zzzzzzzzzzzzzz.'

Hamburger America by George Motz proved to be a particularly entertaining study. Described as a 'State-By-State Guide to 100 Great Burger Joints', it is the result of seven years' research. Typical examples of the prodigious platefuls that Motz took on board were the 'Thurman Burger' of Columbus, Ohio, whose successive strata consist of a twelve-ounce beef patty, grilled onions, lettuce, tomato, sautéd mushrooms, pickle, mayonnaise, half a pound of sliced ham, grilled mozzarella and American cheese, and the 'Seismic Burger' sold in Meers, Oklahoma, with 'one pound of ground longhorn beef topped with cheese, bacon, jalapeño slices …' Surprisingly, photographs of Motz reveal a man of average dimensions. In his introduction, he warns would-be emulators: 'Embrace moderation.'

Mrs H and I aimed for a much pared-down version of these American gut-busters. It would, we agreed, be gratifying to survive the experience. We determined not only to limit the quantity of beef to around 150g per burger but also to diminish the astonishing quantity of stuff that often joins the meat between top and bottom buns. When Heston Blumenthal attempted to produce the ultimate hamburger for his book *Further Adventures in Search of Perfection*, the result was a towering stack of iceberg lettuce, tomato, grilled cheese and pickle. The painstakingly researched Hestonburger was all but lost towards the bottom. With good reason, such efforts are referred to in the US as 'five-napkin burgers'. By chance, I happened to visit one of the spots where Blumenthal studied burgers. It was a faux grungy joint that had been transplanted from the Bowery and installed on the ground floor of a swanky Manhattan hotel called Le Parker Meridien. Being pretty much unsigned, the burger bar took some finding among the mirrors and the large Damien Hirst (one of his spin paintings, not a bovine work) in the glitzy lobby, but a smoky whiff acted as an olfactory signpost. As Blumenthal says, it was 'a great burger'. Unfortunately, he seemed more impressed by 'the effort that had gone into creating a context for that burger' and did not emulate its restraint in salad/pickle accompaniments.

I knew that a piled-up burger would not go down well with Mrs H. 'I always go for a plain hamburger,' she said. 'A load of slippery things piled up together makes it too challenging to eat.' However, she is keen on tomato ketchup with her burger. At least, I thought she was until I quizzed her about this passion. 'Actually, I don't like it with hamburgers,' she blithely asserted. 'I think it detracts from the meatiness of the burger.'

'Well, why do you reach for the ketchup bottle when we have hamburgers?' I inquired with the lethal suavity of a prosecuting QC.

'I might have a bit of ketchup with half the toasted bun.'

'Ha!'

'But I don't put my halves of the bun together – the ketchup doesn't go on the hamburger! So nuts to you, Mr Nosey Parker.' With that, which was accompanied by an impressive length of stuck-out tongue, she considered herself vindicated.

'But you've always liked gherkins with your burger.'

To my astonishment Mrs H said, 'I don't think I ever had a gherkin before I met you.'

'You're constantly buying them. We only go to Ikea so you can buy the sweet Swedish ones.'

'You're the gherkin addict,' she shot back. 'Who else would trail round New York to visit a pickle stall? It was you who made us catch a cab across Manhattan so we could visit Guss Pickles on the Lower East Side. It was very vinegary and full of men in stained aprons fishing things like giant caterpillars out of plastic barrels. You bought a huge willie-sized pickle and went, "Mmm, lovely." It was all very butch.'

'I bought you a Guss Pickle T-shirt that you never wore.'

'That's because you put it in a plastic bag with your leaky

gherkins, so it smelled of vinegar no matter how often I washed it.'

We did, however, agree about the bun. It shouldn't be too big, but it should be sprinkled with sesame seeds. Having discussed the peripherals, it was time to get down to the meat of the matter.

All hamburger authorities agree that you should mince your own beef. You need to know what you're cooking. Somewhat counter-intuitively, this should not be the best steak cuts. 'Fillet, rib-eye, even rump are too lean,' pontificated Mrs H. 'You want a good bit of fat in the mix to provide juiciness and flavour.' Most American hamburger gurus specify chuck beef. Chuck is a term for shoulder beef, also known in the UK as blade. It contains around 18–25 per cent fat, which is deemed more or less perfect for hamburgers.

Unless you have access to a butcher's powerful mincer, the meat has to be trimmed of connective tissue. 'This is it,' said Mrs H, pointing out some white stringy strips in the meat with the tip of her kitchen knife. 'It's tough, non-fatty stuff that surrounds the muscle fibres of the meat.' Tough is the word. According to Richard Wrangham's book *Catching Fire*, 'Connective tissue is slippery, elastic and strong: the tensile strength of tendons can be half that of aluminium.' Fortunately, connective tissue turns to jelly when heated. So why did I have to cut it out?

'If you don't cut it out,' Mrs H explained, 'it wraps itself round the spindle of your mincer.' That's what happened to Jeffrey Steingarten, food guru of US *Vogue*, when he omitted to take this precaution during his attempt to make the perfect burger. 'The Waring electric meat grinder began to make the sound of fingernails scraping on a blackboard, but amplified a hundred times. We had to buy a new one.'

Its connective tissue safely removed, our meat went into the fridge for an hour to chill again. 'This is to ensure that the fat stays hard while being minced,' explained Mrs H in full didactic flow. 'Otherwise, the blade gets covered in fatty gunge and a horrible pink mousse emerges instead of mince speckled with bits of red and white.'

Judy Rogers of the Zuni Café in San Francisco goes further still: 'Refrigerate the grinder to chill thoroughly. A warm grinder can warm the meat.' For mincing we used our KitchenAid food mixer with (pre-chilled) mincing attachment. It's better to mince the meat twice or even three times to ensure the fat is thoroughly amalgamated. Some experts advocate the addition of salt, fried chopped onions and even a spoonful or two of cream. Steingarten found a report in the *US Journal of Food Science* that said the addition of 10 per cent water (about one and a half tablespoons per burger) 'resulted in higher juiciness, tenderness and over-all palatability'. I also came across a suggestion from James Beard, 'the father of American gastronomy', that the inclusion of an ice-cube in the burger ensures a moist, rare interior.

When it comes to forming the burgers, Harold McGee maintains, 'The gently gathered ground beef in a good hamburger has a delicate quality quite unlike even a tender steak.' The gentle gathering is intended to produce a tasty, crumbly burger. When cooking burgers, what you must not do is what you see short-order cooks doing in American films. You must not press the burger on the grill with your spatula. Though powerfully tempting in a mysterious way, it has the effect of squeezing out the juices. You get a dry burger.

Up to our hocks in advice, we decided to start sizzling. For all our tests, we used our Weber gas barbecue (a ribbed, cast-iron griddle on a gas hob also produces good results). About four to five minutes per side at medium-hot heat produces a medium-rare burger. Just to be perverse, we started with a sample of ready-minced beef, though this wasn't just any old mince. It was Galloway shoulder beef or chuck aged for thirty-five days and sold by Farmer Sharp (a cooperative of Cumbrian farmers) at London's Borough Market. Though we approached it with dubious forks, it hit the bull's eye with our first shot. 'This is quite good, actually,' said Mrs H. 'Really flavoursome. A highly beefy burger.'

So much for never using prepared mince. Our second burger was made from Harrods chuck (£8.50 per kilo). The 'gently gathered' business sounds wacky, but the effect on the taste was perceptible. 'It holds together well and the flavour is pretty good,' said Mrs H. For comparative purposes, we tried chuck from our local butcher (£7.80 per kilo). Mrs H expressed misgivings about the smell. 'It reminds me of school dinners.' But she polished it off happily. We also tried burgers made from rump (dry and lacking in flavour) and hanger steak (better but still on the dry side).

It may seem contradictory, but while cheap beef produces a very good hamburger, so does very, very expensive beef. As a result of my commission, I was sent a 600g chunk of Queensland Wagyu from Harrods. Normally, it would have cost £174.95 per kilo for meat that is 30 per cent fat. Peering in awe at this plutocratic lump, we discovered that it was ribboned and streaked with what looked like pink butter. Fortunately for one's arteries, Wagyu fat is high in (relatively) healthy unsaturates. Even when thoroughly chilled, the meat felt to be melting the moment you started handling it. Mincing this plutocratic fillet seemed lese-majesty of a high order, but the resulting burgers were highly acceptable. Very tasty, immaculately moist, each fragment of meat was imbued with gravy-flavoured fat. 'This is very, very good,' said Mrs H as she nibbled her final fragment. 'You just want a bit more.' Our two 125g burgers cost around £45.

Finally, we tried an adapted version of a burger recipe developed by Heston Blumenthal and his Fat Duck team. We minced a mixture of 50 per cent short rib beef (rich in both fat and flavour, this is a cut that lies on top of the big ribs in an area at the centre on each side of the ribcage) with 25 per cent brisket and 25 per cent chuck. In one of the burgers we hid an ice-cube, to the other we added one and a half tablespoons of water. 'A really excellent beefy taste,' said Mrs H, as she nibbled the results. 'Heston's combination is very good if you can find short rib. It produces a pleasing greasiness.' The additional water resulted in a notably juicy burger. So did the ice-cube, which had the additional bonus of ensuring a rare interior, though commercial operations may get customer complaints concerning the resulting hole. 'Hurrah for the Iceburger!' declared my heroic partner as she dabbed a fragment from her lips. 'We must remember to use ice-cubes when we have hamburgers again. Maybe in five or six years.'

THE SOUND OF FALLING SCALES

'IT WAS THE FIRST THING we ever cooked together,' I reminisced in sentimental mood.

'You mean it was the first thing that you ever got roped into,' blurted Mrs H. 'After years and years spending a good chunk of January with crinkly fingers and the whole house covered in sticky stuff, I decided it was time you lent a hand. Very revealing it was too. You just sat there and moaned.'

'I never moaned.'

'You moaned constantly. It was very revealing about your character. I decided I had a lot to put up with.'

Though marmalade-making at home is often regarded as a symbol of domestic bliss, it did not prove to be very blissful in our case. This was the moment when, with a great clatter, the scales fell from Mrs H's eyes. She was only too willing to itemise my shortcomings as a partner in preserving activities.

'You were resistant to my instructions. You didn't see why you had to sterilise the pots or why you had to chop finely. It was obvious that you didn't know anything about making preserves and it was obvious that you were not a patient man.'

'I'm extremely patient.'

'You're extremely cunning. You say, "Ooh, I can't do that," so I have to do it. You couldn't be bothered to chop peel equally. You wanted to do it any old how. You thought the oranges didn't need scrubbing. You couldn't manage to put all the pips in a muslin bag and tie it on to the pan-handle. So I took over. Now I know you're doing it just to get out of things. Ha, ha, ha! Am I right?'

'Not at all.'

'Yes, I am.'

It was all a long way from our cheese-on-toast-in-bed bliss. But even Mrs H concedes that I am not to blame for her devoting many hours each year to making marmalade, something that she does not particularly like. She started making it for a friend of ours, a marmalade devotee of many years standing. Since he gets through a jar every ten days, he requires thirty-six jars a year.

When she started making marmalade for our friend, I began eating this bittersweet elixir myself. Jolly good it is too. Though I'm not such an addict as he is, I still manage to consume a jar every three weeks or so, making an annual requirement of eighteen jars a year. Mrs H's uncomplaining altruism in filling our joint order for fifty-odd jars would make her a candidate for beatification. At least, it would if this were true – not the altruism but the uncomplaining. She complains about the task long and hard. 'Damn! Ergh! Sticky! Ugh! Horrible!' she mutters while stirring her seething cauldron. Shrouded by clouds of pungent vapour, she might be one of the weird sisters in *Macbeth*. I was unwise enough to point this out at a moment when the rolling boil was at its peak. 'Is that so, matey?' replied Mrs H. 'Well, you can do it next year.'

Of course, she'll forget, I thought. But she didn't. Women have an unfortunate tendency not to forget. So when Seville oranges made their brief appearance in the following year, I was roped in. I realised that our first joint culinary endeavour was not going to be without the occasional release of steam, but it did have one advantage. If Mrs H were ever to throw in the towel, I would be able to have a bash at making the stuff myself. Breakfast without homemade marmalade would be lacking in appeal.

6

Infernal rind

'I WISH IT HAD STAYED PUT IN ARAB COUNTRIES,' said Mrs H. This may seem a strange remark to make about marmalade, the great stalwart of the British breakfast table, but I had just been informing her about its unexpected provenance. First recorded in English in 1480, the word comes from the Portuguese *marmelada*, which refers to quince preserve. Since the finest marmalade is made from Seville oranges, there remains a strong link with the Iberian peninsula. According to *The Book of Marmalade* by food historian C. Anne Wilson, the origin of the preserve lies further south: 'It does look as though Arab food customs and recipes were the original source of this confection in Portugal.'

'Well, that's *really* interesting,' Mrs H responded in an unconvincing way. Strangely, she was more occupied with another aspect of the spread. 'I wonder if kitchens in Portugal get covered in the bloody stuff?' She has a point there. Just a few molecules of marmalade have the magical ability to coat an extraordinary area. The transformation of our kitchen into Chez Sticky takes place each January.

Seville oranges have a brief and immutable season (around three weeks). If you want to make marmalade, you should snap them up as soon as you see them. You should also buy preserving sugar in some quantity because that also tends to disappear. And you need jars to put it in. Most marmalade makers collect jam and pickle jars throughout the year, resulting in a pleasing medley of containers for their output. Since such forward planning is impossible in our house, we tend to buy jars, along with lids with a faux gingham design, circles of waxy paper, labels, etc., from the kitchen company Lakeland.

It is a tricky thing to balance the three elements – Seville oranges, jars and sugar. You always seem to have too much or too little of one of them. With an excess of sugar or jars, you can shove them in a cupboard until next year, but the temptation is to buy more Seville oranges. An excess of oranges involves an emergency foray round local supermarkets to buy more preserving sugar. You could freeze the oranges, but what person with sufficient interest in food to make marmalade will have enough room in their freezer? And so January passes in an endless round of shopping, steaming, stirring, potting and complaining from Mrs H ('My fingers have gone like prunes'), all to make something you can buy in any supermarket.

So why does she bother, especially since she is not a great lover of the stuff? (She will occasionally accept a slice of marmalade on toast and show signs of mild enjoyment, but I have never seen her reach for the pot of her own accord.) The main reason for this annual onslaught is the torrent of compliments that Mrs H receives for her preserve. Most marmalade makers think their stuff is pretty hot stuff – C. Anne Wilson remarks that her own is 'matchless' – and they're usually right. It is not something you can buy in the supermarket. A world away from the one-dimensional sweetness of commercial marmalades, the homemade version does a dance on the tastebuds that hardly any other food can match. With a profound bittersweetness that hints at its exotic origins, it delivers a complex and potent combination of flavours.

But there is a price to be paid for such perfection. Instead of using the food processor to chop up the peel, Mrs H sticks to traditional methods, i.e. a sharp knife. 'In order to ensure that your peel is evenly distributed throughout the jar, it has to be of a uniform length and thickness,' she rather grandly explained. This doesn't happen with a food processor. Taking on the role of time-and-motion expert, I once egged her into using this more efficient way of cutting peel and I never heard the end of it. 'It just chops the peel up any old how,' she blurted accusingly. 'That's all right if you want mushy marmalade. Do you want mushy marmalade?'

For the first time, my role in this annual epic was going to be more than advisory. I was going to get my hands dirty or, rather, sticky. But first they had to be clean. 'Make sure you wash them properly!' ordered the Generalissimo. When I was finally allowed to get my hands on an orange, I discovered that there is quite a bit more to marmalade making than I had thought. Seville oranges are often creased, tough-looking jobs – the Tommy Lee Joneses of the citrus world – and washing them is a tedious prelude before you get down to business. You dig out the stalk, a black warty bit at the top. Then you search for fragments of Sevillian soil wedged in the cracks of the peel. Compensation for this dermatological exploration comes with the fresh, astringent perfume of the zest. Having weighed out three pounds of washed oranges, you bisect them and squeeze out the juice. By far the easiest way of doing this is to use an electric juicer. A cheap one works just as well as the hugely expensive Porsche-designed one I bought in a testosterone-induced moment of madness a few years ago.

A fair amount of juice comes out of fresh Seville oranges, but they're also rich in pips and pith. When you've finished squeezing, you collect the pips from the juicer. You may be forcibly reminded to include any pips that might have been left in the halved orange peels. 'You've left three pips behind!' Mrs H pointed out. It might be considered that a few pips in marmalade would add to its homemade credentials – but apparently not. The pips are placed in the centre in a square of buttercloth muslin. You pull the four corners of the muslin together and tie them with a long piece of string. Our muslin also came from Lakeland. 'Very much recommended,' says Mrs H, who has something of an obsession with Lakeland. 'Their muslin squares are just the right size for the pips.' (Apparently, a clean J-cloth – well, you wouldn't use a dirty one – is also effective.) The resulting little sack goes into the jam pan along with the orange juice. This is because pips are rich in the natural gelling agent known as pectin, which trips off the tongue more easily than its other name, heteropolysaccharide. The pips should save you having to use the commercial pectin known, rather splendidly, as Certo. 'I bet you don't know how to rescue the sack of pips at the end of the boil,' said Mrs H.

'Er, no.'

'I knew you wouldn't. You'd never think of tying the string to the handle of the jam pan. That's why you need a long piece.'

The next step was, to me at least, a surprise. You add six pints of water to the juice. Who would have thought there was water in marmalade? 'You add it to jam as well,' said Mrs H.

'You didn't add it when you were making strawberry jam.'

'Well, that's different. Get on with chopping the peel.'

Ah, yes, I'd forgotten that bit. Unlike normal orange consumption when the peel is chucked away, unless you shove a chunk in each cheek to do a Marlon Brando impression ('You don't even think to call me Godfather'), marmalade-making is a very satisfactory activity for those who detest waste. To chop the peel, you need a short, sharp knife, a chopping board and Radio 4. Bisect each squeezed hemisphere, so you get the peel of a quarter-orange. You then slice this wedge to create ten strips of peel. At least that's how I was directed, but just to show the old anarchic spirit wasn't entirely dead I sometimes did a random amount with some bigger chunks.

'Jolly good fun making marmalade, isn't it?' I announced with resolute buoyancy.

Silence.

Actually, it does get a bit wearing around the tenth quarter-orange peel.

'I knew you'd get fed up,' said Mrs H when she caught me taking a breather. 'And these bits are too big. You'll have to halve them.' I discovered that you need to do the peel-chopping in phases. A cup of coffee or a stare into space with your mouth open is required at regular intervals. It takes maybe an hour – thirty minutes for more dedicated types – to convert the hollow hemispheres from three pounds of oranges into a heap of two-tone strips. The sliced peel goes into the pan of diluted orange juice (with tethered bag of pips), which is brought to the boil on the hob at full blast, then turned down to a simmer for a couple of hours until the peel is soft (it should break up when you press it).

If you nibble the cooked peel at this stage, the effect is a wake-up call for your tastebuds; a profound, startling bitterness with an aftertaste that goes on and on. This orangey bitterness is the backbone of Seville orange marmalade. It is also the zesty powerhouse that propels Cointreau, Grand Marnier and most gins. At the Beefeater gin distillery in London, I once saw sackfuls of dried peel from bitter Spanish oranges that join juniper, orris root and what-have-you among the botanical flavourings. Each year, the company imports three tons of dried orange peel and that is a lot of peel, since it is virtually weightless. Pared from the fruit immediately after picking, the peel is dried on washing lines in the orange grove.

But back to marmalade. When the peel has simmered to softness, you are advised by some authorities, including Mrs H, to leave it in the juice to steep overnight. Or you can just press on. Either way, you have to squeeze the pectin from the bag of pips into the orange juice. After squeezing, Mrs H simmers the bag of pips in a small saucepan of water to extract the last molecule of pectin. This also goes in with the juice. Now comes the moment to add the preserving sugar. Tate & Lyle says it has a larger crystal that 'dissolves more slowly to help make a better product.' Mrs H says it 'helps with the clarity – you don't get so much scum', but some marmalade makers I know achieve excellent results with bog-standard granulated. If you start with three pounds of oranges, the quantity required is six pounds of preserving sugar. Don't add the sugar before the peel is soft. I am earnestly assured by Mrs H that the peel will never get one jot softer from that moment.

While heating the sugary, peel-laden juice to the boil, you have to stir constantly and you have to stir in a certain way. 'Slowly does it,' ordered Mrs H in a parade-ground 'Wait-for-it' growl. 'If you whirl it round in your fine, manly way, you're going to start smashing the peel.' So I stopped whirling. 'But you haven't dissolved the sugar properly.' I started whirling again.

'I think it's dissolved now,' I said after a bit.

'I bet it isn't,' said Mrs H, pinching my spoon. 'There!' she said triumphantly. 'I can feel great crunchy bits at the bottom. You may think it's fine, but do you know what would happen if you didn't dissolve all the sugar?"

'Er, no.'

'It would turn crystalline. That's not good. It might have been fine when you were growing copper sulphate crystals at school but it's not what you want in marmalade. You can tell when the sugar's nearly dissolved because the peel starts to look different. It becomes slightly glassy. That's the fruit hardening up. Also the liquid becomes more transparent.' When the sugar has fully dissolved, the marmalade undergoes the thrilling phase known as the 'rolling boil'. This is quite a bit more than a simmer but somewhat less than a full-blown volcanic boil. It might take some fiddling to achieve the right temperature. 'Do you see it rising up the side?' asked the Generalissimo. 'Well, it shouldn't be doing that.'

The rolling boil in a big pan is rather impressive and a bit scary. The golden goo churns and seethes with hundreds of little bubbles. It's the sort of thing that used to be poured on besieging forces from the top of battlements. Had that thought ever occurred to Mrs H?

'No.'

A foam forms amid the churning orangey boil. The effect is a bit like a film of the surface of the sun. Had that ever struck Mrs H?

'No. Are you stirring properly? You should be stirring with a figure-of-eight movement.' Blimey! Hovering over a steamy pan doing figure-of-eight movements with my wooden spoon was not why I came into the kitchen.

There might have been the possibility of a Spartacus-style revolt by the kitchen slave, but for the fact that you don't have to stir constantly during the rolling boil. Once every five minutes is enough to make sure the bottom bit of the marmalade does not burn, though you have to set the timer to make sure you don't forget. The wonderful bittersweet smell compensates for the tedium of the task. In fact, there are wonderful citrus smells of various kinds throughout the marmalade-making process. (Oil from bergamot, an inedible orange, is used in perfumes and Earl Grey tea.) However, this olfactory magic seems to have palled on Mrs H.

'I find the whole thing extremely banal,' she huffed.

But how long does the rolling boil go on for? C. Anne Wilson and other marmalade authorities say fifteen to twenty minutes. A breeze. But Mrs H says, 'Until it's done.'

'Oh.'

'It depends how much pectin there is in the oranges. This seems to vary with the age of the fruit.'

The procedure to tell if it's done, known as 'the wrinkle test', is like something from the age of alchemy. You put a plate in the fridge to get cold. After, say, fifteen minutes, when you think the marmalade might be done, you dribble a small, golden splat on the plate and shove it back in the fridge to get cold. If the dribble forms wrinkles when you push one edge with your finger, the marmalade is done. If there are no wrinkles, the rolling boil goes on. And on. And on. To the accompaniment of increasingly vehement cussing, Mrs H splats and chills and prods. A deep gloom descends. In the case of the most recalcitrant batches, she reaches for the Certo. Sometimes two bottles go in. She glumly insists that it won't set, but it always seems to. There is a danger during this period that the marmalade will burn or, at any rate, caramelise a bit. The result is a dark, opaque preserve approaching mahogany in hue. In common with other aficionados, particularly males, I favour dark-coloured marmalade, but Mrs H doesn't agree. 'It should be clear and golden. Dark marmalade tastes burnt to me.' After a mere hour or so, which involved twelve lots of figure-of-eight stirs, my marmalade obligingly wrinkled. 'Now we start potting!' I said, with the gung-ho enthusiasm of a wet-behind-the-ears greenhorn.

'Not so fast!' barked the boss. 'First we stir in a bit of butter, which takes away the foam and stops bubbles appearing in the finished marmalade. Then leave it to cool for at least twenty minutes or your peel will rise to the top of the jar when you pot it. Marmalade judges don't like uneven distribution of peel.' Quite right too. Neither do I. I forgot to mention that during the rolling boil you also have to get busy with the jam jars. These have to be thoroughly washed, even if new from Lakeland. A dishwasher helps here. Then the jars are sterilised in the oven at 80°C for half an hour or so to kill off any surviving nasties. All v. tedious, not to mention painful when juggling hot jars from the oven, but v. important in order to avoid green mould growing on top of your marmalade. That doesn't go down well with marmalade judges either. Additionally, Mrs H pointed out, if you pot hot marmalade in cold jars, the dread crystallisation can result.

After twenty minutes has expired, you can start potting. This is where the real stickiness starts. After giving the marmalade a final distributive stir, you start bailing with a jug. To ensure that most of the hot syrup gets into the jar, a wide-mouthed funnel is recommended. The marmalade has a slurry-like quality by this stage, so it doesn't so much pour as tumble from the mug into the funnel. Inevitably, there are many sticky spillages. In the case of my batch, three pounds of oranges and six pounds of sugar (plus the water) produced enough marmalade to fill ten one-pound jars. Mrs H complimented me on the efficiency of my output. 'I was only getting eight jars.' When the jars have cooled, you put a little waxed disc of paper on the surface of the marmalade. This may seem like a needless fussiness, but it helps to prevent product contraction.

After the waxed paper discs, you screw on the gingham-patterned lids. Peering at my jars, Mrs H was impressed by the bright, light gold oranginess of my product. Me too. Its clean tang has converted me from my preference for the mahogany-coloured version. A box of homemade Seville orange marmalade is a highly satisfactory thing to have achieved. It is, however, a dangerous thing to boast to chums about. As soon as you mention your marvellous preserve, the other party invariably says, 'Oh, but I love homemade marmalade!' Or, less politely, 'I could take some of that off your hands.' Before you know where you are, your box has declined to a single jar. On the other hand, it's hard to stay shtum when you've converted fruit to gold.

How to eat marmalade

For some time, I was keen on untoasted brown bread and butter as the foundation for my breakfast marmalade. The combination produces a nice puddingy sensation in the mouth. But I've come round to the more orthodox view that marmalade is best on toast. Spreading it thickly – you can scarcely spread a chunky preserve thinly – on well-buttered toast made from good bread produces a sensational combination of textures and tastes – crunchy, chewy, tart, sweet, luxurious, astringent. It is a grown-up way to start the day.

Marmalade does not have to be the gastronomic equivalent of an alarm clock (though the lure of marmalade on toast is very effective in getting me out of bed). It is possible to enjoy its taste at other times and in other ways than the familiar breakfast spread. A few years ago, I held a competition in my column for the best use for marmalade in recipes or snacks as a way of inducing Mrs H to consume her own output.

Despite the measly prize of one pot of Mrs H's marmalade, the entries flowed in by the sackload. Several of the suggestions, though doubtless highly regarded by the entrants, were less than tempting. I didn't feel any great urge to try Shredded Wheat 'carefully prised open', then spread with marmalade and 'eaten like a sandwich'. Same went for marmalade on bread fried in bacon fat. Someone expressed the view that 'marmalade is quite interesting with lemon-marinaded mackerel fillets fried in butter'. Another suggested spreading marmalade on hot cheese on toast. The combination of marmalade and kippers had several advocates ('lovely!'), who were subsequently supported by David Dimbleby, once shown eagerly tucking into this curious gastronomic partnership on television.

The most frequent and plausible suggestion was for the addition of marmalade to bread and butter pudding. Moreover, it worked with Mrs H, who was finally induced to take on board her own product with some eagerness. The winner was a steamy memory from Arundel: 'One of the ways to my heart in the early days of courtship was for my husband to make a bread and butter pudding. Along with the butter, he would spread the bread with marmalade and shavings of stem ginger. The added zip and zest made it into an erotic delight.'

Though it might not compare for arousal, my favourite dessert incorporating marmalade is ice-cream. I first encountered marmalade ice-cream made by Criterion Ices of Suffolk. Accompanied by a warning ('Beware: It bites back a bit'), this excellent product is flavoured with Frank Cooper's Vintage Marmalade. It prompted me to make ice-cream with Mrs H's marmalade. The palate-tingling result, generously laden with frozen chunks of peel, was one of the best grown-up ice-creams I've ever licked. But you don't have to make Seville orange marmalade to enjoy this treat. 'You can use anything from Rose's lime marmalade to ginger marmalade,' the ice-cream expert Robin Weir once told me. 'Even quite nasty marmalades make great ice-creams.'

Mrs H adored marmalade ice-cream but there is another

marmalade item that she likes even more. The marmalade cocktail was a Twenties invention that has recently been revived as the breakfast cocktail. This may seem a bit early for a drink propelled by a hefty slug of gin and a touch of Cointreau, but Mrs H thinks otherwise. 'It's lovely,' she said. 'What a way to start the day.'

Mrs H's recipe for Seville orange marmalade

If you are a marmalade maker, there is no time in the early part of the year for complacency. You have to be up and at it in no uncertain terms. Seville oranges usually make an appearance around the second or third week in January, but they are around for only four weeks. Try to buy the plumpest-looking fruit, as the pith will contain more pectin and therefore will set better. Our marmalade challenges have occurred when we used drier, end-of-season fruit. When it won't set, I reach for pectin, a natural setting agent. Certo is the leading brand.

I use preserving sugar, as it produces a scum-free set with a brighter colour. Because we make marmalade regularly and in quite large quantities, we have a proper preserving pan, but I also use a large stockpot to boil the water and oranges. Whatever you use, make sure it is tall and wide enough to accommodate the rather frightening 'rolling boil', a bubbling, swirling mass of marmalade that is apt to rise up the sides.

Squeezing the juice can be a laborious task. For years I used one of those wooden squeezers, but then I had a

present of an electric juicer – so now this part is easy-peasy
(and quite enjoyable). A wide-mouthed jam-making funnel
is a useful aid for safely transferring the marmalade into a jar
and saves wiping off the dribbles on the outside should you
have an unsteady hand.

You will also need the phone number for Lakeland. You
will probably run out of jars, lids, wax discs, labels, string or
muslin. (In our case, we are likely to have left most of these
items in Yorkshire.) Lakeland usually has all these in stock.
It also offers an emergency next-day delivery service. As you
will see from the recipe, marmalade making takes an age –
so set aside plenty of time.

This is a pretty standard recipe that you will find, with a
few small variations, in most cookbooks that include
marmalade or on bags of preserving sugar. Tried and tested
over a century or more, it is based on Imperial weights, so I
have included them here. It should make between eight to
ten 450g (1lb) jars.

1.4kg Seville oranges (3lb)
juice of 2 lemons
3.4 litres water (6 pints)
2.7kg preserving sugar (6lb)
a small knob of butter

First make sure you have enough glass jars and lids and that
they are washed and clean. If you don't want a recipient to
discover a little fur coat of mould in your marmalade, you
must wash the jars thoroughly in very hot soapy water.

Rinse them well and allow them to dry naturally, or, better still, use a dishwasher. It is also a good idea to place a small plate in the fridge for later use when testing for a set. And make sure you have a sharpened knife for slicing the peel.

Wash the oranges and remove the stalks. Give them a scrub if required. Next, halve the oranges and squeeze out the juice and pips. Do the same with the lemons. Reserve the pips and tie them in a piece of muslin, together with any membrane that has been produced during the squeezing process. Use a long length of string so that you can tie the muslin bag on to the handle of the preserving pan.

The next stage involves slicing the orange peel. (Discard the lemon.) Try to get the segments of peel as even as possible and the same length. I find it easier if I cut each orange in half and then half again. A sharp knife really helps to speed things up. Now place the peel, fruit juices and water in the preserving pan. Tie the muslin bag containing the pips to the handle and plop it into the pan.

Simmer the peel gently until it becomes very soft and the liquid has reduced by about half. It should take about 2 hours to reach this stage. If you can squidge a piece of peel between your finger and thumb, it is soft enough. Remove the muslin bag using its piece of string. Squeeze it well and allow the juice and jelly-like pectin to run into the pan. (At this stage, I warm the clean jars in the oven at 80°C. Cold jars and hot marmalade can result in crystallisation.)

Add the sugar to the pan, heating it gently and stirring until the sugar has completely dissolved. Bring the marmalade to a rolling boil (there should be lots of little bubbles). Maintain this until the setting point has been reached – it should take around 15 minutes. Test for a set by placing a small amount of marmalade on a plate you have chilled in the fridge. Replace in the fridge and check the plate after a minute. If the splat runs all over the plate, the marmalade needs further boiling. If it forms a wrinkle when you press the splat with a finger, you're done.

Take the marmalade off the heat. Stir in a small knob of butter, which has the effect of removing any scum that has formed on the surface. Now let it stand for 20 minutes before potting. Fill the jars right up to the rim – I use a jug and a jam funnel. This can be a very sticky phase, but you have to fill the jars as much as possible. Marmalade shrinks as it cools and you do not want to create a large air space. When it has cooled sufficiently, screw the lids on tightly, and if required, add a label. Then all you have to do is wash up and find somewhere to store all the jars until you are able to give them away. I am compelled to keep a few, since someone in our house likes a bit of marmalade with his breakfast. I rarely eat it – too sticky on the fingers.

Marmalade bread and butter pudding

85g butter, softened
225g good quality white bread, sliced
1 x 454g jar good quality Seville orange marmalade
15g fresh ginger root, peeled and grated
2 large eggs
2 egg yolks
a pinch of salt
1 heaped tablespoon caster sugar
275ml full cream milk
125ml double cream

Butter the bread and spread with marmalade (you will
probably use about half a jar). Sprinkle grated ginger over
the marmalade. Lay the slices in a buttered baking dish so
they overlap. Beat together the eggs and yolks with the salt
and sugar and mix in the milk and cream. Pour the egg
mixture over the bread slices and leave to soak for 20
minutes. Put into the oven, preheated to 180°C/Gas Mark
4, and bake for 40 minutes until golden brown. This
pudding should serve four people.

Marmalade ice-cream

Since this recipe uses raw egg, you should be certain of the
freshness and quality of your eggs. It should not be eaten by
people who are pregnant or susceptible to infection. To
avoid any risk you should first make the egg, sugar and
cream into a custard (details in any ice-cream book) and
allow to cool. This recipe makes about 1 litre of ice-cream.

3 fresh, free-range egg yolks
300g marmalade
   (chunky Seville orange marmalade works best)
2 tablespoons orange juice
500ml whipping cream
30g caster sugar

Thoroughly amalgamate the egg yolks, marmalade, orange
juice, cream and sugar by stirring in a bowl. Pour the
contents of the bowl into an ice-cream maker and churn
until the mixture has thickened to the consistency of soft
whipped cream. Scoop into a plastic container and freeze.
Remove from the freezer 20 minutes before serving.

Breakfast cocktail

1 teaspoon orange marmalade
50ml gin
15ml Cointreau
juice of ½ a lemon

To make one cocktail, stir the marmalade with the gin in
the base of the shaker until dissolved. Add the other
ingredients and shake very vigorously, with ice. Strain into a
cocktail glass. The suggestion in one cocktail guide to
garnish with a slice of toast on the rim takes the breakfast
metaphor too literally.

THE LURE OF THE COOKBOOK

IF MRS H WAS IRKED by the sticky slog of marmalade, a more chronic irritant was my burgeoning collection of cookbooks, which clogged her formerly tidy domain. Alongside her well-thumbed classics appeared works from distant and little known areas of gastronomy. Elizabeth David had to budge over for *Noshe Djan: Afghan Food & Cookery*. Delia was elbowed aside for *The International Squid Cookbook*. Robert Carrier rubbed shoulders with the *Ava Gardner Cookbook* (very sound on macaroni cheese).

'Do we really need a book of recipes from the eighteenth-century navy?' Mrs H grizzled one day. 'I don't really fancy boiled shit.' I should explain that this was not a cloacal expletive from my wife. It is the name of a dish in *Lobscouse & Spotted Dog* by Anne Chotzinoff Grossman and Lisa Grossman Thomas, a gastronomic companion to the seafaring novels of Patrick O'Brian. Boiled shit is exactly what its name suggests: '1oz assorted seabird guano, ¼ cup rainwater. Gather the guano in a large clam shell. Gradually add the water, stirring constantly. Set in a hot sun until it boils. Serves one.' The authors of the book say, 'We made it, but we do not claim to have drunk it.'

In my view, every decent cookbook collection should find room for items that, while not being exactly appetising, are still of interest. Irritatingly preoccupied with the practical, my wife feels differently. In order to dispel Mrs H's urge to ditch *Lobscouse & Spotted Dog*, which happens to be a highly enjoyable culinary adventure, I made lobscouse, a dish that gave the name 'Scouser' to Liverpudlians and is also popular in the ports of the Baltic. (Spotted dog is spotted dick by another name.) With one exception, the ingredients for lobscouse – corned beef, smoked ham, onion, leek, potato and spices – were easily obtained. What I couldn't get hold of was '8 ounces Ship's Biscuit', incorporated in the recipe in crumb form. Though tempted by a tip for beating the dough ('put in a stout bag and repeatedly drive a car over it'), I settled instead for Bath Oliver biscuits. The lobscouse, which proved to be a rather superior version of corned beef hash, went down well with Mrs H. She is a big fan of corned beef hash.

The problem about finding room for several hundred food books was exacerbated by their bulk. Cookbooks tend to be on the big size and the bigger the cook (at least in reputation), the bigger the book. It proved particularly difficult to persuade Mrs H about the merits of my three largest cookbooks. There isn't a single recipe in their collective 2,137 pages that anyone but a mad culinary obsessive would want to attempt. Mrs H staggered when a deliveryman handed over *A Day at elBulli*, by the Spanish culinary genius Ferran Adrià. Unfortunately, its practical value was less than staggering. The 528 pages are bulked out by double-page spreads of dubious value including:

    a) a collection of model bulldogs (*bulli* means bulldog);

    b) the raking of gravel at the entrance to the restaurant;

    c) the delivery of bottles to the recycling bin.

Though the book contains thirty recipes, including such treats as 'preserved tuna oil air' and 'freeze-dried cold white miso foam', a note explained that they were not intended to be attempted by the likes of us: 'The technical level requires specialist equipment … and professional experience to achieve good results.'

Like the Chrysler Building being overshadowed by the Empire State Building, Adrià's monster was outsized by the 529 pages of Heston Blumenthal's *The Big Fat Duck Cookbook*. Having already essayed his recipes for snail porridge for a newspaper (when we were faxed the recipe from Blumenthal's kitchen, it omitted any indication of when to add the snails) and Black Forest gateau (see page 291), we felt scant desire to have a bash at salmon poached in a liquorice gel, radish ravioli of oyster, etc.

Bigger even than Blumenthal's behemoth was Alain Ducasse's scarcely liftable *Culinary Encyclopaedia*. Contrary to the title, there was very little in its 1,080 pages that appeared feasible for the amateur (even the simplest are complicated in some way – 'crispy country bacon with a truffled salad of pig's head') and an entire section is possibly illegal in the UK, not that I had any desire to eat thrush, whether accompanied by apples, giblet canapés, chanterelles or polenta. It would take a particularly greedy and ruthless gastronome to buy songbirds for the pot.

'You did buy some little birds – very probably songbirds – to eat once,' interjects Mrs H undiplomatically. 'Do you remember that tin?'

Thank you, dear. I'm glad you brought that up. It happened during a brief infatuation with Chinese food. In a rash moment, I bought a tin from a Chinese supermarket that carried not a word of any European language on the label. It felt a bit light. I opened it with a trepidation that turned out to be well merited. Inside, there were half a dozen little birds standing in something congealed.

'Why did you buy it?' asked my wife. 'There's a picture of a nest of birds on the label.'

'I thought it was a trademark.'

No, we didn't, since you ask. The Oriental birds went in the bin untasted.

Anyway, back to books. Instead of the outré and challenging dishes proposed by the three modern masters, I felt the urge to try some recipes from another compendious work. Pioneering but solidly middle-class, it became the foundation stone of British cooking when first published in 1861. But where was I going to find scope for adventure in *Mrs Beeton's Book of Household Management?* Turtle soup was possibly too adventurous ('To make this soup with less difficulty, cut off the head of the turtle the preceding day'). Even mock turtle soup was rather demanding ('half a calf's head'). Prince of Wales's soup with '12 turnips, 1 lump of sugar, 2 spoonfuls of strong veal stock …' was ruled out due to Ms H's aversion to turnips. Sago soup? Mutton pudding? Not quite right for persuading Mrs H about the merits of Mrs B. I'd almost given up hope of turning the culinary clock back 150 years when in section 1,408 I struck gold or, to be precise, white.

Mrs H recalled the moment. '"Blancmange," you said. "Let's do blancmange!" You got out Mrs Beeton and showed me ancient pictures of jellies and blancmange. You got so excited that you took Mrs Beeton off to bed with you. Good grief, I thought, what kind of person gets excited by blancmange?'

7

The joy of blancmange

I CONCEDE THAT THERE may have been more alluring chapter headings in food literature. The word sort of sits there like the substance it describes. Mrs H's reaction when I conceived a desire to make blancmange after coming across several tempting recipes in Mrs Beeton was not encouraging. 'Oh, no, not that horrible cornfloury stuff. I must have been eight when I last had it. I remember that the chocolate one was particularly bad. Brown & Polson have a lot to answer for …'

'No, I want to do a proper one, a little castle with turrets, like you see in Mrs Beeton.'

'Turrets?'

'Yes, look here. You do it in a mould with sweet and bitter almonds. Where do we get isinglass?'

'Isinglass? Have you come unhinged?' Thus began an epic exploration of blancmange, which went beyond the pages of Mrs Beeton.

Blancmange is the laughing stock of the dinner table. George & Weedon Grossmith utilised the dessert to torment Charles Pooter, the baffled hero of their 1892 masterpiece *The Diary of a Nobody*. 'November 18. I told Sarah not to bring up the BLANC-MANGE for breakfast ... In spite of my instructions, that BLANC-MANGE was brought up for supper. To make things worse, there had been an attempt to disguise it, by placing it in a glass bowl with jam round it. I told Carrie, when we were alone, if that BLANC-MANGE were placed on the table again, I would walk out of the home.' Poor Mr Pooter, hounded out by a pud.

Yet the hilarity is misplaced. A properly made blancmange is an impressive and tasty dessert. Tinged with almond and lemon, it is certainly the equal of trendy pannacotta. Moreover, blancmange is endowed with a mysterious and exotic lineage. The word is obviously French – their version is *blancmanger* – and, though it arrived in medieval times, we continue to pronounce this white-food in the French manner.

Blancmange originally referred to a family of substantial medieval dishes, often, though not necessarily, sweetened and usually containing chicken or fish. They were white, but not jellified. According to *Cooking and Dining in Medieval England* by Peter Brears, the recipes all included 'rice cooked to softness, ground with almond milks and either hen or capon, or fish such as lobster, haddock, carp, dace, ray, pike, perch or tench, the whole being ... a smooth paste, dished and garnished.' The pale, unresisting result would have been welcome in a pre-denture era. It seems that the French borrowed the word from the Italian *biancomangiare*. The almond element of the dish suggests an Arab origin, but regiments of food historians have tried without success to track down the provenance of blanc-mange. *The Oxford Companion to Food* hedges its bets: 'It seems likely that *blancmanger* does reflect eastern influence, but the exact source and path are obscure.'

Befitting a nation of gastronomic traditionalists, the Italians still eat a *biancomangiare* soup. Pulverised chicken breast is stirred into chicken stock thickened with cream, rice flour and fresh ground almonds. The result is garnished with strips of chicken breast, chopped dill and a few pomegranate seeds. I made this pallid broth for Mrs H and it went down a storm. 'Very good chicken soup,' she said, gazing at the steamy white pond with its gem-like archipelago of pomegranate. 'Very rich and creamy, with an interesting range of flavours. Rather memorable. Well worth doing again.'

Blanc-Mange (A Supper Dish)

Despite the merits of this medieval meal-in-itself, blanc-mange (at least in Britain) became identified with the familiar jelly pudding. With the exception of Charles Pooter, the Victorians could not get enough of it. Rightly ignoring Brown & Polson's dire cornflour version invented in 1854, *Mrs Beeton's Book of Household Management* (1861) included a social hierarchy of three tiers of blancmange: 'Blanc-Mange (A Supper Dish)', 'Arrowroot Blanc-Mange (An Inexpensive Supper Dish)' and 'Cheap Blanc-Mange'.

In a moment of rash extravagance, we plumped for

Blanc-Mange (A Supper Dish). Mrs B's recipe requires isinglass, obtained from the swimming bladders of fish, particularly sturgeon, to impart the requisite stiffness, but we sacrificed authenticity and went for gelatine. This is a similar jellifying agent extracted from the bones of cattle and horses. Pig skin also makes a contribution. The transmutation of such gruesome items into the pure transparency of gelatine is one of the stranger gastronomic metamorphoses. (Vegetarians may prefer to try out the carrageen moss pudding described on page 130.) Since Mrs H is an old hand with gelatine, she guided me through the mysteries of blancmange-making.

'Have you got clean hands?' The inquiry might have come from Mrs Beeton herself. (See page 988 of her *Household Management*: '"Cleanliness is next to godliness," saith the proverb.')

'No. I got them specially dirty before I came into the kitchen.'

'I didn't know that we had Mr Clever-Clever in the kitchen.'

You start Blanc-Mange (A Supper Dish) by warming a pint of milk with 'the rind of half a lemon' (we used a zester). The smell was sensational. Calculating the proportion of gelatine to liquid proved problematic, though at first it seemed straightforward. The packet contained fifteen leaves of gelatine – they are moulded with a diamond pattern like very small mullion windows – sufficient to jellify two pints of liquid. So, we needed seven and a half leaves. You chop up the little panes, then soak them and squeeze – a strange, clammy sensation that somehow hints at the organic origin of this ingredient. It was only after completing this task that one of us ('It was me,' says Mrs H) remembered that the recipe also contained one pint of cream, which is added at a later stage. 'So we have to use all fifteen leaves,' I pointed out.

'Doh!' said Mrs H.

When these had been soaked and squeezed, the flaccid gelatine was added to the lemon-infused milk. 'I generally add it in small quantities,' advised Mrs H. 'NOT A GREAT LUMP!' I reduced my speed of addition but not sufficiently. 'You're still putting in great wodges!' Mrs H said the milk should be gently warmed to ensure the gelatine dissolves. This, she added, applies particularly to gelatine in great wodges.

When the gelatine has dissolved, you add pounded almonds, which provides a pleasing link with the dish's medieval prototype. Mrs Beeton's recipe calls for both sweet and bitter almonds. You can buy the sweet ones anywhere, and we acquired the latter in a Chinese supermarket. While I was pounding them in a mortar and pestle (damned hard work – has no one thought of bringing out an electric version?), I was reminded of an expostulation frequently seen in detective yarns when the sleuth would sniff the lips of a corpse: 'The tell-tale smell of bitter almonds. Prussic acid!' This is an old term for hydrogen cyanide. Less lethally, bitter almonds also smell a bit like marzipan. The mixture of pounded bitter almonds and ordinary ground almonds was stirred into the milk. 'I want you to taste the

flavour before we slowly bring it to the boil,' said Mrs H.
Never averse to sampling, I had a go. It tasted lemony
and almondy. This is only what you would expect, but still
rather good. 'Can you see here?' Mrs H added, a few minutes later. 'These little bubbles starting to appear – that
means it's just starting to boil.'

'Ah, how interesting. I'd never associated bubbles with
boiling before.' But my sarcasm was lost on Mrs H.

'They're not the big bubbles you get when something's
boiling. It's *tiny* foam because it's just below boiling. If
we were to bung in a thermometer it would be 200°F or
something.' (Mrs H shows her age.) She then strained the
mixture through a muslin-lined sieve. It emerged in a slow,
reluctant stream. 'Just let it drain through.' When the
trickle ceased, Mrs H picked up the edges of the muslin so
it formed a sort of bag and squeezed out the last remaining
drops of milk. I then measured a pint of cream and added
it to the strained milk. 'Stir the mixture occasionally until
nearly cold,' says Mrs Beeton.

At this point, the recipe entered my specialist area. Mrs
Beeton says 'noyeau, maraschino, curaçao or any favourite
liqueur, added in small proportions, very much enhances
this always favourite dish'. Though we were plumb out of
crème de noyeau (an almond liqueur), we happened to have
both maraschino (a sweet cherry liqueur) and Cointreau (a
variant of curaçao). Since we were using two plastic moulds
– somewhat like castles though lacking in turrets – I was
able to try out both forms of alcoholic enhancement.

All was going swimmingly until Mrs H picked up the

measuring jug. 'Which scale did you use for the milk and cream?'

'That one for half a pint,' I said pointing to a Plimsoll line on the side. 'I did each one twice over.'

'That measures a third of a pint,' she said icily.

'Oh. How will that affect it?'

'I don't know.'

Using two-thirds of the correct quantity of liquid certainly ensured a firm set after a few hours in the fridge. Mrs H picked up one of the moulds, inverted it over a plate and shook it to extract the blancmange. Nothing happened. She shook harder, then harder still. Vibrating in every molecule, she resembled a road-digger with an old-fashioned pneumatic drill. Even though she had taken care to lubricate the mould with almond oil before filling with blancmange mix, as Mrs Beeton suggested, the shaking was singularly unproductive. 'Hmm,' I mused. 'Mrs Beeton says, "It should come out easily."'

'Does she now?'

I took over the shaking. Nothing. Mrs H applied a knife round the side, at first delicately, which still had no effect when she shook, then she really put the knife in, which did the job. Neither of our blancmange castles was quite intact after being coaxed from their moulds, but I maintained that the slightly battered appearance added to their appeal. 'Not too bad,' said Mrs H. 'A little bit chewy. The maraschino blancmange tastes quite strong. I actually prefer the Cointreau. It complements the almond and lemon without taking over.'

Our Victorian dessert worked well when combined with a mixture of soft fruits, though Mrs H thought we had made too much blancmange. 'Two large blancmanges for two people is a bit overwhelming.' We managed to get through quite a lot of these super-strength puds before waving the *blanc* flag. Like Mr Pooter, we found it not quite so appealing on the second day. 'I think blancmange should be eaten on the day you make it,' said Mrs H. 'After that, it shrinks and gets a bit hard.' When we did it again for a dinner party, Mrs H used individual silicone moulds, which performed perfectly at the evacuation stage. Served with a sprinkling of raspberries, the little blancmanges were a huge success with our guests. 'This one is a bit less stiff on account of me putting in the right quantity of milk and cream,' she explained.

Seaside blancmange

There is only one dessert to be found in the 512 pages of Alan Davidson's book *North Atlantic Seafood*. The solitary seafaring pud utilises carrageen (*Chondrus crispus*), a handsome seaweed found particularly in the south-west of Ireland, where the village of Carragheen donated its name (though the spelling changed a bit). You can buy little packets of dried carrageen, which are usually accompanied by a sprinkling of tiny shells. One of the best things about making this dish is watching the desiccated tangles reconstitute as gorgeous fronds of cream and purple in tepid water. It is as though you were gazing into a particularly clean and wholesome rock pool. However, as we shall see, this ingredient can have a certain shock value.

Davidson's recipe is for chocolate carrageen, but I was more interested in carrageen moss pudding, which I had enjoyed at the end of a boozy lunch at Ballymaloe House, near Cork. I remember the carrageen pudding made by Myrtle Allen, doyenne of Hibernian cuisine, as a light, but distinctive blancmange. Maybe I detected a very slight maritime tinge, but, given the circs, my recollection might not be all that accurate.

You don't need much carrageen to make carrageen moss pudding. According to *Irish Traditional Cooking* by Myrtle's daughter-in-law Darina Allen, 'The success of this dish lies in using only just enough carrageen needed to get a set – so you don't taste it in the pudding.' She recommends '8 grams (1 semi-closed fistful)'. Davidson suggested 'two good handfuls', but he described the seaweed tang as 'delicious'. Of course, all this depends on the size of your fist. Mine are on the big side, so one sufficed. I suppose we put 10–12g in the tepid water.

Most recipes tell you to fish out the shells but Mrs H pooh-poohed all that: 'We're going to strain it anyway.' After ten minutes in tepid water, you recover the softened fronds and use them to jellify 900ml milk. The recipe (see page 135) is a bit of a palaver, involving simmering, sieving, adding egg yolk, leaving to cool and folding in egg white. 'It's a leisurely pudding,' observed Mrs H. 'You do something, then you go away, then you come back and do something else, then comes the worrying bit when you see if the wretched thing has set.'

While it was cooling, I tried a bit of the jellified milk. This did not go down well with Mrs H. 'I want that. I want that. That bit you've put in your mouth. There won't be any left.' My explanation that the sampling was purely for research purposes did little to mollify her. But she got even more agitated after accidentally putting her hand on a frond of softened carrageen that had escaped into the sink. 'ARGH!' If she had encountered Tennyson's monstrous Kraken ('Far, far beneath in the abysmal sea,/His ancient, dreamless, uninvaded sleep/The Kraken sleepeth'), the effect could scarcely have been more momentous. 'I did not like that. It felt all slippery, like something horrid you see at the seaside.' This is not a problem you get with Brown & Polson.

After a few hours in the fridge, the carrageen had achieved a light set. 'It doesn't exactly shimmy in the bowl but it does slither around,' said Mrs H. It was a vanilla-speckled mousse without the slightest marine taint. Darina Allen would have approved. 'Do you like it?' inquired Mrs H.

'Well, yes.'

'What's wrong?'

'I expected it to be more assertive.'

'It's very melt-in-the-mouth. There are little puffs of air in it. It's very nice and not too sweet.'

'That's all very well, but little puffs of air are not my idea of pud. I might have preferred more of a seaweed taste. We'll try that next time.'

'Who says there's going to be a next time?'

Mrs H on Mrs Beeton's blancmange

Erase any memories of childhood blancmanges; this dish
turned out to be a wonderful surprise. With a subtle, grown-
up taste, it has become a favourite dessert. Any berried fruit
will go well with it. Use the most Victorian-looking jelly
mould you can find for that impressive turreted look. You
just can't pull off the same effect with a rabbit shape.

The ingredients listed will be enough to fill a 1.1litre jelly
mould. You should be able to buy almond oil from a
chemist or a health food shop. This oil aids the release of the
blancmange from the mould. You only need a little but
make sure any tricky bits are well coated. This recipe was
originally based on Imperial weights, so I have included
them here.

**rind from ½ a large lemon (wash and scrub it well if it is
    unwaxed)**
600ml milk (1 pint)
110g caster sugar (4 oz)
**35g fine leaf gelatine (or enough to set 600ml/
    1 pint of liquid)**
**15g ground almonds (½ oz) (or a mixture of sweet and
    bitter almonds, which Mrs Beeton recommends)**
600ml double cream (1 pint)
a little almond oil to lubricate the mould

There is quite a leisurely start to the recipe, so begin by
taking the rind from the lemon (I use a potato peeler). Pour
the milk into a saucepan, add the lemon rind and sugar and
place it over a *very* low heat until the milk is well flavoured.
You can have a little taste to check. Turn off the heat when
you are satisfied with the taste. You should get the smell and
tang of the lemon rind.

Next prepare the gelatine according to the instructions on
the packet. When it has softened, add the gelatine to the
milk mix, making sure it is well dissolved. Then stir in the
ground almonds. (Either blanch whole almonds and
vigorously pound to a paste, or purchase ready-ground
almonds. Both work well.)

Returning the pan to the heat, allow the milk to just
come to the boil. Then remove from the heat and strain the
liquid through a fine sieve lined with muslin into a jug.
(Discard the lemon rind and almond gunk.)

Add the cream and stir the mixture occasionally until it is
nearly cold. Let it stand for a few minutes for the mixture to
settle. Then carefully pour the mixture into the mould,
which should be previously oiled with the almond oil. Avoid
pouring in the sediment that has collected in the bottom of
the jug (this would spoil the appearance of the blancmange
with gritty-looking bits). Put the filled mould into the fridge
to firm up.

When the blancmange has set, turn it out of the mould
by loosening the edges a little with a knife. Then, placing
your serving plate on the top of the mould, invert it, give a

vigorous shake and out it should plop. The almond oil gives a glisten to the finished dish.

Mrs Beeton suggests that the flavour of the blancmange can be varied by substituting vanilla or bay leaves for the lemon and almonds. You can also add liqueurs such as Cointreau or maraschino.

Mrs H's recipe for carrageen moss pudding

This is such a surprising dish. How something that looks like a bird's nest can so quickly be transformed into a dish with a delicate sweetened hint of the sea always amazes me. It is a raw egg recipe – so you will have to miss out if you cannot eat eggs in this form. This pudding serves four to six people.

1 tablespoon dried carrageen moss
900ml whole milk
1 fresh, free-range egg
1 tablespoon caster sugar
½ teaspoon vanilla extract

Soak the carrageen in tepid water for 10 minutes. Then strain, put it into a saucepan with the milk and bring slowly to the boil. Put a lid on the saucepan and simmer the carrageen and milk for 20 minutes.

Separate the egg and place the yolk in a bowl. Add the sugar and vanilla essence and whisk together for a few seconds, then pour the milk and carrageen through a strainer on to the egg yolk mixture, whisking all the time. You will need to rub the jelly exuded by the carrageen through the strainer and beat it into the liquid. This should thicken as you beat. Test a sample for set on a saucer. It should set in a couple of minutes. If not, rub more jelly through the strainer. Finally, whisk the egg white to a good stiffness and fold it in gently. Leave the pudding to cool.

Serve chilled with soft brown sugar and cream or some kind of poached fruit compote. Rhubarb works well. Yum.

TOOLS FOR THE JOB

WHILE I MAY BE TO BLAME (mostly) for the accumulation of food books that line the walls of three rooms in our house, I am relatively innocent – well, not quite so guilty – concerning the vast quantity of utensils and cutlery that fills every one of our kitchen cupboards and drawers to bursting. The spectacle of the man of the house swearing furiously, with veins sticking out on his forehead as he tries to heave open a jammed drawer, is a frequent *divertissement* in our house.

Adopting the role of Grand Inquisitor, I put Mrs H in the dock concerning our excess of equipment. 'Why do we have three woks when we rarely, if ever, eat stir-fry?'

'One arrived by default.'

'What do you mean "by default"?'

'I bought the Le Creuset wok in a mad moment. It's a bit too big and heavy for everyday use. The other one is a rather posh Chinese wok. I use it all the time, but not as a wok. I use it for steaming asparagus.'

'And the other wok?'

'I don't count that as a wok. It's more of a saucepan that looks like a wok.'

'What about that metal mallet thing for bashing out steaks? We never use it on steaks.'

'No, but we use it for beef olives.'

'When have we ever had a beef olive?'

Though she admits inheriting a gadget gene from her father, Mrs H sturdily defended her acquisitions. 'I quite like the potato ricer and the jar key for popping the lids off jars. I couldn't live without the slotted spoon, kitchen tongs, digital scales or scissors.'

'But why do we need four pairs of kitchen scissors?'

'We just do. Don't worry about it. After the stick blender, my most important gadget is a skewer. There's no better way of seeing if fish or chicken is done. Anyway, my gadgets are small. Yours are huge, like the electric meat slicer.'

'It's very useful.'

'We only got it because you brought back a ton of salami and cured meat from Italy. And you were responsible for the ice-cream maker and the food mixer and the bread maker and the espresso machine.'

'But we use all those.'

'How about the cataplana thing you brought back from Portugal?'

Well, yes, there was that. When I was on a press trip to Portugal I became obsessed with the desire to acquire a cataplana. Somewhat like a small wok but with a high, hinged lid that is clamped shut during cooking to conserve flavour, it is primarily used for *ameijoas na cataplana*, an excellent stew of pork and clams. When I tracked down a cataplana, my friend Rose Prince, who was also on the trip, predicted: 'You'll never use it.' To prove her wrong, I made *ameijoas na cataplana* the instant I returned. Admittedly, I've never used the cataplana since then, but its day will come.

'Its day will come, huh?' scoffed Mrs H. 'Just like the conical strainer you brought back from Spain to make fish soup. I'm still waiting for my first bowlful. Or the chestnut pan you brought back from France.'

'How can its day come when you chucked it out? '

'We had it for six years and you never used it once. It was purely decorative. Well, as decorative as a rusty frying pan with lots of holes can be.'

Rarely a day passes when I don't regret the loss of the chestnut pan, which you can also use for smoking mussels over a certain kind of pine needle. I feel its lack constantly. Same goes for the salamander that I saw in Languedoc. This is the somewhat fanciful name for a long-handled iron disc that you heat in the fire or on a gas ring. When warmed to red heat, it is used for caramelising the top of the dessert known as *crème catalan*. Outside the shop, I pondered endlessly over this item but was dissuaded by Mrs H. Madness. What could be more vital? I would far sooner have a salamander than our two weedy blowtorches that take an aeon to scorch a crème brûlée. Not that we ever have crème brûlée.

In truth, neither of us feels much restraint where kitchen

gadgets are concerned. We may not have a decent screw-driver in the house, but I know that somewhere (it may take a bit of finding) we have the precise implement to pit an olive, scale a sea bass, shuck an oyster, bisect a lobster, zest a lime, julienne a carrot and extract the pinbones from a trout. Though justified on the erroneous premise that the right tool will transform prowess, these items have a mysterious appeal that is not necessarily linked to practicality. This is evident from Mrs H's wish list. 'Apart from an outdoor hot tub [not strictly speaking a culinary device], I'd really like an outdoor smoker and one of those things for grilling a dozen sardines at the same time, but they're fantastically expensive. And I'd like one of those French hinged moulds for raised pies but they're even more expensive than the sardine rack.'

We may be nuts about kitchen gizmos, but there are a few we don't want. We have survived without toaster, microwave or pressure cooker. Toast seems to have more character when done under the grill. Anyway, it's im-possible to do Welsh rabbit in a toaster. Both of us are indifferent to microwaves, which are more to do with heating than with cooking. Though some people swear by pressure cookers, Mrs H has yet to recover from childhood trauma caused by one. 'My mother had one that scared the living daylights out of me, hissing away like a mad swan.' And I was put off the damn things after a depressing experience in Brittany. We were staying in a holiday cottage with our Parisian friends. One day, I spent a fortune on a free-range, organic poulet noir. Unfortunately, the cottage was not equipped with an oven (a fairly vital culinary gadget in my view), but there was a pressure cooker. A wonderfully fragrant blast of steam emerged when I released the valve. Opening the cooker, I speared the chicken with a fork and lifted it out. The bird was so tender that it tore free of the fork and fell – PLOP! – on to the floor. Our friends looked at each other: '*Cuisine rosbif!*' I recovered an untainted breast of poulet noir and took a nibble. It was utterly tasteless. All the flavour was in the steam.

There is one gadget that, above all others, manages to be irresistibly alluring (at least to foodies) but is scarcely ever used. The idea of a machine to make pasta has a powerful appeal for the food-obsessed, though there is an equally strong reason for not going through the fag of actually using it. You may just have noticed that most supermarkets carry a vast range of pasta. I once heard someone express an eternal truth concerning the pasta machine: 'The first week, you use it three times. The second week, you use it twice. The third week, you use it once. After that, it disappears into a cupboard and you go back to buying pasta from the supermarket.'

The Hirst household didn't even achieve this. We only managed to make pasta twice. The first time, Mrs H's tagliatelle resembled a collection of very short, fat, twisted twigs. They looked like Jiminy Cricket's furled umbrella. The second time, Mrs H attempted to make spinach and ricotta ravioli, which resulted in half a dozen squashed triangles of such unearthly bizarreness that I burst out laughing. Mrs H was so miffed that the pasta machines disappeared into the cupboard. Yes, the plural is intentional. Machines. We managed not to make pasta even though we have two pasta machines. Even in a household that makes a speciality of superfluous culinary equipment, this was ridiculous. Eventually, sheer weight of machinery won the case for homemade pasta. When Mrs H's dudgeon subsided, we returned to the knotty problem of spaghetti, tagliatelle, linguine etc.

8

Slower pasta

THIS IS HOW WE MANAGED to acquire two pasta machines. Mrs H bought me a pasta machine as a birthday present. 'You said you always wanted one,' she said, though I had no memory of ever making such a request. Anyway, I had one now. In its favour, the pasta machine has a pleasing heft. It gleams in a meaningful way and has a solid handle for turning. A very satisfactory gadget – as long as you actually use it. This culinary hurdy-gurdy has two functions. First, there is a stainless steel wringer whose ever-decreasing settings are used for squeezing pasta dough into sheets. Second, rollers can be fitted to cut the sheets into tagliatelle, fettuccine and, less successfully, ravioli. Soon after receiving this unexpected gift, I was given a second pasta machine, which came as an accessory with our KitchenAid food mixer. It works along the same lines as the first, except that it attaches to the drive shaft of the mixer, much like the power take-off on a tractor.

Notwithstanding this excess of pasta machines, we continued buying dried pasta. The chef Rowley Leigh is all in favour of this intransigence. 'The mystery to me is why

anybody bothers at all since the results are usually so dire,'
he wrote about homemade pasta. 'The packet stuff is
usually much better.' Moreover, buying it is a bit easier than
making it. Others have felt the same over the years. In the
eighteenth century, Naples had 280 pasta shops and many
more mobile pasta sellers. It is a shame that the Neapolitan
method of eating spaghetti in the street has died out. It
involved 'raising the strands at arm's length and gradually
lowering them into one's mouth'.

Yet, powerful, even imperative arguments for DIY pasta
have been advanced by two of the finest Italian cooks. 'In
about half an hour you can have [pasta] that has real
personality and you have the satisfaction of knowing all the
ingredients that went into it,' urges Giorgio Locatelli. 'I
promise you, once you get the feel of it, it will seem like
therapy, not a job.' Marcella Hazan goes even further. 'I
don't know of anything you can make in your kitchen that
yields such generous returns on as modest an investment of
time and effort as egg pasta.' I don't think I've encountered
a more persuasive statement in the whole of gastronomy.

Despite feeling Rowley's sceptical eye over my shoulder,
I determined to master homemade pasta. Mrs H, who had
been on a pasta-making course since the Jiminy Cricket
debacle, directed operations. The first step is to make the
dough, which involved sieving 250g of '00' (extra-fine)
pasta flour to make it even more extra fine. This is piled
in a mound in the centre of your work surface. You need
a good deal of work surface when making pasta. The
charming Italian name for this mound is *fontana di farina*

(fountain of flour). You make a well in the middle of the *fontana* and form a little lake by cracking in two eggs and the yolk from a third.

Everything was fine so far, but that was about to change. 'You're not going to like this bit,' Mrs H cackled horribly. 'You're going to go, "Urgh!"' The mixing technique involves plunging a hand into the middle of the lake in order to combine the eggs and the flour. I once saw Locatelli do it with effortless brio. He whirled his fingers a few times like a human whisk and, a moment or two later, the result was a nice, clean blob of dough. When I did it, the flour fountain exploded across the work surface, while the eggs overflowed their crater and headed for freedom. 'Looks rather like Mount Etna,' said Mrs H. This was probably accurate, since she once saw the volcano in eruption, but not very helpful. I managed to dam the yolky rivulets with flour and attempted to start making the dough, but the materials proved remarkably reluctant to combine. Very quickly, my fingers became impossibly caked with egg and flour. I went, 'Urgh!'

My advice in such circs is to use a knife (preferably blunt) to peel your fingers. In order to counter the stickiness, Marcella Hazan has a wise suggestion. (It comes as no surprise to learn she has two PhDs.) She recommends using a fork to scramble the eggs lightly and mix with the flour 'until these are no longer runny'. So do I.

Just when you have given up all hope, the eggs and flour cohere. At this point, you can start kneading. 'First spread a little flour over your work surface and put the dough in the middle,' said Mrs H. 'Use the heels of your palms to press the dough. You have to press and push so you're stretching the dough. Fold it in half from the top, then push and press again. Push, press, fold. Push, press, fold.' The chant might have come from a slave-master on a galley. Had this been the case, there would have been a spot of whip-cracking at this stage, for my efforts were regarded as inadequate. 'No, not like that,' Mrs H tutted. 'At present, you're just pressing down on the dough as if you want to push it through the table. You want to push it from the shoulders rather than the elbows – like a cat having a stretch.'

It took me a while to get the knack. What you have to do is push at the midway point of the lump with the heels of both palms – you push it away, but at the same time slightly downwards – before folding and doing it again. 'That's exactly what I said,' huffed Mrs H. 'Push, press, fold.'

In order to stretch the gluten in the flour, which makes the pasta both strong and elastic, you have to do this for at least ten minutes, which feels like half an hour. But I can see what Locatelli means by 'therapy'. In the end, it is quite satisfying. You feel you've achieved something when the dough suddenly transforms under your hands into a firm, smooth lump with a silky sheen on its surface. For the first time in years, I had learned a new skill. But you don't want to overdo the kneading. Locatelli warns that if you continue beyond this moment, 'You can break the gluten strands.' I felt no urge to keep going one second longer than necessary. When the dough is in tip-top nick, you wrap it in clingfilm and leave it to rest for an hour. (Don't leave it overnight like we did with a second batch. The pasta becomes too relaxed and badly behaved.)

At this point, you have a choice. You can either use a machine to roll out the pasta or tackle it with a vast rolling pin (thirty-two inches is the recommended length). Marcella Hazan says mastering the latter method will endow you with 'one of the most precious skills that a cook can command' and the result will have 'a succulence that no other pasta can match', but it's not simple. She devotes five pages to describing the technique. When I suggested it as a possibility to Mrs H, she rolled her eyes skyward.

We were going to use one of our pasta machines. They are somewhat less demanding than a thirty-two-inch rolling pin. After considering the matter for all of two seconds, Mrs H plumped for the electric-powered pasta roller. (If you haven't got one, you may be better off. Our friend Giorgio Alessio, who makes the best pasta I've ever tasted at his restaurant La Lanterna in Scarborough, advocates the hand-turned machine: 'It give you far more control.') You start by cutting your kneaded lump into a number of manageable pieces. Hazan suggests three times the number of eggs you have used. Though we had used three eggs, we settled for eight bits – yes, I know it should be nine – though six seemed to work OK as well. You flatten your first lump with the palm of your hand until it is about a centimetre thick and feed it into the machine at the No.1 setting. Then you fold the dough in half and feed it in again. According to the KitchenAid instruction book, this stage is repeated 'several times or until the dough is smooth and pliable'. In practice this means three or four times, or you might get fed up with the whole business.

When each lump has been squashed at the No.1 setting, you lay them on a clean tea towel with a *cordon sanitaire* between them to prevent sticking. After this, you simply push each piece through the rollers at progressively higher settings, which produce a progressive diminution of the gaps between the rollers. As we fed the yellow dough through the ever-closer rollers, it resembled first a shirt collar, then a Sixties kipper tie. Occasionally, the dough released a bubble-gum-style pop. When the dough became a silk evening scarf, at setting No.5, it was time to switch to the cutter. This works in much the same way as the roller. For our first batch, we made narrow ribbons of fettuccine. Using the palm of my hand to hold the blonde tresses as they emerged from the cutter, I felt like a hairdresser in some posh salon.

If making pasta became a worthwhile exercise at this point, it was even more persuasive after a brief simmer. Wonderfully resilient on the palate, springy and full of life, it is far superior to shop-bought pasta, whether fresh or dried. In fact, it is so staggeringly good that you pledge never to eat shop-bought pasta again (though, of course, you will). Gillian Riley is probably right when she writes, 'Freshly-made pasta has a delicate flavour and needs little more than a few chopped herbs and a knob of butter, nothing else, not even Parmesan,' though no Parmesan is a step too far for some of us.

In similar vein, Marcella Hazan warns us off coloured pasta, which 'depends for its hues on colouring agents that either communicate no flavour, and therefore have no gastronomic interest, or else impart flavour that lacks freshness'. But sometimes you have to question the dictates of even the greatest gurus. This is especially so if you happen to have a packet of squid ink in the fridge. *Tagliatelle al nero di seppia* is one of the most impressive of all pastas. I mixed the little sachet of cephalopod smokescreen with the eggs before adding to the *fontina di farina*. This startling mixture of hellish black and heavenly white is even messier than the standard *fontina*. Again, you give up all hope it will ever amalgamate but it does eventually. The resulting lump of dough resembles a granite boulder you might find on the beach. 'Lovely squidy flavour,' said Mrs H as she slurped up a strand of Bible-black tagliatelle.

After that, there was no stopping us with coloured pasta. For the green version, you substitute 50g of spinach purée for one egg yolk. As the verdant lumps of dough went into the rollers, it looked as though we were making squashed frog. When the pasta emerged from the roller at the No. 5 setting, it might have been a tie for a particularly decadent club. Red pasta was even more dramatic. This calls for 25g of beetroot purée instead of an egg yolk. The resulting ruby-red tagliatelle is the prettiest food imaginable. Though it faded to a pale pink when boiled (the green pasta is more colour-fast), it was still a most attractive morsel. Combining good looks and great taste, homemade pasta is surprisingly sensual. With the possible exception of the spaghetti scene in *The Lady and the Tramp*, I'd never previously seen pasta as sexy.

Puttanesca sauce

Even if you don't do homemade pasta, you can do home-made pasta sauce. If I may release a bee from my bonnet: NEVER BUY BOTTLED PASTA SAUCE. It is so easy, cheap and enjoyable to make that it is madness to pay money to some TV celeb for his picture on the label. Mrs H prefers the following sauce, which she humorously terms 'whore's drawers', to anything else in my culinary repertoire. The celebrated explanation of 'puttanesca' is that it was a fast cupboard sauce cooked by the prostitutes (*puttana*) of Naples prior to a night on the streets. Unfortunately, the Wikipedia entry scotches this colourful yarn. The sauce was apparently invented in the Fifties by a restaurateur called Sandro Petti on the island of Ischia. He came up with this classic in response to the request of some late-night diners: '*Facci una puttanata qualsiasi*' ('Make any kind of rubbish'). The noun '*puttanata*' means trash or rubbish. Despite this persuasive rebuttal of a carefully nutured myth, this fast, warming sauce is still pretty good if you're heading out for the night. It's best with the narrow spaghetti called spaghettini, but penne also works well. The quantities given below will feed two, rather generously.

1 clove of garlic
1 tin of anchovies in oil
about 24 Kalamata olives
1 dessertspoon capers
¼ teaspoon cayenne pepper
2 x 400g tins of good plum tomatoes
olive oil
250g spaghettini or penne

You make it in a large saucepan (or wok). Finely chop the garlic and anchovies. Gently fry the garlic in the olive oil poured from the tin of anchovies. When the garlic has softened, add the chopped anchovies and fry until dissolved. Then add the olives (de-stoning prevents subsequent counting of stones and your partner complaining about her unfair share), capers, cayenne, the tomatoes and a splash of olive oil. Bring to the boil, stir, then reduce to a simmer. Cook over a low heat, stirring occasionally, for an hour or so (while taking on board a glass or two of Chianti). This should have the effect of reducing and thickening the sauce. In another pan, boil the dried pasta according to the instructions on the packet. When cooked, drain the pasta and put into a large bowl. Add the puttanesca sauce, mix thoroughly and serve.

WALKING DOWN THE AISLES

A FEW YEARS AGO, the excessive nature of our food-buying habits was brought home to me by a curious incident that took place in a supermarket near our home. I was hovering round the deli counter, buying a tranche of this and a soupçon of that, when I was addressed by a young fellow behind the counter. 'Excuse me, it's my last day working here,' he announced. 'I'm off to medical school next week. Do you mind if I ask you a question?'

'Well, no, as long as it's not medical.'

'What do you do for a living?'

'I'm a journalist.'

'Oh.'

'Why do you ask?'

'Well, you come in here so often and spend so much on food that we thought ...'

'What?'

'We thought that you must be an eccentric millionaire.'

Yes, we do spend a lot of time and, worse, money in supermarkets. There isn't much alternative to supermarkets if you need to buy food in our bit of London, though there are plenty of them to choose from. I didn't spend so much time there before I met Mrs H. She remembers being bemused by my priorities. 'You would take me to a shop just to look at a jar of Mrs Adler's Old Jerusalem Gefilte Fish. They were horrid floating things that reminded me of specimens in the Path Lab at the Middlesex Hospital. I thought it was very odd.'

And here was me thinking she'd found a kindred spirit. Though we go to the supermarket as a couple, our paths diverge immediately we're inside. Mrs H is more interested in vegetables than me. 'I always follow my little routine,' she says. 'Vegetables, coffee, cat food, milk, cleaning stuff.' Well, where's the fun in that? No wonder I deviate for pleasure and excitement. My little routine goes: oysters, fish, paté, salami, olive oil, cheese, baguettes, wine. It is a banquet that Lucullus might have envied. I bet you wouldn't have found the great Roman gourmet deliberating over Whiskas and Vanish.

After following our well-worn paths like creatures in the forest, we then spend an amazing amount of time looking for each other. That bad-tempered man you've seen furiously stalking up and down the aisles is me. Curiously, Mrs H claims she does exactly the same. 'When we shop together, it takes ages,' she moans. 'I can always track you down eventually. You're either fondling wine bottles or gazing dreamily at the fish counter.'

I do occasionally venture into the veg patch at the supermarket, but Mrs H scrutinises my acquisitions with an eagle eye. 'No, you don't want them,' she said the other day.

'Yes, I do. They're only 49p.'

'We've got tons of shallots, both round ones and banana.'

'I can't spend 49p?'

'No.'

'How come you can spend £70 on a leg of ham and I can't spend 49p?'

'It wasn't £70, it was £57.'

'Well, that's all right, then.'

The whole Serrano ham, which dangled by a hoof in our loft for several months, was a somewhat unusual purchase. We don't buy legs of cured ham all the time. Mrs H bought it for a party. When we eventually tackled it, the ham was a triumph. This was due partly to its quality, but also, if I may say so, to the impressive carving of exquisitely slender rashers (you are supposed to see the knife through the slice) by the author of these words. I would particularly recommend the purchase of a whole Serrano – and the arched wooden gadget that holds it in place – for the man in the kitchen. While engaged in carving, you are briefly transformed into the patrician proprietor of one of the great Sevillian tapas bars like El Rinconcillo or Sol y Sombra, though I'm not sure that I matched their technique. Restaurant critic Terry Durack noted how the owners of the bars did the task 'holding the leg like a cello, gracefully pulling the slender knife across as if it were a bow'.

But the enhancement of my ego was not the main reason

that prompted Mrs H's Iberian investment. The ham was on sale in the cut-price supermarket Lidl, which took over the Safeway premises near us. It might not be the supermarket that we'd choose to have as a neighbour, but it is an *interesting* shop. Mrs H says it's a bit like buying food in Moscow during the Communist era. 'The way it is stocked is highly erratic. You can't rely on finding celery there.' On the other hand, there aren't many supermarkets where you can buy both bratwurst and a unicycle ('the ultimate one-wheeled fun'). I was once tempted by a soldering set. Considering the urban location of this branch, the most bizarre display was an assortment of equestrian equipment. Lidl did not manage to dispose of many horse blankets, though I noticed that the entire stock of training whips (£2.99) had sold out.

One day, while gazing at the blossom-laden elder tree in the churchyard opposite our house, it occurred to me that we were missing out on the biggest supermarket of all. Better still, it is completely free. I decided that we were going to acquire our food from the hedgerow rather than the supermarket. Farewell neon, hello sunlight. Bizarrely, Mrs H did not share my newfound passion for hunter-gathering in the wild – both the wild of North Yorkshire and the slightly less wild of suburban London. 'This hunter-gathering business sends you a bit bonkers,' she grizzled, while probing a bush for blackberries. 'We seem to have spent half the summer falling into ditches.'

There was a scintilla of truth in this outburst. Despite the concomitant stings, scratches and insect bites, foraging is an addictive occupation. Nettles lead to wild garlic, which leads to elderflowers, which lead to blackberries, which lead to hawthorn berries. After discovering how good the results are – nettle and potato soup, wild garlic mayonnaise, elderflower cordial – you go back for more while the picking is good. Eventually you get used to the bemused glances of passers-by.

Aside from abrasions and the expenditure of much amount of time in processing the fruits of your labours, the main drawback of foraging is the astounding number of pots that result. Though picturesque, the regiment of jars turns a reasonably well-ordered kitchen into a wizard's lair, especially if you have to let them mature for seven years (the recommended maturing period for the elderberry-based Pontack sauce). Still, I'm pretty sure we'll be back in the hedgerow next year – and that's not just because it's free. Try finding nettles or wild garlic leaves in the supermarket. 'Yes, I'd go back,' Mrs H grudgingly agreed. 'But I'd prefer not to do the picking in the park on a Sunday. Wandering round in outsize Marigold gloves looks a bit odd.'

9

A bite on the wild side

Nettles

'I'll be stung to bits. They'll taste gritty and horrid and we'll be going to the lavatory for ages.' Mrs H was not all that desperate to go nettle-hunting, but this reluctance is a mystery to Italians. The food writer Anna Del Conte gives us all a ticking-off: 'It seems a sad waste that these eminently edible weeds should hardly be eaten in a country where they grow in such profusion.' Same goes for Giorgio Locatelli, who once told me about his nation's love of the nettle: 'Italians love getting something for free.'

I used the old silvery tongue to weaken my wife's intransigence. 'No, you won't be stung. Where are your kitchen gloves?'

'Why don't you go picking the wretched things if you're so keen on them?'

For that inquiry I had an answer at the end of my arms. Big hands, you see. Marigolds won't fit. And it was, of course, impossible to go picking these vindictive plants, appropriately known in Somerset as Devil's Leaf, without gloves. The nettle's defence mechanism, ingenious enough for a Bond villain, is a cocktail of poisons including formic acid, which is injected via needles made of silica. This Rosa Klebb of the botanical world wields a glass hypodermic.

Mrs H broadened her attack to the whole notion of foraging. 'Wild food! We'll end up tree hugging and painting ourselves with woad and dancing round the Rollright Stones. Anyway, I bet you can get kitchen gloves to fit even your giant mitts.' She was right, dammit, but the acquisition of my first-ever rubber gloves disproved Richard Mabey's classic text *Food for Free*. I was 75p down before I'd picked a single leaf.

Despite Mabey's observation that nettles are 'widespread and abundant', it proved rather difficult to find a patch in suburban London that met Mrs H's demanding criteria. Those at the roadside were ruled out due to the generous spicing of exhaust fumes, while park nettles were stigmatised by possible canine contributions. No wonder Giorgio Locatelli grows them in his restaurant's garden in Virginia Water, though the suggestion in his book *Made in Italy* that 'the stalks are the part with the sting' suggests that the maestro hasn't had a close encounter with a nettle leaf recently. When we eventually found a thicket of nettles in a dog-free area of our local park, Mrs H insisted on asking permission from the wardens before we started snipping, which scarcely seemed to be in the ruthless survivalist spirit of our forebears.

In the end, it was Mrs H who donned my supersized

Marigolds and did the snipping (more dextrous, don't you know), though I helped by pointing out 'the tops and the young pale green leaves' recommended by Mabey. My invaluable indication of tempting examples of *Urtica dioica* drew a volley of appropriately stinging remarks from the harvester. 'Thanks for pointing that one out. I'd never have spotted a nettle by myself. Ouch! One's got me on the leg. Can't you bring the bag a bit nearer?'

Back home, it was my turn with the rubber gloves. It is very strange to prepare a vegetable that bites back. Each leaf has to be removed from the stalks, which are so fibrous that they were once grown to make cloth. Our bag of nettles required an hour of fastidious pruning. Food for free is only for the time rich. In the course of this activity, I managed to snip a hole in one of the fingers of my new Marigolds. Dealing with this tough, ragged, very untamed plant has a curiously medieval quality. In Pamela Michael's book *Edible Wild Plants & Herbs*, we learn that they were used to treat '30 or 40 ailments of extreme diversity'. Brother Cadfael would have been big on nettles, but how did he manage without rubber gloves?

Left to soak in the kitchen sink, our haul resembled a mini Sargasso Sea. Eerily, the water turned pale pink. Nettle blood. Like our own haemoglobin, the nettle is rich in iron, which constitutes 2.3 per cent of its weight. I washed the soggy leaves two or three times to rid them of grit. Cold water steadily seeped through the hole in my glove. Eventually, the nettles matched the demanding hygiene standards of Mrs H, who regarded food found in the park with deep suspicion. But what the devil should we do with the devil's leaf now?

Most nettle recipes start by making a purée. You boil them for two or three minutes with a splash of salted water in a pan with the lid on, then drain and either purée in the food processor or use the potato masher to mash them with butter. When cooked the nettle loses its sting and darkens to British Racing Green. The result on the palate is hardly earth-shaking. According to Anna Del Conte, the flavour is 'sweet', 'delicate' and 'just discernible' in risotto. Mabey goes further, claiming nettle purée by itself is 'rather insipid – don't expect it to taste like spinach, as is sometimes suggested'. Our nettles tasted mildly herby with a slight, not displeasing metallic tang.

But when incorporated with other ingredients, the well-hidden charm of the nettle emerges. Nettle purée spread on buttered toast topped with a poached egg placated my disgruntled picker. 'What a nice taste – and the colours are lovely.' Nettle risotto, flecked with the plant's intense green, was equally pleasing, but my nettle and potato soup received an even more rapturous reception. I should point out that our substantial intake of nettles did not provoke the dire intestinal consequences predicted by Mrs H, but there was something in what she said. Mabey warns that nettle leaves become 'coarse, unpleasantly bitter and decidedly laxative' after the end of June. By Midsummer Day, you'd better dash if you want to avoid the trots.

Wild garlic

Sometimes, even keen food lovers show reluctance when foraging for certain foodstuffs. This was the case with Mrs H and wild garlic. 'Cor blimey,' she announced in her delicate, lady-like way. 'Talk about a pong. The whiff from that lot would fell an ox.' It wouldn't really, but it would taste quite nice with a bit of braised beef. 'That lot' was a bank of wild garlic in the same park where we got the nettles. Smell aside, it is rather an attractive plant – in his *Dictionary of English Plant Names*, Geoffrey Grigson says it produces 'one of the most beautiful floorings' – with strap-like, pointy leaves and balls of tiny, white, star-shaped flowers that could make an appearance in wedding bouquets, were it not for their distinctive fragrance.

This is indeed very powerful. Especially when you tread on the leaves, it is like the most garlicky dish you've ever eaten, possibly with a top-note of house gas. I remember coming across this assault on the schnoz when roaming as a child in Yorkshire. No, we didn't eat it, though the plant has a long history of adding interest to stews and salads. Its alternative name of ramsons derives from the Old English word *hramsa*. Ramsey in Essex and Ramsbottom in Lancashire were named after wild garlic.

We are so led by the nose that wild garlic smells im-possibly rank to use as a foodstuff. Yet the taste of the leaves is surprisingly delicate, exactly the tinge of garlic that ambitious cooks want to attain with cultivated garlic bulbs. Everyone who has seen Scorsese's *GoodFellas* remembers the scene where razor-cut slivers of garlic bulb are gently sautéd for a prison meal. The idea is that the translucent particles melt into the oil. Apparently it was the technique used by Scorsese's mother, but in my experience the tiny strands always shrivel and burn before achieving deliquescence.

Mrs H was unpersuaded about wild garlic or ramsons. 'You can go and pick those smelly things yourself.' So I did. I returned to the park with a plastic bag for more PYO. It began raining heavily, a possibility that is omitted from most accounts of foraging. This had the advantage of removing observers who might have thought that I was snaffling hyacinths. Fortunately, wild garlic is the easiest of all wild plants to harvest. It is profuse and lacking in stings and thorns. I suppose the pong is meant to repel prospective consumers, though Pamela Michael notes that cows aren't put off. 'The only disaster I ever experienced with ramsons,' she writes, 'was on a farm where I worked during the war, when the cows got into a patch and the whole day's milk was ruined by the pungent taint of garlic.' After a minute or two of foraging – just about the ideal length of time for this task – I'd gathered a bulging bag of leaves. You can also eat the flowers, stalks (a bit like chives) and bulbs of wild garlic, though I'm not sure if you should be seen wielding a trowel in a public park.

For canine and other reasons, it's best to give the leaves a wipe. (Don't tell Mrs H, but I didn't bother when I found wild garlic in the middle of a wood, miles from anywhere.) You can use the leaves for many of the same jobs as bulb garlic. More, in fact, because the leaves can be used as a salad or for stuffing baked fish. Richard Mabey suggests cutting them in long strips and laying them over sliced tomato. He also conveys the recommendation that they can be added to peanut butter sandwiches, though he doesn't seem to have tried that. Me neither.

The first thing I did with them was garlic bread. Here, wild garlic does the combined work of chopped bulb garlic and parsley. Mrs H admired the appearance of the garlic butter prior to spreading in the baguettes. 'How lovely.' Baked to a crisp gold in the oven, the garlic bread was a definitive version of this venerable dinner party starter. 'Rather excellent,' said Mrs H. 'None of that aggressive bite you get from garlic cloves.'

Following this success, we did no end of wild garlic dishes. It makes a very decent pesto and can be chopped into tomato sauce for pasta. Mrs H used it in a lamb casserole to impressive effect. Wild garlic risotto is outstanding. No wonder the weed has sprouted in food columns and on the menus of posh restaurants. John Gerard's *Herbal* of 1597 suggested that wild garlic 'maye very well be eaten in April and Maie with butter, of such as are of a strong constitution, and labouring men'. Not being among the latter, Mrs H obviously has a strong constitution.

With a fairly long season (Gerard was right there), there seems to be only one problem with wild garlic or ramsons. Since it is free and profuse, you tend to be a bit greedy. I picked bag after bag. We ate wild garlic with pasta, in salads, with couscous and with roast chicken. Mixing the chopped leaves with mayonnaise produces a delicate aioli. If you do the same with soft goat's cheese the result is akin to Boursin, though with a delicate green tinge. V. delish on toast. But mostly I made more and more wild garlic pesto. You can fill your fridge with jars for future use, though this may bring some pungent comments from others who share the fridge.

Elderflower

Going by appearances, few would associate Mrs H with the cocaine trade. Yet this paradigm of middle-class rectitude attracted attention in a local pharmacy by purchasing significant quantities of a substance commonly associated with the purveyors of jazz talc. In case the Metropolitan Police feels the urge to pay a surprise visit to Hirst HQ with a battering ram, I should explain that her acquisition was associated with our research into the consumption of wild plants. The plant in question was not *Erythroxylum coca*, found on the eastern slopes of the Andes, but *Sambucus nigra*, found pretty much everywhere in the UK.

In early summer, this deciduous tree advertises its presence with a gaudy display of creamy-white blooms and an olfactory trumpeting of a heady aroma variously described as 'almost Oriental' and 'muscat-like'. These are the flowers of the elder, for which, as Richard Mabey points out, 'there are probably more uses than any other species of blossom'. It was concentrated elderflower cordial that caused Mrs H to come under the eye of suspicion, but we'll come to that later.

For three weeks or so in early summer, elderflower is everywhere. It must be one of the most profuse shrubs in Britain. Our nearest elder is in the grounds of the church across the road from our house in London. This is not entirely appropriate, since the elder was the object of heathen veneration – the tree was associated with the White Goddess who enraptured Robert Graves – and was therefore anathematised by early Christians. However, it was the luxuriance of the flowery interloper, rather than its pagan significance, that prompted Steve the verger to welcome my appearance with Mrs H's florists' shears. He even offered some empty Communion wine bottles to contain the fruits of our labours.

Five minutes after setting out, I returned with a basket filled with a froth of umbels. My first production run concerned the elderflower drink eulogised by Pamela Michael: 'The best wild flower drink ever.' The first instruction in her recipe is rarely seen in cookbooks: 'Shake the flowers free of insects …' Shaking the blooms, I felt a little like a priest wielding an aspergillum – the device used for sprinkling holy water – though my blessing failed to disperse the inhabitants. The tiny flies clung on tight and had to be dispatched by the flick of a finger. Soon I had twelve flower heads gyrating in four litres of sugary water sharpened with white wine vinegar and flecked with lemon peel. The effect of this swirling, psychedelic blur of white blossoms, was almost hypnotic. Maybe the elder's pagan reputation is not without justification. Somewhat brusquely, Mrs H roused me from my flower-induced trance.

'What are you peering at?'

'Oh, nothing.'

After twenty-four hours' steeping, I strained my potion. 'So refreshing,' said Mrs H. 'Perfect for a summer day.' After this success, I became a regular sight at the church, snipping the goddess's blooms. I made elder vinegar (I'm still waiting to find a use for this astringent infusion). We had elderflower fritters (not bad but a bit lumpy). Mrs H made elderflower and rhubarb jam. 'Very impressive if you don't mind your jam on the runny side,' she said. 'A lovely pink conserve. It would be great with ice-cream or yogurt.' Her elderflower jelly, which achieved a more resilient set, went well with pork and lamb. Before we had it as a condiment, I sneaked a spoonful and the aftertaste lingered happily for minutes afterwards.

Though very generous in supply, there is a time limit on elderflowers. They should be picked soon after the flowers open. The eighteenth-century cook John Nott wrote: 'Gather your bunches of Elder Flowers just as they are beginning to open, for that is the time of their Perfection … afterwards they grow dead and faint.' Dead and faint isn't quite right. The scent of the mature elderflower is pungent and blowsy. One horticulturalist recommends that they should be picked 'before they develop the feline fragrance of middle age'. Elderflowers are best when they have just opened and the delicately perfumed little flowers are the colour of Cornish cream. Don't bother when they have turned white and whiffy.

I was worried that I'd left it too late when I made my most expensive elderflower product. Elderflower liqueur sounds like one of those drinks made by Miss Marple types in thatched cottages. Such refreshments have the reputation of being ferociously potent and honey-sweetened elder-flower liqueur is no exception. Making one bottle of elderflower liqueur requires one bottle of vodka. For some reason that eludes me now, possibly greed, I decided to make two bottles of elderflower liqueur. When I sampled it after making, the taste was worrying.

It was very stalky and powerful. Maybe even a bit feline. Pretty much undrinkable, in fact. It looked like my investment was going down the drain, but one authority recommended storing in the dark for at least two months before drinking. Two months afterwards to the day, I offered a lunchtime sample to Mrs H. 'A fantastic sweet smell like hay.' But was that just to cheer me up? 'It's a nice, straw-coloured liquid.' Then she took a sip. After swallowing, her mouth dropped open and her eyes rolled skywards. This was not because she had been poisoned. It is merely Mrs H's indication of alcoholic strength. 'It's very pleasant and fresh,' she eventually declared. 'Grassy, meadowsweet, outdoorsy – but not like a dung heap.'

'Gratifying to know.'

'Quite summer-like. It would be lovely poured over fruit.' I took a sip. Yes, it was drinkable, just about. It did seem fantastically potent, but that might have been because it was lunchtime. At a subsequent sampling, doubts began to set in. Probably due to an extended steeping of the elderflower in the vodka, it was still a bit stalky. A lot stalky, actually. Still, I pondered, it might be OK in a cocktail. After considerable experimentation, I came up with a successful application. If you ever find yourself stuck with a large quantity of rather rustic elderflower vodka, your best course is to make an elderflower caipirinha. This is quite fitting, since the national drink of Brazil is a rural potion (the name is a diminutive of *caipira*, meaning 'countryman') made with cachaça, agricultural rum. Mrs H claimed that the real caipirinha is 'slightly straw-like', so it seemed a fair bet that my rustic product would work OK. It certainly did with Mrs H. 'Don't suppose there's any chance of another?' Despite this plaudit, we still have one and a half bottles of elderflower vodka lurking in the drinks cupboard.

The greatest success we had with elderflower was a concentrated cordial. Diluted with still or fizzy water, it tasted better – or at least as good – as any of the commercially available versions and was considerably cheaper. So alluring was this quintessence of summer that we decided to make another batch. It was then that Mrs H strayed, very slightly, into the murky world of narcotics.

The recipe involves dissolving 1 kilo of sugar in a pint of boiling water and adding ten elderflower heads and a sliced lemon, along with 25g citric acid, which is required to neutralise the sugar. You just stir it well, leave for 24 hours, strain and bottle. What could be simpler? Except when

Mrs H tried buying citric acid at our local Boots she was informed that the shop didn't stock this harmless ingredient. 'Try an independent chemist,' a Boots salesperson helpfully suggested. At one of those, there was a stock of maybe thirty packets of citric acid. Returning a few days later, when we were making the second batch, Mrs H found three packets remaining. 'Why do you want it?' asked a shop assistant.

'For making elderflower cordial,' said Mrs H. 'Has everyone been making it?'

'You can use citric acid for de-scaling the kettle as well.'

'There must be a lot of de-scaling going on.'

'Well, there may be another reason …'

'What's that?' inquired Mrs H.

'Citric acid is often used for cutting cocaine. That's why Boots don't sell it.'

Blackberries

'One, two, three, four, five,' Mrs H seethed. Her fingers darted into the tangle of a blackberry bush, but she was not counting the fruits of her labours. 'I've now had five nettle stings. Whose idea was this?' I'm sorry to admit that the impetus to go brambling stemmed from a newspaper article about cutting food bills. 'Dine like a king, spend like a pauper,' urged the headline. I'm even sorrier to reveal that the author was a certain C. Hirst. 'September brings blackberries for the hunter-gatherer,' wrote this culinary tightwad. 'This most generous of wild fruits is excellent in crumble, mousse and junket, but never better than when infusing apples in a pie.'

As often transpires with the torrent of advice that pours from newspapers, my well-intentioned words, which happened to be written in the comfort of my London office, turned out to be somewhat wide of the mark when put into practice at a hedgerow in North Yorkshire. Though they looked big and tempting when we spotted the patch a few days earlier, the blackberries had been ruptured and mangled by subsequent downpours.

Moreover, they were not quite as easy to pick as a certain newspaper article suggested. 'The best ones are always just out of reach,' grizzled Mrs H, as she edged through the springy tussocks fringing the bramble. 'It's like walking on an ice floe that might conceal a crevasse. You wouldn't want to fall in.' No, indeed. A few years ago, a helicopter was called in to rescue a North Yorkshire man who had been trapped in a bramble thicket near the sea for two days. The circumstances of this strange ordeal were somewhat mysterious, since it was too early to go brambling. (It emerged that the victim, who had spent some hours in the pub prior to his misadventure, was 'known to the police'.) Despite our endeavours, which resulted in numerous abrasions and an impressive purple smear on my T-shirt, our basket remained depressingly slow to fill. Desirable fruit hung temptingly inches out of reach amid a fearsome forest of thorns. While I was brushing away a cluster of blue-arsed flies, which share the human appetite for black-berries, a gleaming new 4 x 4 drew up alongside. 'They

won't be much good after that rain,' announced the driver.
'I need a machete,' I huffed.

'You need someone else to do it for you,' noted my
unsought adviser, who roared off chortling at his pleasantry.

After an hour of picking and cussing, we accumulated a
kilo of the world's mankiest blackberries. A second stop
proved equally unsatisfactory. Displaying an imaginative
morbidity that is, I'd venture, not uncommon among
females, Mrs H expressed concern about treading on a
hidden corpse in the long grass. We managed to increase
our haul by another half kilo of equally battered fruit. But
it's worth persisting with blackberries. Depending on
location, some bushes ripen later than others. Two weeks
later, I came across a spot that was glutted with perfect
blackberries, which went into a blackberry and apple pie.
Since it was on a busy path to the beach, I was puzzled that
the irresistible (at least to me), glistening fruit had not been
picked. The same indifference seems to apply to apples. Are
children now so insulated from nature that they simply
don't know that these things are edible? Or does fruit hold
no appeal nowadays? How strange that scrumping has to
be encouraged.

As well as being free and profuse (sometimes), wild
blackberries have much to be said in their favour. They are
pleasing in appearance and have an appealing subtle taste.
I'm a big fan of crème de mure, the blackberry equivalent
of the blackcurrant liqueur crème de cassis. Though lacking
the acid tang of blackcurrants, it makes an excellent kir.
Wherever you use blackberries – pies, crumbles, jellies,

jams, ice cream, sorbet, sauces – an additional splash of crème de mure intensifies the flavour.

Did you know that the blackberry played a part in destroying the TV career of Fanny Cradock? She behaved intolerably to Devon housewife Gwen Troake in Esther Rantzen's 1976 TV programme *The Big Time*. Mrs Troake had won a competition to provide dinner for various bigwigs and wanted to serve duckling with bramble sauce. The belligerent Cradock snapped at this ('What's a bramble?') and everything else that poor Mrs Troake suggested. The viewing public was so offended that the mad old bat was booted off TV for good. In her *Fruit Book*, Jane Grigson says Mrs Troake's sauce goes better with puds.

Our 'runty' (Mrs H's word) blackberries went into a chutney. The bubbling purple stew of blackberry and apple looked more suited to a magician's cauldron than a saucepan. The result was then sieved by Mrs H, our resident sieving specialist, before being simmered with sugar. Her five hours' labour in hedgerow and kitchen produced two and a half jars of velvety goo, but it was time well spent – at least in my view.

Hawthorn

Hawthorn berries stood up to the summer storms far better than blackberries. By early September, North Yorkshire hedgerows were aflame with bright red haws. It was only after poring through literature on wild food that I realised they were edible. In my childhood, I had presumed that their main function was to serve as missiles. My father was the usual target, poor chap. However, you can also use them to make a jelly, though reviews are lukewarm. It is variously described as 'moderate' (Richard Mabey) and 'insipid without lemon juice' (Pamela Michael). Chutney appears to be the best bet. Pamela Michael says it is 'delicious with all cold meats and poultry'. We rapidly filled a large punnet with berry-laden twigs. Snip the haws from their stalks, simmer with vinegar for an hour, rub the contents through a sieve, then simmer again with spices and dried fruit. What could be easier? Except that separating a kilo of berries from their stems took us almost two hours.

'Us?' erupted Mrs H. 'You did half an ounce and spent the entire time huffing and puffing and complaining that it was fiddly women's work before packing it in.' When that task was finished, we washed the berries. Floating in the sink, the ruby-like haws reminded me of cranberries I saw being harvested by pump from flooded bogs in Massachusetts. Boiling removed the bright scarlet coats of the haws. Underneath, they were a dull khaki. The task of 'rubbing through a sieve', so easily described, was perhaps the least rewarding culinary task I've ever attempted. Five minutes rubbing the boiled berries into a sieve with a wooden spoon produced less than a teaspoon of purée.

Mrs H proved to be of sterner stuff. After pummelling away for two hours, the haws were transformed into a small pile of brown pulp. 'Cat puke,' she observed. The resulting chutney (two small jars) was a shiny brown, densely granular in texture and pleasantly tasty. You could envisage it being served with fine cheese in a posh restaurant. Only posh joints could afford the labour. While undeniably cheap, hawthorn chutney is the ultimate in Slow Food. 'Would you do them again?' I asked Mrs H.

'Never. Too much fuss.' Then she nibbled the haw condiment with a fragment of blue goat's cheese. 'Well, I might ...'

Elderberry

As with elderflowers in spring, we tend to ignore the early autumnal deliveries of elderberries on hedgerows and waste ground. Though there are a host of applications – chutney, wine, ketchup, jelly, autumn pudding – most of the tart fruit tends to go down the throats of birds, particularly starlings. There was one celebrated recipe that I particularly wanted to try. A long-matured elderberry condiment called Pontack sauce is said to be particularly good with liver, though it also goes with game and pork and can be used to bolster gravies. In her book *Preserves*, Pam Corbin describes Pontack sauce as 'kitchen alchemy at its most exciting and rewarding ... a secret weapon for the store cupboard that I don't like to be without'.

Its curious name derives from the Pontack's Head, the first de luxe French restaurant in London. This was established in the late seventeenth century by the owner of Château Haut-Brion. For this reason, Richard Mabey suggests that the original recipe for Pontack sauce would have been wine-based, but the cost of Haut-Brion argues against this theory. It wasn't cheap when Jonathan Swift bought a bottle for seven shillings. Today, the 2006 vintage will set you back £348. We decided to use cider vinegar, but there remained a more significant problem. Despite the extraordinary profusion of elder trees in this country – when they're in flower you see one every fifty yards along the side of the A1 – we managed to miss out on the entire crop of elderberries.

We would have picked them in at our place in Yorkshire, but due to deluges they were still dark green when it was time to travel back down south. 'Not to worry,' I said. 'I still have a secret stock down south.' I was thinking of the ecclesiastical tree in London that I plundered for elder-flowers. With berries in mind, I had been somewhat restrained when snipping the blooms. A fat lot of good it did me. The birds had got there first, blast their pecky little beaks. Eventually in the Kent countryside we came across a single bush that had escaped the attention of local starlings. The reason became evident when we tried picking the berries. The tree was at the side of the busiest byway in the Home Counties. Since there was no pavement, the traffic was obliged to detour round the pickers. Many drivers scarcely bothered. Foraging isn't always as healthy a pastime as its advocates suggest.

We ended up with a small bowl of elderberries. Mrs H undertook the somewhat involved process of making Pontack sauce. Her efforts filled a tiny bottle like the one Alice found with the label 'DRINK ME'.

'Is that it?' I said somewhat ungratefully. 'We'll have another bash next year.'

'You mean you'll have a bash next year,' said Mrs H.

Next summer, we extended our summer break in Yorkshire long enough for the elderberries to ripen. On a glorious September day, we saw a bush burdened with gleaming black bunches. Then we found another and another and another. It was a fantastic year for elderberries. Snip, snip, snip went our secateurs. Our harvest was anxiously observed by a flock of starlings perched on power lines like notes on a stave. Back in our house, Mrs H repeated that her involvement with Pontack sauce was at an end. As I've said before, it's funny how women tend not to forget.

'I did it last year,' she announced in a non-negotiable manner.

'But you only made the world's teensiest bottle.'

'Doesn't matter. It's your turn.'

Accepting the unfairness of fate's roulette, I discovered the mysteries of Pontack sauce for myself. The first step is to strip the berries from their fronds. This is not too hard (you use the tines of a dinner fork) as long as you do it outside so the carpet does not gain an archipelago of elder-berry blotches. You wash the result, place in a non-reactive container, cover with cider vinegar and leave overnight in an oven at the lowest temperature. In the morning, you strain the marinade through a sieve, mashing the berries with a wooden spoon. The deep maroon extract is more dye than foodstuff. This is simmered with chopped shallots, ginger root and spices for half an hour. Pam Corbin suggests 'perhaps muttering some magic charm while you watch over the dark, bubbling potion'.

'It *does* look like a witch's brew,' said Mrs H. 'Have you done any incantations over it?'

'No, I haven't done any bloody incantations over it.' The one thing I could do without at this stage was humorous comments from non-participants.

After straining again, the murky juice is given a final boil for five minutes, then poured into the empty vinegar bottles, which you have washed, de-labelled, washed again with very hot water and dried in a hot oven to sterilise. In recipes for Pontack sauce, no one mentions the phenomenal amount of washing up involved. Even Sisyphus would find it a bit repetitive.

Mrs H lolled reading on the sofa with the cat on her lap while I strained and washed and huffed and puffed. 'Funny,' she remarked. 'Our usual positions are reversed. You usually sit reading books while I scurry round. How do you like it?'

'Bah!'

'Look, you've frightened the cat.'

My production of Pontack sauce had a final sting in the tail. As I mentioned earlier, it has to be matured before use. Seven years is the traditional period, though Pam Corbin admitted she was 'hard pushed to keep it for seven months'. We tried a spoonful of the tiny bottle that Mrs H made last year. It had become much thicker.

'Crikey!' she said. 'Looks like cough mixture. It tastes

a bit like Worcester sauce. Spicy and tart, but it's got potential.'

Beef gravy enriched with immature Pontack sauce was transformed into something fruity, spicy and rich. 'Rather good,' said Mrs H. 'Nice and Christmassy. I think it's the cloves. It will be brilliant with game.'

Touch wood, it will continue to improve as the years go by. Since I made three litres, we should be able to test this out. As long as I can remember where I put it.

Mushrooms

Mushrooms take up the lion's share of the space in most books on wild food, but in my experience they are not all that easy to find. They are not as profuse as blackberries and do not advertise their presence with the same gaudy display as the elderflower. But this was not the reason that Mrs H resisted my proposal of a wild mushroom hunt. 'Do we have to?' she wailed. 'I've grown quite attached to my liver. I don't want to risk it by eating deathcap.' Pooh-poohing this trifling objection, I loaded the car with penknife, trug, Edmund Garnweidner's *Mushrooms & Toadstools of Britain & Europe* and Mrs H. Though mushroom foraging may have become a popular hobby in the foodie community, our search surprised the genial rustics of Surrey.

'Searchin' for your breakfast?' barked a plum-faced cove from his Jag.

'How lucky you are knowing about mushrooms,' said a

svelte equestrienne. This was some way from the truth, but I do know one or two. After peering at any number of stones, decaying golf balls and other less savoury items, we eventually filled the trug with examples of three unambiguous mushrooms. The Parasol mushroom looks exactly like one of those fashion accessories that appear on the Quality Street tin, while the Penny Bun (the same as the prized Italian porcini) has a close resemblance to the tiny, tasteless rolls that once accompanied soup in restaurants. I yelped like a prospector finding a nugget when we came across one of these mycological treasures, though it had already been extensively nibbled. I took this as confirmation of wholesomeness.

No one would have trouble identifying a Giant Puffball, described by Antonio Carluccio as 'one of the most rewarding as well as the most distinctive' species. In his book *A Passion for Mushrooms*, the great man is pictured carrying several dozen of these monsters. He even found a supermarket basket to carry them home. We found just the one. Though small, it was perfectly oval and gratifyingly heavy.

Back home, I was put in charge of cooking our mushroom feast. 'I'm having nothing to do with them,' declared Mrs H. This was just as well, since a host of wriggling forest fauna fell from the deep gills of the Parasols. Cooked in the manner prescribed by Carluccio – sliced, dipped in beaten egg then breadcrumbs and fried in olive oil – they were light, delicate and juicy. The sautéd Penny Bun was even better, a fungal triumph. For the highlight of our feast,

I decided to fry the Giant Puffball in garlic butter. But when I started slicing it up, I got a surprise. Instead of the pure white flesh I was expecting, it was filled with a stiff, translucent jelly. In the middle, a pale, glaucomatous eye stared back at me. It was my most disturbing encounter with any vegetable life form.

'Come and look at this,' I said to Mrs H.

When she had recovered, we tracked the thing down in the pages of Roger Phillips's pictorial book *Mushrooms*. 'The outer wall of the egg is white to pinkish but there is a thick, gelatinous middle layer held between the membranous inner and outer layers.' I had picked an immature stinkhorn, more graphically described by its Latin name, *Phallus impudicus*. When adult, it would assume its distinctive anthropomorphism and emit 'a strong, sickly offensive smell which attracts flies from large distances'. But this one wasn't going to get the chance to be Lord of the Flies. Despite Phillips's less-than-tempting note, 'The egg stage, which lacks the disgusting smell, is edible though not tasty,' it went in the bin. As the thing stared blankly back at me, I felt like John Hurt. I had brought home the Alien. Oddly enough, Mrs H has preferred to gather her mushrooms in the supermarket since then.

Mrs H's recipe for wild blackberry chutney

This recipe follows a traditional chutney formula and is based on a recipe in Pamela Michael's *Edible Wild Plants & Herbs*. However, because wild blackberries are quite pippy, the chutney is sieved – producing a smooth and glossy product. Pamela Michael recommends this chutney spread thinly in a ham sandwich and she is right. So chuck away the Branston and try this. It is also rather good with game.

Remember to inspect the fruit for spiders or little wormy things that may be lurking. They usually float out after you wash the fruit. The best pan to use for chutney is a preserving pan, as the size allows the necessary evaporation to take place, but a stockpot large enough to take all the ingredients will do.

The test for the 'done-ness' of a chutney occurs when you can pull a wooden spoon across the base of the pan and the chutney momentarily remains where it is (think of Moses parting the Red Sea). Finally, if you wish to use a lid to seal the chutney, it is worth investing in a supply of new ones. The vinegar in chutney can easily eat into the seal if old lids are used.

1.5kg blackberries gathered from the hedgerow
500g onions
500g apples (Bramleys are recommended – if you're using windfall apples, you'll need 1kg because of the brown bits)
1 teaspoon sea salt
1 teaspoon powdered mustard
1 teaspoon ground ginger
1 teaspoon ground mace
¼ teaspoon cayenne pepper
1 litre cider vinegar (I prefer this to malt)
500g soft brown sugar

I always start making jams, marmalade and chutneys with the ritual of washing and warming the glass jars. So wash six to eight jars in hot soapy water and dry in an oven at 70°C. Wash and de-stalk the blackberries, keeping an eye out for any unbidden wildlife and rejecting any runty, unripe or over-ripe fruit. Leave the fruit to drain in a colander. Onions and apples are next: de-skin the onions and peel and core the apples. Chop both into small pieces and place in a large pan along with the salt, spices and blackberries. Finally, add the vinegar. Bring everything to the boil, then turn the heat down and cook gently for around an hour, stirring the chutney occasionally.

Remove the pan from the stove and let the chutney cool a little. Then rub the mixture through a fine sieve or a mouli food mill. Return the blended mix to the pan and add the sugar, heating slowly and stirring the chutney until the sugar is fully dissolved. Now bring the chutney to the boil and cook for 10–15 minutes, or until the chutney is done (see test above).

Pour the chutney into the clean warm jars right up to the rim. Place a waxed disc on the top and either seal with the cellophane and rubber band method or use a new bought lid when the chutney is cold.

Mrs H's recipe for nettle soup

Strip the leaves from the stalks and wash thoroughly. Use kitchen gloves. (Special note in case gentlemen make excuses: yellow rubber gloves in large sizes are widely available.) Fill a saucepan with nettle leaves and add 100ml salted water. Cover the pan and bring the water to the boil for 2 minutes. Then, using a tea towel, hold the lid on to the pan and shake. Return to boil for another minute when the nettles should be wilted. Pour off the water. Add a knob of butter and mash the nettles with a potato masher until pureéd. The rest is a doddle, since it follows the customary way of making soup. I prefer using a stick blender for soups. Soups containing potato can go gluey if you whizz them up in a food processor. This should serve four to six people.

1 onion, finely chopped
50g butter
4 tablespoons nettle purée (prepared as described above)
1 litre chicken stock
1 floury potato such as King Edward, peeled, roughly
    chopped and washed
salt and pepper
1 tablespoon crème fraîche or double cream
freshly grated nutmeg

Start by gently frying the onion in the butter until transparent and slightly browning, then stir in the nettle purée. Now add the stock and the potato. Simmer until the potato is soft, then liquidise with a stick blender. I prefer to do this briefly so the soup is slightly grainy, but you may like to do it longer for a smoother soup. Finally, season the soup to taste and pour into bowls. Swirl in a dollop of cream or crème fraîche and add a little grated nutmeg to each bowl before serving.

Mrs H's recipe for Pontack sauce

We have high hopes for this sauce. It seems to be a versatile product that can accompany pork, liver, duck and game and can impart flavour to casseroles and gravies. This recipe makes about 1 litre and if you have a small kitchen, open the windows when you reach the boiling stage – the vapours can be eye-watering.

750g elderberries
750ml cider vinegar or red wine (something more
    modestly priced than Château Haut-Brion)
300g shallots, finely chopped
1 teaspoon salt
1 heaped tablespoon black peppercorns
12 whole cloves
4 allspice berries
1 blade of mace
20g root ginger, peeled and finely chopped

After spending a happy hour or two separating the elderberries from their stalks with a fork, give them a good wash and place them in a casserole or large dish with a lid. Pour the vinegar (or wine) over the berries. Cover and leave overnight in a low oven (130°C/Gas Mark ½). The following day, strain the berries through a sieve, pressing with a wooden spoon to extract the maximum juice from the fruits.

Put the juice into a pan with the shallots, salt, peppercorns, spices and ginger. Bring the sauce gently to the boil, then turn down and simmer for 20–30 minutes to reduce the sauce a little.

Remove the pan from the heat and again strain the sauce through a sieve and return to the boil, this time for 5–10 minutes, by which time the sauce should have thickened more. Pour it into a sterilised bottle or jar with a lid and leave it to mature for as long as possible. The prescribed period is seven years, though twelve months can produce a good sauce.

WHINING AND DINING

WE MAY ARGUE OVER AUBERGINES, squabble about
shallots and cross swords over cucumbers, but there is one
culinary area where peace and harmony reign. We scarcely
ever have a heated debate about where we are going out to
eat. That's because we don't go eating out ...

'Whoa, hold it there,' chips in Mrs H. 'You eat out all
the time.'

'I certainly do not.'

'What about you going to Corrigan's last Thursday? Or
Café Anglais the week before? And you're never away from
St John or the Blue Print. You roll home from lunch in
Moro and say, "Have we to have a light supper?" It's usually
when I'm absolutely starving.'

'Well, you go out as well.'

'I go to a little Turkish place in Waterloo at Christmas
with friends from work. I don't call that incessant going
out.'

Anyway, as I was saying, we don't go eating out together
as much as we once did. After our early days eating at
Poon's, our taste for Chinese meals declined to a once-a-year

visit to Chinatown. Same applies to Indian food. We never have takeaways. It seems insane to have an expensive meal made for you when your kitchen cupboards are crammed to overflowing with comestibles.

'I used to like doner kebabs from that place in Croydon,' Mrs H mused wistfully.

'That was before I entered your life. How come you can never remember me taking you out?'

'I do remember you taking me out. You used to buy me a hotdog at Ikea when we were buying stuff for the kitchen. It cost 50p. Wow, how generous. And you'd bite the end off my frankfurter and try and convince me that that was how they came.'

'You believed me as well.'

'I couldn't believe anyone would be so greedy. Why did you do it?'

'Because I like the ends.'

'You like the bit in the middle as well. I'm surprised I got any sausage at all, Mr G. Guts!'

There is, however, one fast-food chain that we have consistently patronised over the years. We used to visit our local Pizza Express after attending a film club that briefly flourished in our area. A pizza and a bottle of Montepulciano was the ideal accompaniment when we discussed *The Seventh Seal* or *À Bout de Souffle* in an earnest, roll-neck jumper sort of way. It went particularly well with *L'Avventura, Rocco and His Brothers* and *La Dolce Vita*. We were usually the only people in there and the manageress smiled benignly at her late arrivals as they tucked into a

Four Seasons (me) and a Margherita (Mrs H). We carried on eating there most weeks even though the film club packed up (there is not a big audience down our way for art house cinema, though a dozen turned up for *Belle de Jour*). The main reason was that, like the doner kebab, pizza is a tricky dish to do at home.

Two things made me change my mind about trying to do pizza myself. The first was a revelatory trip to Naples, where we discovered just how stupendous this simple snack could be. 'They are melt-in-the-mouth pizzas,' announced Mrs H after we dined at Da Michele, a Neapolitan shrine to the purist pizza. The second was a nudging remark in the entry on pizza in *The Oxford Companion to Italian Food* by Gillian Riley. Together they started us on the long, hot road to Margheritaville.

10

Pizza excess

'WHY CAN'T WE JUST GO OUT FOR ONE?' said Mrs H when I announced my decision to make pizza at home. 'I suppose I'd better join in or the kitchen will never be usable again.' Her reluctant acquiescence turned to horrified anguish when I added that, in a rash moment of over-confidence, I had asked Pasquale Speziano, the Naples-born chef of Pizza Rustica in Richmond, Surrey, which topped the pizza section in *Restaurant* magazine's 'UK Best Dishes Awards', to assay the results of our heated endeavours. He was visiting Hirst HQ in five days' time.

'You *haven't!*' gasped Mrs H.

But I had. Mrs H was about to receive daily pizza deliveries without even having to pick up the phone.

In case you've ever wondered, the consequence of eating twenty-odd pizzas in five days is a slight but persistent groaning. Our weird diet was inspired by a comment in *The Oxford Companion to Italian Food*. Gillian Riley's entry on pizza, 'a flattened lump of bread dough, usually round, flavoured with whatever comes to hand', concludes with a wagging finger in the direction of her slothful compatriots.

While admitting that pizza should 'really be cooked by professionals in a wood-fired oven', she adds that the dish is 'so easy and cheap to make at home that sending out for a far-from-cheap imitation of the real thing is something to think twice about.'

I have never been tempted to have a pizza from a delivery chain and can count on the fingers of one hand the number of supermarket pizzas that have entered our house. (I grew up in a pre-pizza era that must seem as distant as silent films to the young of today.) Until my recent spell of pizza madness, we have always gone out to eat pizza. This is because my previous attempt at homemade pizza was not, to be brutally honest, a great success. Believing that it might be possible to short-circuit the tedious, messy business of dough-making, I bought a pizza base manufactured by the Napolina food company. Though not quite a genuine homemade pizza, Napolina declared it to be *'produtto in Italia'*, so I had high hopes.

It was also my first chance to use the pizza stone that came with our Fisher & Paykel oven. Like the oven, it had travelled all the way from New Zealand, so it seemed a shame not to use it. The stone had been in the oven at max (around 300°C) for an hour before I slid on my virtually homemade pizza, coated with tomato purée and dotted with sliced mozzarella. Five minutes later, I presented it to Mrs H. It looked fairly plausible, even if its perfect circularity gave away its factory origin. 'Er …' said Mrs H, after taking her first nibble of my construction. 'It tastes like a digestive biscuit and the topping is completely wrong.

Can we throw it away?' Not all food made in Italy is wonderful.

But that was not the end of the disaster. On the following day, Mrs H asked: 'Did you damp the pizza stone and heat it up very slowly the first time you used it?'

'Eh?'

'You have to prove it so it won't crack.'

'Of course it won't crack,' I said, lifting the much-travelled stone out of the oven. It snapped in two in my hands, again very much like a digestive biscuit. 'I suppose you'd like another?'

'Yes.'

'You know the pizza stone came from New Zealand? It won't be cheap. Are you sure?'

'Yes.'

For my return bout with pizza, I was going to make proper dough and an authentic topping. I also planned to be a bit more careful when heating the replacement stone, which cost in the vicinity of £90. Even so, 'heating' is the operative word when making pizza. You've got to achieve an inferno to make this dish from the land of Dante. When the American food writer Jeffrey Steingarten tried to make the perfect pizza, he was stymied by his oven thermostat, which restricted the temperature to 260°C. His solution was to freeze wet paper towels, which he then wrapped around his oven's heat sensor. 'My oven, believing incorrectly that its temperature was near freezing point, went full blast until thick waves of smoke billowed from every crack, vent and pore,' reported Steingarten in his book *It Must've Been Something I Ate*. 'Inside the oven was a blackened disc of dough pocked with puddles of flaming cheese. I had succeeded beyond all expectations.'

The reason that Steingarten induced his oven to an unfeasible temperature is that he was trying to bake a Neapolitan-style pizza, which requires an oven surface temperature of at least 485°C. Heston Blumenthal's attempt to make the perfect pizza for his book and TV series *In Search of Perfection* was scuppered by his Gaggenau cooker, which threw in the towel at a mere 370°C. His solution was to 'preheat a cast-iron frying pan over a high heat for at least twenty minutes', while simultaneously 'preheating a grill to the highest possible temperature'. He cooked his 'perfect pizza' on the inverted frying pan, which was placed under the grill for ninety seconds. This arrangement sounded more than a little risky to me. Having destroyed my wife's pizza stone in my first endeavour, I didn't fancy destroying our house in my second.

On the other hand, I can understand the motivation behind the unhinged experiments of Steingarten and Blumenthal. It was at Da Michele (1–3 Via Cesare Sersale, Naples) that I ate the best pizza of my life. A hellishly hot, wood-fired stove occupies a good chunk of the white-tiled premises. During Heston Blumenthal's visit to Da Michele (we pizza researchers tend to follow the same well-trodden route), his industrial thermometer merely registered 'Error' when he tried to take the temperature of the oven. It gave up the ghost because the heat topped 500°C. Whipped out after about three or four minutes, my Margherita had an undulating surface like a good Yorkshire pudding. The nodule-like uplands of this landscape were slightly carbonised by the intense heat of the oven, while the valleys were relatively soft. It was the contrasting textures of this miraculously light pizza, along with the sparse, though richly flavoured topping of puréed San Marzano tomatoes (grown in the volcanic Neapolitan soil, they have no peer for flavour) dotted with basil and molten mozzarella that produced such a sublime result.

In fact, it was so good that I followed the example of the gent seated opposite me and ordered a second pizza. This time I went for a Marinara with a topping of tomato purée, sliced garlic, dried oregano and a few anchovy fillets. Having consumed this equally transcendental treat, I stopped ordering pizzas since I had consumed almost the entire menu of Da Michele. With exemplary restraint, it only does three kinds of pizza. Ever since my visit, I have had mild regrets about not having the third type, the folded Margherita or Marinara called calzone (trouser leg), but I'll be back.

During my pizza-making odyssey, I followed Da Michele's example and made nothing but the Marinara (alleged to have sustained Neapolitan mariners on their voyages) and the Margherita (named after the Italian queen who tucked into one in Naples in 1889, a brave snack since the city was racked by cholera at the time). In his introduction to Nikko Amandonico's book *La Pizza*, Ian Thomson insists: 'These [two] are the only authentic pizzas. Everything else is dross.' (Amandonico does not agree or it would have been a very slim volume.)

For our pizza, Mrs H made a dough from reconstituted dried yeast, organic Italian '00' flour (soft and low in fibre), salt and warm water. Left to ferment for an hour, it obligingly rose to twice its size. Mrs H then kneaded it again and left it to rise for a further fifteen minutes. Now came the moment when the ball of dough was transformed into a pizza base. I rolled it out with a rolling pin, turning frequently, though any *pizzaiolo* worth his salt would use his fingers. Perversely, the dough contracted slightly after being rolled, as if shrinking from its fiery fate. Eventually, the slender disc assumed an acceptable shape, like a wonky circle drawn by a toddler.

For the Marinara topping, Mrs H drained a tin of tomatoes, which she pulverised by squeezing. The resulting fragments were distributed over the pizza base. I added a sprinkling of dried oregano, the magical savoury of pizza cuisine, along with a pinch of salt and an anointment of olive oil. The oven containing our new (and proved) pizza stone had been preheated for an hour at its maximum temperature of 300°C and I induced further heat by switching on the oven fan. Using a short-handled pizza shovel, I carefully edged the raw pizza on to the hot stone. Eight minutes later, we nibbled the result. It looked OK, though the crust was cooked to a dark brown. 'Hmm,' said Mrs H, crunching the crisp circumference. 'It looks a bit like a water biscuit.' Yes, it would have been quite a good water biscuit. Unfortunately, it was quite a bad pizza.

On the following day, we went back to the drawing board – or, rather, the nearest Italian deli. We bought a type of Italian '00' flour called Cuor d'Italia made specifically for pizzas, buffalo milk mozzarella, some La Fiammante tinned tomatoes (we were assured that they were akin to the legendary San Marzano), fresh basil and fresh oregano. We also bought a chunk of fresh yeast that smelled like the pub of your dreams. Though not precisely circular – its shape was closer to the Iberian peninsula – our second pizza looked marginally better than No.1 when it came out of the electric oven. This time, the outer crust was a mid-tan, but the base proved to be a bit doughy in the middle. Moreover, the Margherita topping – tomato and mozzarella with a few basil leaves to complete the Italian *tricolore* – displayed a dismaying tendency to slide off the pizza when I lifted it to my mouth. 'I don't remember this happening when I've had pizzas in restaurants,' I said morosely.

'The dough is a bit thicker this time,' Mrs H pointed out. 'I don't think you cooked it enough. There don't seem to be any air bubbles in the base.' More experimentation was called for. We made pizzas with fresh and dried yeast, with buffalo and cows' milk mozzarella (various authorities recommend both kinds), with olive oil in the dough and without, with fresh oregano and dried, with tinned tomatoes, fresh cherry tomatoes and a costly tomato sauce made by the Cipriani company of Harry's Bar fame. Slowly, I gained the knack of making dough (the dough hook on our food mixer helped no end). My topping technique also steadily improved. The pizzette recipe from Giorgio Locatelli's book *Made in Italy* was particularly successful. Topped with the anchovy sauce known as bagna cauda and sliced cherry tomatoes, the mini pizzas swelled up nicely in the oven. 'Absolutely delicious,' said Mrs H. 'But it's more like a crisp Roman pizza than a soft Naples one.' Was lack of heat the problem?

At this point, I decided that it was time to play my trump card. Sitting in our garden is a small wood-fired oven. Made of terracotta, it is called a Beehive. Though not quite the brick stove stipulated by the Associazione Verace Pizza Napoletana, it has been known to produce fairly impressive temperatures. For our next attempt, I got a good blaze going in the Beehive with two bags of logs. While the heat was building to a Vesuvian level, I wielded the rolling pin on my pizza base (shape: Tasmania) and dotted it with halved cherry tomatoes, snipped mozzarella and a splat of oil. When the wood had converted to white ash, I scraped it to one side of the stove. Using a pizza shovel, I introduced my classy-looking pizza on to the floor of the stove with a flashy élan that any Neapolitan *pizzaiolo* might have envied. Everything was going fine until I tried extracting my pizza from the Beehive. One edge brushed against some hot charcoal and burst into flames.

With much huffing and puffing, I managed to quell the blaze. Despite extensive charring round its periphery, the centre of the pizza seemed strangely undercooked. 'I don't think the mozzarella has melted,' said Mrs H, while prodding the tepid cheese.

'Yes, I know that.'

'The dough is not quite cooked under the tomatoes. Do we need to get the heat up?'

'I've been trying to get the heat up, darling,' I said through gritted teeth.

'I wonder if the logs were damp?' Cursing somewhat, I packed the stove with logs carefully selected for irreproachable dryness. This time, it became far hotter, though still nowhere near the incandescence of the hearth in Da Michele. A second pizza (shape: Antarctica) with a Marinara topping fared somewhat better, producing the requisite slightly charred nodules and an undulating base. 'That's a bit more like it,' said Mrs H.

Since Britain's top pizza chef was coming round on the following day, I dashed back to the deli for more supplies. It was not a time for economies. We cleared the entire stock of '00' pizza flour, along with another six tins of La Fiammante tomatoes and six buffalo milk mozzarella (it seemed to work better than cow's milk). In order to guarantee combustion, we bought a small forest of kiln-dried logs from a specialist supplier. In the evening, we drove round to Pizza Rustica in Richmond to taste Pasquale Speziano's prize-winning pizza. Though it was the champ's night off, his deputy's effort was very impressive. 'It's got a lovely texture,' said Mrs H, who, considering the monotony of her recent diet, munched her Margherita with surprising enthusiasm. 'The edges are nice and springy like the pizza we had in Naples.' Peering round the small, open kitchen, I was astonished to find no wood-burning stove. Deaf to the requirements of the Neapolitan pizza, the Richmond authorities had refused to allow a wood oven in the restaurant. The best pizza in the UK had been cooked by electricity.

For Pasquale Speziano's sampling, we decided to make pizzas cooked with both electricity and wood. Prior to his arrival, I loaded the Beehive with logs with the fury of a stoker on an Atlantic liner racing for the Blue Riband. My luxury, kiln-dried wood produced a rather scary heat. Smoke seeped from fissures in the Beehive. Even Steingarten would have been impressed. I was just welcoming the pizza judge into our house when I heard a curious whooping from Mrs H in the garden. Dashing to investigate this alarm call, I found her playing a hose over the Beehive, which was swathed in billows of black smoke. The heat required for the Neapolitan pizza had proved too much for the wooden base supplied with the oven. 'I've remembered why we stopped using it,' said my dripping partner. 'The base caught fire once before.' When the smoke had been quenched apart from a few tenacious eddies, we continued cooking.

Pasquale was elegant, polite and generous. 'Is very good,' said this prince of the pizza when he tried our wood-fired version, which emerged from a somewhat less intense heat than we intended. The pizza from our electric oven drew similar plaudits. 'Very nice.' Pasquale said, 'It is not necessary to use a wood-fired stove for a good pizza.' The dough was the important part, particularly what he charmingly referred to as 'the levitation'. He did not need much urging to give a practical demonstration. In fact, it was impossible to stop him. He whirled a handful or two of flour with a fingernail-sized bit of yeast, a splash of warm water, a dash of olive oil ('Because your London water is too hard!') and a pinch of salt in a bowl. After furious pummelling at blurry speed, a ball of dough magically appeared. More water, more pummelling and the ball of dough was left in its bowl under a damp cloth for about twenty minutes. He then kneaded the expanded dough for a minute, made it into a sphere again and covered it for a further twenty minutes. 'The more levitation you have, the quicker it cooks and the lighter your pizza.'

Instead of using a rolling pin to make the base, Pasquale spread the dough by hand in the prescribed manner of the Associazione Verace Pizza Napoletana. After a few moments of aerial whirling, the pizza base was magically formed. The result was almost perfectly circular. Pasquale pressed his knuckles gently around the circumference to form a raised crust, known as the *cornicione*. 'The shape doesn't matter,' said Pasquale reassuringly as he installed a Margherita topping at lightning speed. 'It's the taste that counts.' His pizza was light, springy and exceedingly edible. 'I have a Margherita for lunch most days,' said Pasquale. And on other days? 'I have a Margherita with a salad on top.'

Though we could not match Pasquale's masterpiece, our pizzas were better than most I've had from pizzerias in Britain. If you can find a deli that stocks the wonderfully silky '00' pizza flour and good tinned tomatoes, you don't need Neapolitan heat to make a quite acceptable pizza. It is a bit more trouble than dialling for a takeaway, but the sight of a homemade pizza, fragrant and steaming from the oven, is considerably more magical than something that arrives on the back of a moped. It transforms a humdrum snack into a thrilling event. We will be making more pizzas, though not on our new pizza stone. I managed to crack that one as well.

Basic pizza dough

This is a recipe where you use your kitchen worktop for making the pizza dough. It makes four medium-sized pizzas. Using an Italian '00' flour manufactured especially for pizzas will give you a dough with a super-smooth texture. It has a fine grind and high gluten content (12–14 per cent protein) and should be available from a good Italian delicatessen. The local Italian deli where we buy the flour also sells fresh yeast, which I prefer to dried (I think it has a faster fermentation). Heat is everything for a pizza – so crank up your oven to its highest point and if you use a pizza stone make sure you prove it beforehand, according to the instructions.

15g fresh yeast
1 teaspoon granulated sugar
250ml lukewarm water
1 tablespoon olive oil
500g Italian pizza flour Tipo '00'
½ teaspoon sea salt

Set your oven temperature as high as it will go (250°C plus, if you can get it).

Start making the pizza dough by first taking a small bowl and mixing the fresh yeast and sugar together until it liquifies, then adding the warm water and olive oil. Put it aside for a few minutes in order to set the fermentation process off. (If using dried yeast, follow the instructions on the packet or tin.) While you are waiting for the lovely yeasty smells to perfume your kitchen, sieve the flour and salt on to a clean work surface. Form it into a mound and make a well in the middle big enough to hold the liquid yeast.

When it is ready, pour the yeasty mix into the well in the flour and either using your hands or a fork bring the flour gradually in from the sides. I quite like using my hands – using a twisty, swirling motion with my fingers – rather like opening a door handle. If using the fork method, finish off by using your hands when the mixture starts to come together (you can dust them to prevent too much sticking). Knead the dough fairly vigorously with both hands, using a stretch and fold method (good exercise for your shoulders) until you have a soft springy dough.

Transfer the dough into a large bowl. Sprinkle a little flour over the top to prevent a crust forming and cover the bowl with a damp tea towel. Leave the dough in a warm place until it has doubled in size. If the temperature is right this should take about 1–2 hours.

When the dough is nicely risen, remove it to a flour-dusted surface and knead it a little more to push the air out (2 minutes). Then divide it up into four small balls and roll, using a rolling pin, or hand form (better because it stretches the gluten) the pizza into a roughly circular shape about 0.5cm thick. Now is the time to turn to your topping. The two simplest – and best – follow.

Pizza Margherita

1 x 400g tin of good plum tomatoes (San Marzano
   tomatoes work best)
5–6 slices of fresh mozzarella (preferably buffalo)
a handful of fresh basil leaves
sea salt and black pepper
olive oil
pizza base (see above)

Preheat your oven as high as it will go. Prove your pizza
stone by dampening it with a wet cloth and placing it in the
oven. (If you haven't a pizza stone, just use an oven tray,
though there is no need to preheat it.)

Drain the tin of tomatoes and crush them with your
hand. Slice the mozzarella and tear the basil leaves.

Assemble the pizza in the following order: spread the
crushed drained tomatoes over the pizza base; arrange the
sliced mozzarella over the tomatoes; top with a scattering of
basil leaves, a scrunch of sea salt and black pepper and a
drizzle of olive oil.

Slide the pizza on to the pizza stone (or oven tray) and
bake in the oven until the cheese has melted, the edges are
golden and the base has crisped up. Add more olive oil and
basil before serving.

Tip: dusting your work surface and the pizza stone with
semolina acts as a non-stick agent and makes transferring
the pizza easier.

Pizza Marinara

1 x 400g tin of good plum tomatoes (San Marzano
    tomatoes work best)
1 clove of garlic, finely chopped
1 teaspoon fresh oregano leaves, roughly chopped or
    ½ teaspoon dried oregano
salt
4 anchovy fillets
2 tablespoons extra virgin olive oil
pizza base (see above)

Preheat your oven as high as it will go and spread the
crushed tomatoes on the pizza base as described in the
previous recipe. Scatter with chopped garlic, oregano and a
good pinch of salt. Add the anchovy fillets and drizzle over
the extra virgin olive oil.

Slide the pizza on to the pizza stone (or oven tray) and
bake in the oven until the edges are golden and the base has
crisped up. Add more olive oil before serving.

DINNER PARTY DUST-UP

WHY IS IT THAT WE HAVE NEVER had a dinner party that was not preceded by a spat, dispute or full-blown eruption? It had been my intention to ponder this phenomenon silently, but I accidentally voiced my query within the hearing of Mrs H. This turned out to be a mistake.

'I'll tell you why,' she announced, after perhaps a thousandth of a second's pause for meditation. 'For some reason, I've got it in my head that a dinner party should be a joint effort. But at the moment when there are a million things to do, you blithely announce that you're going off for a swim or a little nap. This means I get into a dither. Maybe it's because we're not very good at planning. I'm always coming across recipes that say you should start two days ahead, but we usually start in the afternoon of the same day so there is a mad trot round the supermarket. And then you say you have an urgent appointment with the swimming pool or the bed and that's why we have a row.'

'Other people don't seem to have a terrific bust-up before their dinner parties,' I pointed out.

'I can't work out how other people manage to greet you

with a calm smile,' said Mrs H. 'Usually we've just been screeching at one another when the doorbell rings. I suppose we greet people with calm smiles. Except you don't. You tell people, "It's been sheer hell. Never again!"'

If you ask me – not that anyone does – the reason for the stormy atmosphere that boils up before our dinner parties has less to do with preparing the food than with the cleaning and tidying that Mrs H requires. At other people's dinner parties, I'm quite happy whatever the state of the surroundings as long as the food – and, oh yes, the wine – is OK and plentiful. I've been to fine dinner parties where it was necessary to clear the dining table of a thick accretion of newspapers and books before sitting down. Our house, however, has to be scrubbed, polished and burnished to within an inch of its life before the guests arrive.

One mandatory task strikes me as being particularly curious, so I decided to have it out with the Generalissimo. 'Why the hell do I always have to vacuum the stair carpet?'

'It's because I'm usually at work and don't clean up during the week.'

'But why the stairs?'

'Maybe people will want to use the upstairs loo. It's like a throwback to wearing clean knickers in case you're knocked down by an ambulance.'

'Bus.'

'Eh?'

'You mean bus, not ambulance.'

Ignoring my correction, Mrs H pressed on with her analysis. 'One reason I'm obsessed with cleaning up is that people are always expressing opinions about our house in a way that I wouldn't dream of talking about their house. I still remember your friend who looked at our dining room and sniffed, "Well, it's scarcely minimalist."'

I'd argue the point except for the fact that Mrs H is right. On the very day of this discussion, a dinner guest began her critique even before she'd got through the front door: 'The dandelions in your garden are letting the side down.'

'They weren't dandelions, they were aquilegia,' huffed Mrs H in the post-party analysis.

Ironically, flowers can be a cause of dispute between Mrs H and me. 'I like having flowers on the table, but you're always moving them to odd places,' said Mrs H. 'I've sometimes found them in the broom cupboard. And you always pick the wrong time to do things. At the very moment that I'm up to my ears in batter mix, you'll say, "Have I to open the oysters?"'

Once the dinner party is under way, things usually go OK. Though there was the time when the spiced beef wouldn't carve and we ended up with a pile of beefy fragments. And the time when we invited a famous chef and the roast potatoes burnt and the beef went grey because we had one drink too many before the meal. And the time when some guests from west London arrived in a furious temper because south-east London, where we happen to live, is so far from west London. (Of course, it is far nearer from south-east London to west London.) Then there was the time that someone crashed into every car in our street during the cheese course. But even that was a negligible disturbance compared to the ring on the door just as I was carving the pork. The street was full of fire engines. 'Don't worry,' said our neighbour, 'but I thought you should know that the house next door is on fire.'

Customarily, however, the blemishes at our festivities are less cataclysmic.

'You're always putting the wrong cutlery out,' Mrs H recalled. 'We're just sitting down and I'll notice that people have been given serving spoons instead of dessertspoons.'

'Well, you're always forgetting vegetables. How many times have I found a terrine of celeriac mash or pommes dauphinoise in the oven when the meal is finished?'

'Ha! I don't think that you've got much room to talk. How come the wine is ALWAYS at your end of the table? And you never make sure that everyone's glass is filled – except your own, of course.'

'I don't remember people complaining very much.'

'No,' Mrs H was compelled to agree. 'Usually they say it's been very nice.' After a momentary reflection, she added, 'Except for the evening in France when you made everyone eat those shellfish that look like doggy doo.'

Ah, yes, there was that.

11

A selfish feast

IN RETROSPECT, IT MAY HAVE BEEN unwise to entrust me with the food kitty when we stayed with our friends Malcolm and Eileen, who had been lent a villa in southwest France. Let loose amid the oceanic cornucopia of the Toulouse fish market, I instantly dispersed our collective funds of eighty euros on a large quantity of langoustines, crevettes, the small whelks known as *bulots*, crabs, oysters, mussels, scallops and rococo-shelled murex. But my greatest prize was a generous quantity of the Mediterranean sea creature that the *Oxford Companion to Food* says does 'not have a current English name, though it may sometimes be referred to as a "sea squirt".' Known in France as *violets*, their brown, wrinkled appearance has also produced the appellations *figue de mer* and even the oxymoronic *pomme de terre de mer*. These names are on the euphemistic side. Mrs H, who had been the unappreciative recipient of *violets* in the past, insists their brown, wrinkled appearance resembles a canine calling card.

My mountain of shellfish was greeted with amazement and approbation (possibly more the former than the latter).

Apart, that is, from the *violets*, which were regarded with undisguised revulsion by the womenfolk. However, Malcolm expressed wary interest: 'They look a bit like the things inside Daleks.'

'Not to worry, you don't eat the skins,' I cheerily urged. 'You eat the bit inside that looks like scrambled egg.' Enlarging on my theme, I pointed out that smaller *violets* taste sweet with a slight iodine tang, though big ones (they can be twenty centimetres in length) are like solid TCP. In his book *Mediterranean Seafood*, Alan Davidson says, 'It is eaten raw and is pleasant washed down with dry white wine … I have never faced up to a big one.' Edouard Loubet even offers a recipe for 'sea squirts in a germander marinade' in his book *A Chef in Provence*. 'Pretty yummy, huh?' I cajoled. Despite my PR campaign for these gnarly inhabitants of the littoral, the others showed zero sign of being persuaded.

Hacking through the leathery skin of a *violet*, it lived up to its English nickname. Dripping somewhat, I passed an opened sea squirt to Malcolm, who tackled it with a degree of trepidation. 'I like to think of myself as an adventurous eater, but this may be a step too far,' he said. Malcolm's subsequent grimace suggested that the experience had not been one of life's gastronomic highlights. 'It reminds me of something left in a wardrobe with mothballs for many years,' he reported. 'Bloody horrible.'

I tried one just to show that they were 'pleasant washed down with dry white wine'.

'Well, did you enjoy it?' asked Mrs H.

'Not really.'

Far from sympathising, Mrs H stuck the knife in, just as I did to the *violets*. 'Only a silly man would try to inflict such things on his friends,' she said. 'Only a very silly man would buy two dozen of them.' I suggested that they might have been a bit elderly. Even in Languedoc, there seem to be few takers for this Mediterranean treat. I recalled that the *poissonnière* appeared delighted by my desire to corner the Toulouse *violet* market. *The Oxford Companion to Food* concedes that the *violet* is 'not everywhere regarded as edible' and twenty-first century France appears to be heading in this direction. When I suggested to my companions that we should 'get back on that high wire' and buy another batch, the response was a firm negative. Indeed, divorce appeared a distinct prospect.

It grieves me to say that this is not the only occasion when my fervour for all things piscine has produced disharmony. It is not going too far to say that a tug o' war between my tendency to head for the fishmonger's slab in pursuit of the scaly, tentacled and armour-clad and Mrs H's desire to lug me away typifies our relationship. Looking bemused, she has accompanied me on tours of fish markets around the world. We've viewed inky swirls of cephalopods in Athens, mounds of gesticulating crabs in Barcelona, rustling piles of dried haddock in Reykjavik and shoals of tiddlers in Venice. In the spectacular fish market of Muscat, the fish were so fresh they were leaping from the slabs. As far as I am concerned, these are places of the utmost bliss. Our salty blood and tears indicate mankind's marine origins and, if the decision had been left to me, we would never have left. Discovering the mind-boggling variety of sea creatures – and, better still, eating them – takes us back to our murky, primeval origins. Unfortunately, my partner has not been persuaded to share my passion for strange things found in the sea.

This can be literally the case, as with the impressive fish we came across on the beach at Filey, North Yorkshire. It was large, silver and oval, with the big eyes characteristic of deep-ocean dwellers. It was also very dead. Some people had propped it up and were taking photographs of this unusual visitor. I was gazing awestruck when a more knowledgeable pair of strollers arrived. 'That's a Ray's bream,' said one of them. 'Old George caught one and said it was the best fish he'd ever eaten.' With that, his companion snatched up the fish, sniffed it and marched off with it.

I had been formulating the same move, but was restrained by Mrs H. Disappointment turned to consolation when we came across another dead Ray's bream a bit further along the beach. This was also in quite good nick despite being nibbled by seagulls. 'I wonder if …' I started.

'No. Absolutely not. NO!'

Weirdly, she displayed a similar antipathy toward some items sold by Filey's fishmonger, despite their irreproachable freshness. 'You are NOT buying those horrible rubbery things. NO!'

'Rick Stein says "they taste almost like lobster".'

'They're like off-cuts from a tyre factory.'

'Does that mean they're in *Michelin*?'

'Ha! Well, you're not having them.'

'Are you two having a domestic?' inquired the lady behind the counter.

With that, I accepted defeat. I must admit that Rick Stein's tribute to the whelk, which appears in his first book, *English Seafood Cookery* (published in 1988 when he was still 'Richard Stein'), is heavily qualified: 'When freshly boiled in salt water they can taste almost like lobster, albeit a bit tough. But the flavour is variable; sometimes they taste frightful … I can't say I'm an enthusiast.'

By the time Rick Stein's *Fruits of the Sea* appeared in 1997, he had gained a more wholehearted appreciation of this mollusc. 'I've got a lot of time for whelks,' he confides, before introducing his legion of fans to whelk fritters. A few pages earlier, there is a dish called Chinese whelks with bean sprouts and button mushrooms. 'Thinly sliced and stirred into a Chinese stir-fry,' Stein insists, 'whelks are incredibly good.'

It was this paean that sent me scuttling, alone this time, back to the fishmonger in Filey. I snapped up half a pound of boiled, de-shelled whelks for a couple of quid. Admittedly, the price of Stein's dish began to soar as I acquired other ingredients. Along with the mushrooms and bean sprouts, it required oyster sauce, dry sherry, pak choi, root ginger and hot peppers. Mrs H's response to my whelk-laden shopping trip would have registered high on the Richter scale, but Stein's 'incredibly good' promise placated her, at least temporarily. After slicing and stir-frying as directed, the result didn't look too bad, while the smell was positively tempting. Moreover, the taste was OK – with the exception of one ingredient.

Even when pared into slivers, the whelks remained resolutely whelkish. A couple of minutes after taking her first mouthful, Mrs H announced: 'I'm still chewing.' At my insistence, we chomped on and on. 'Just like school dinners,' said Mrs H. Nearing the bottom of her bowl, she laid aside her spoon. 'I'm feeling a bit queasy,' she groaned. I was forced to admit that I was feeling not unqueasy myself.

Twenty-four hours later, the whelks were still making their presence felt. Rick Stein may have come to venerate the blighters, but as far as I'm concerned, these hardy gastropods crossed the cusp into inedibility. For some reason, the British whelk tends to be a monster. We seem to be so impressed by their mature dimensions that edibility is of little consequence. Maybe British whelk addicts train themselves to absorb these giants in the same way that it is possible to build up a tolerance for arsenic. In France, they sensibly stick to smaller whelks. The *bulots* in garlic sauce I once had in Lille were highly acceptable, even to Mrs H.

It is, I feel, a tribute to the resilience of the human spirit that little more than a year after this episode, I once again found myself seriously contemplating the consumption of a whelk. The reason was a meeting with Fergus Henderson of St John restaurant in Smithfield. In the course of our conversation, the topic of whelks came up (as it might in any discourse between two red-blooded fellows). 'I'm very keen on whelks, but people are reluctant to eat them,' he declared. 'It's very hard to speak for whelks. They have to speak for themselves. People who try them usually like them. You just put some in salty water and get simmering. Can't remember how long. Quite a while. By the end they should be soft and tender and sweet.'

This planted a seed. A week or so later, I came back to Fergus with my proposal for an all-whelk lunch. The chef generously acceded to my proposal, though there was a slight problem. 'We haven't had whelks on the menu for the past year or so. I was sampling one from a new batch when I had a bad moment. You know: Mmmm – errrr – urggh. Luckily, I spat it out. Maybe it's time for them to come back. I've had some quite nice whelk moments.'

Many – possibly most – people may feel that there is no such thing as a nice whelk moment, though someone must be scoffing them because Fergus had a bit of trouble finding some for the Whelkathon, as it came to be known. 'I phoned round the whelkhouses to secure the finest possible whelks. Unfortunately, the south coast didn't have any, but we've got some from Bristol and some more from Ireland. We ended up with about twelve kilos,' he announced, as a small mountain of the blighters was placed before my tasting panel. This consisted of Jeremy Lee of the Blueprint Café and (after being lured with the promise of a bottle of Jo Malone scent) Mrs H.

Boiled briefly then allowed to cool in their own liquor, the whelks were the colour of Cornish cream when prised from their handsome shells. 'A certain amount of chewiness is no bad thing,' declared Fergus. 'But they're terribly sweet and lovely. A quintessentially English dish.'

'They're far more tender than the ones we had in York-shire,' said Mrs H, when she had steeled herself sufficiently to take a nibble. 'But I'm not getting a huge amount of flavour from them.'

'Obviously, you have to develop a relationship with the whelk,' suggested Jeremy. 'I'm very impressed. I like this very well indeed.'

Though we had made scant inroads into the shoal of whelks *au naturel*, the first of the warm whelk dishes arrived. Piled on slices of toast fried in duck fat, this was a dark green slurry of whelks, bacon and laver bread. 'Bacon is a good addition to most things,' said Fergus. 'This is from Old Spot pigs. Very happy bacon.'

'A triumph. I'm very pleasantly surprised,' said Jeremy. 'It may make a few converts. It will certainly refresh memories for old friends of the whelk.'

'I like the bacon,' said Mrs H.

The second dish was described by Fergus as 'chickpeas braised with whelks, chorizo, pig's trotter and a bit of rocket to mix in and keep scurvy at bay'. He assessed a mouthful: 'Hmm. Quite harmonious. There are no bullies here.'

'Very good,' rhapsodised Jeremy. 'The whelk should be ennobled. It's far better than those big clams or Canadian lobsters that are tough as old boots.'

'If you're desperate you could eat whelks,' groaned Mrs H. 'But you'd never choose them before lamb.'

Though there was a lengthy interval before our next encounter with maritime oddities, Mrs H still objected with impressive vigour. 'Good grief! What on earth are those?'

she yelped after seeing the dozen molluscs I had acquired at London's New Billingsgate Market. 'Don't they look rude? I don't like to go near them. CHRIS! One's moving! It's expanding! Eek! I'm off!'

To be fair to Mrs H, the geoduck clam lacks the allure of other shellfish. Our intended supper came in oval, grey shells about fourteen centimetres in length, held shut in rubber-band bondage. At one end of each bivalve, a thick, long cylindrical siphon emerged from between the shells. The floppy protuberance was undeniably, even alarmingly phallic. Cutting off the tumescent siphon and skinning it was one of the more disturbing culinary activities I've ever engaged in. A good deal of disassociation was required. But the anthropomorphic connotations declined as I sliced the siphon into a pile of fleshy rings. Served with soy sauce and wasabi horseradish, the dissected phallus would surely prove irresistible when the moment arrived for supper.

Not everyone does a runner when presented with a geoduck. Pronounced 'gooey-duck', it derives from a word meaning 'dig deep' in the language of the Nisqually tribe of north-west America, who presumably must be fond of eating the creatures. It is also regarded as a delicacy in some Asian cuisines. The ones sold at Billingsgate, which were diver-caught in Scotland, mostly go to Chinese restaurants. Living to an age of 150 or more, geoducks can weigh seven kilos, with a siphon that is a metre in length. The web page devoted to these creatures on Google images, which includes some spectacularly big ones, is jaw-dropping.

Along with the X-rated geoducks lolling in tumescent

splendour, my haul from Billingsgate included a kilo of Indian Ocean anchovies (a kilo is an awful lot of anchovies), a doctor fish, a moonfish (cartoon imperious with an up-thrust jaw, it is also known as the Mussolini fish), a silver pomfret and some home-grown treats in the form of a big bundle of razor clams, a half-kilo of sea-urchins and a large cuttlefish. In the kitchen of Hirst HQ, I started work on the Indian Ocean anchovies, which proved quite a bit harder to deal with than their Mediterranean cousins. For each tiny fish, you had to split open the stomach with your thumbnail, remove the backbone, then take off the head and tail and a spiky dorsal fin. The result was two gorgeous fillets decorated with twin stripes of silver like the chrome trim on a '59 Chevy. Unfortunately, I had 100-odd fish to tackle.

'Time well spent,' said Mrs H when I presented her with anchovy fillets sautéd in butter. 'Mmm, they taste so good. They have a lovely, buttery, caramelised flavour that doesn't really taste of fish.' The fillets were equally excellent after being marinaded overnight in white wine vinegar and a little salt. We ate them as a ceviche with olive oil, slivers of garlic, chopped parsley and lemon zest.

Having previously consumed sea urchins in the Aegean, Mrs H happily tucked in. They are best eaten raw. You snip a hole in the top of the spiny shell, remove the stomach sac and use a teaspoon to eat the five streaks of yellow gonads lining the inside of the shell. They have a delicious, slightly metallic taste of oceanic freshness, akin to oysters, but more profound.

'There's a phenolic hint,' mused Mrs H. 'But it's not unpleasant.' I might also have served the razor clams live, but Mrs H was resolutely opposed to the idea. 'You must cook them. When we ate them live, they wriggled round the plate. It was most off-putting.' Even when they were steamed open and grilled with garlic butter, she had mixed feelings. 'My last one was too big. It's made me feel funny. The smaller one I had before was better. More girly, lovely and sweet.'

The grilled cuttlefish was almost as sweet as a razor clam, but more succulent and satisfying. Perfect barbecue food. The surgeon fish was a disappointment – a bit tasteless, with lots of bones. ('Maybe it's an orthopaedic surgeon fish,' said Mrs H – a joke that may go down well in medical circles.) The Mussolini fish was creamy and delicate, though not as fleshy as its infamous namesake. Firm and sweet, the flesh of the pomfret was like a more solid lemon sole. It also fell off the bone like a flat fish, though it isn't. This treat from the Indian Ocean is worth the trip to Billingsgate in itself. But is it worth purchasing geoducks while you're there? We had the sliced siphon both raw as sashimi and steamed in white wine. I thought the results were OK in a chewy sort of way, but scarcely worth the trauma involved in its preparation. Mrs H was less ambivalent. 'That was disgusting,' she said, after nibbling a geoduck ring in desultory fashion.

'So you wouldn't like it again?'

'What do you think?'

SUET AND STEEL

IN CASE THE *violet*/whelk/geoduck saga gives the impression that I have spent much of our relationship inflicting horrifying foods on my wife, I might point out that it could have been a lot worse for her.

'What about the dumplings?' Mrs H points out.

Ah, yes. At least my obsession was short-lived. We only ate dumplings for a week. Yes, I know it sounds strange, but there was a reason (indignation at an American volume called *A World of Dumplings* that included beef ravioli, Jamaican fish patties, won-ton soup and even Cornish pasty but omitted the British dumpling). We munched away at dumplings both savoury and sweet for lunch and supper, but in my kindly way I spared Mrs H other treats that I discovered in an ancient booklet from the suet-maker Atora. I did not insist on sampling such suety treats as liver-and-rice mould or giblet pudding. Looking back, I'm surprised at my restraint in not serving up Buckinghamshire dumpling (stuffed with liver and bacon) with rice croquettes ('when cold form into attractive shapes'). Despite suffering from a troublesome cough, Mrs H refused another suggestion from the book: 'A teaspoon of Atora, taken in a glass of hot milk at bedtime, is a very soothing and beneficial treatment in the case of a cough or sore throat.'

I knew from bitter experience that an Atora confection called tongue roll would not go down well with Mrs H. She conceived an antipathy towards this tasty offal in student days when her landlady cooked ox-tongue on a regular basis. 'I don't think I've ever got over it,' she recalls with a shudder. 'I once looked in the pan and there was this vast tongue rising and falling in the boiling water. It went gloop, gloop, gloop.' Her attitude is disappointing, since I am fond of ox tongue with a green sauce made from parsley, oil and anchovies. Our friend Jeremy Lee of the Blueprint Café contributed an enticing recipe for this dish to a book called *Eat London*: 'You can steep a few tongues at a time as they don't go off … A modicum of patience is required as the tongues must steep for four or five weeks.' Strangely enough, the idea of having several ox tongues occupying her fridge for a month did not appeal to Mrs H.

In her unreasonable way, Mrs H also jibbed at such tempting dishes as Excited Pig ('a whole skinned salami served upright on a dish containing some very hot coffee mixed with a good deal of eau de cologne'), Simultaneous Ice-Cream ('dairy cream and little squares of raw onion frozen together') and Sicilian Headland (a paste of tuna, apples, olives and nuts spread on cold jam omelette). All come from the *Futurist Cookbook* by Filippo Marinetti (1932). Fortunately, there are less challenging dishes in this work of revolutionary cuisine. I decided that it was necessary and vital to try them at Hirst HQ.

Futurist cuisine is food as manifesto. Iconoclastic, wealthy and belligerent, Marinetti was a preposterous poseur like his hero Mussolini, though his campaigns were knowingly ironic. The Futurist movement came into being when Marinetti crashed his car in 1909. Much like Mr Toad's transformative collision in *The Wind in the Willows* ('Poop-poop!'), he was intoxicated by the experience: 'When I came up – torn, filthy and stinking – from under the capsized car, I felt the white-hot iron of joy deliciously pass through my heart.' Aiming for the polar reverse of the Italy loved by tourists – antique, picturesque, rural – the Futurists adored urban clamour and modernity: 'Long Live Steel!' Their plans encompassed avant-garde headwear (made of cork, glass, sponge and neon tubing), feather-weight aluminium trains and the abolition of cutlery. Their repudiation of pasta caused punch-ups in Italian communities around the world.

Swept up by Marinetti's 100 mph prose ('sing of the vibrant nightly fervour of arsenals and shipyards blazing with violent electric moons …'), I made a Futurist meal that exalted 'the geometric splendour of speed' and 'the aesthetics of the machine'. First course was the Cubist Vegetable Patch (a demanding arrangement of fried carrots, fried celery, pickled silverskin onions and cold boiled peas). 'At least it kept you quiet for an hour while you arranged the ingredients,' said Mrs H. 'The taste wasn't quite as interesting as it looked. Heinz Russian salad without the mayonnaise.' This was followed by the Bombardment of

Adrianopolis (deep-fried rice balls, each containing half an anchovy, three capers, a slice of mozzarella and two olives). 'Quite acceptable, rather like arancini rice balls.'

The dessert course was my *pièce de résistance*. 'Oh,' said Mrs H when she caught a glimpse. 'I was hoping you were not going to do that ridiculous sexist pud.' It was a disappointing reaction. The two impressive mounds of Campari-tinged ricotta, each with a strawberry peeping through at the summit, were, in my opinion, a most persuasive rendition of the dish called Strawberry Breasts. If the spectacle was eye-catching, the taste was slightly odd. 'Er, quite nice,' said Mrs H, 'though I prefer my Campari in Campari and soda.' (Coincidentally, the irresistible little conical bottles containing pre-mixed Campari Soda you see in Italian bars were conceived by Futurist designer Fortunato Depero in 1932.)

In Mrs H's deflating opinion, Futurist dishes were 'the kind of thing a child might make if let loose in the kitchen. They're like recipes from the *Funny Face Cookbook*.' For that reason, I chose not to proceed with Marinetti's recipe for Steel Chicken, which is cold roast chicken filled with '200gms of silver hundreds and thousands'. The nearest I could find in our locale was a cake decoration called Pink 'n' Pretty Sparkles, which was scarcely in keeping with the 'courage and audacity' of Futurism. Still, they might come in handy for our next joint effort in the kitchen. What could be more audacious and courageous than baking a cake?

12

A cake is not just for Christmas

Christmas cake

'Would you like a Christmas cake?' Mrs H's inquiry came as a surprise. We had never made a Christmas cake before, though I am partial to the odd slice. Come to think, I must have eaten several hundredweight of it over the years, mostly made by my mother. Anyway, my response was a big 'YES'.

I have a soft spot for Christmas cake. To be precise, I like the cake bit of the Christmas cake, especially when it is accompanied Yorkshire-style by a chunk of Wensleydale. I'm not desperate about the strata that go on top, though for many people the marzipan and the crunchy icing are the whole point of the thing. I like the gleaming, moist texture of the cake with its whiff of old grog and generous abundance of macerated raisins and sultanas. Not that anyone thinks twice about it, but there is something magical about dried fruit. I dare say I would feel rather differently about these little packages of the warm south if I had to remove the seeds from each fruit as, until quite recently, the cook was obliged to do. Elizabeth David blasted sentimentalists who rhapsodised about the old-fashioned Christmas: 'Have they ever stoned bunch after bunch of raisins hardly yet dry on the stalk, and each one as sticky as a piece of warm toffee?'

But why was Mrs H so inspired by a Waitrose recipe card for Christmas cake with Drambuie-soaked fruits? It would have involved a sudden conversion for her to share my Pickwickian appreciation of Christmas cake. 'I knew that you'd like one,' she said selflessly. Hmm. This did not ring true to me. I like lots of things that she refuses point blank to make. *Tripes à la mode de Caen* is just one example. After close questioning, the truth emerged. It was the 'Drambuie' bit of the recipe that prompted her suggestion. Ever since I wrote a regular column on cocktails, our house has been awash with bottles. She saw the Christmas cake as being a way of empty-ing at least one bottle. Since the cake only required 100ml or one-fifth of a 50cl bottle of Drambuie plus a small amount of the spirit for weekly 'feeding' of the finished cake, her Highland clearance was going to have a pretty marginal effect on my grog hoard. Still, every little helps.

We started with the rather sticky job of quartering soft apricots and prunes and halving glacé cherries. (Actually, it was Mrs H who wielded the scissors: 'A lot quicker and less sticky than a knife.') These went into a big bowl with vine fruit, mixed peel and the juice and zest of an orange. My main job was finding the Drambuie in our over-crowded drinks cabinet. Having only seen service in the production of one cocktail (the Rusty Nail, a favourite refreshment of

Frank Sinatra and The Rat Pack), the bottle was pretty much full. I added 100ml to the fruit for overnight maceration. An alcoholic, orangey aroma rose from the bowl. It smelled so good that I wondered if we should stop the Christmas cake right there.

Ructions started on the following day when Mrs H tried to line the baking tin with baking parchment. 'A bit tricky,' she grizzled. 'My maths let me down when working out the amount of paper I needed.' Worse came when the recipe recommended 'a double thickness of baking parchment round the outside of the tin. This will prevent the cake drying out during cooking.' Though I donated a finger to hold the string in place while Mrs H tied a knot, the paper refused to stay in place. It ruffled like a badly made bed. 'Bloody thing,' huffed Mrs H. 'Hopeless, but I suppose it will do.'

When the butter was creamed with dark muscovado sugar, the result had a pleasant rummy smell like molasses with maybe a hint of pipe baccy. Mrs H was not so fond. 'Not a sweet smell, is it? It's a bit smoky. Poo! I'm a bit suspicious of it.' This last, inadvertent expostulation indicated her true feelings towards the whole project. She was driven more by cupboard cleaning than desire for cake. But I found myself gaining interest as the project advanced. There's a lot to be said for muscovado sugar – tarry, dark, complex. The flavour comes from unrefined sugar cane juice. According to the *OED*, 'muscovado' derives from the Portuguese *mascabado*, meaning 'badly made'. In that case, I for one would not want the sugar made one jot better.

I was caught tasting the macerated fruit. 'That's a glacé cherry you owe me from one of your slices,' said Mrs H. The fruit tasted even better when chopped walnuts were added. For many years I had an antipathy to nuts. 'I think it's a mistake they were ever regarded as edible,' I would blithely assert. 'Really they're bits of wood.' But now I can see the point of nuts. The combination of alcoholic raisins and the dryness of walnut works very well.

I was recalled from my nutty reverie by a crack across the knuckles with the business end of a wooden spoon. 'We're going to add the beaten eggs by degrees into the sugar and butter,' observed Mrs H. 'There's a danger of the mixture curdling if you add eggs too fast. It's a basic thing with cakes. Can you see it looking like sick? Those lumpy-looking bits mean it has curdled. I'll bung in a spoonful of flour.' This antidote arrested the curdling.

The next step was to add the fruit and walnuts. 'Then mix well. Fold in the rest of the flour.' This simple instruction brings to mind the archetypal image of a cook. With one arm she encircles a bowl, while her free hand rotates a spoon like an outboard motor. Looks easy, doesn't it? 'Do you want to have a go?' inquired Mrs H. 'You'll moan. I now know why my mother wanted everyone to stir the Christmas cake. You need a breather from time to time.'

At first it was OK, then it got painful quite quickly. I realised, not for the first time, that I lacked cook's muscles. 'Have you made a wish?' asked Mrs H (though purists might say this only applies to Christmas pud).

'I wish this was finished.'

'There, you've wasted your wish now.'

My wish wasn't answered anyway. I had to carry on stirring.

'Oi! You're just smoothing the top. You're not mixing it. You're just pushing the flour down. You need to sort of twist the spoon. And you have to raise your elbow and twist your wrist. Use your shoulder.' After all this, my arm was really aching. Fortunately, our mix was completed, though Mrs H did a bit more stirring just to indicate the inadequacy of my efforts. Eventually, she shovelled the mixture into the lined cake tin with a silicone spatula. 'The great advantage of silicone,' said Mrs H, 'is that it gathers up every fragment of cake mix so there's not much for anyone to lick out.' Fortunately, she didn't scrape out *every* bit. Sweet and rich, the raw cake tasted of Drambuie, orange and lots of other good things. It might have been a pudding made by a particularly inventive chef. Why the bowl scrapings taste so much better than the finished cake is one of the great mysteries of gastronomy. Using a palette knife, Mrs H smoothed the surface of this luxurious aggregate in the cake tin. 'A bit like a brickie spreading cement on a line of bricks,' I said.

'Well,' retorted Mrs H. 'I've never made a brick wall and neither have you.'

With that, the cake went into the oven. Three to four hours at 150°C. It came out looking brown and happy. (It's funny how a fruit cake seems to smile at you.) For two months, we fed the cake with a dessertspoon of Drambuie on a weekly basis, then it fed us. But first there was the essential task of decoration. Ignoring my offer of Pink 'n' Pretty Sparkles, Mrs H installed a jewel-like encrustation of glacé fruit bought at Fortnum & Mason. The cost must have been eye-watering. 'I won't tell you how much,' she said, which is always a bad sign. 'It's your own fault for not liking icing.' Both Christmas cake and plutocratic topping were delicious beyond words. Sliver by sliver, this opulent creation saw us through the cruellest month of January, accompanied, of course, by a wedge of cheese.

The Victoria sponge sandwich

An entry on Wikipedia says that the name came about because Queen Victoria used to 'favour a slice of the sponge cake for her afternoon tea', though *The Oxford Companion to Food* is more guarded in its explanation, 'named after Queen Victoria'. Mrs H was confident of success since she made one as part of her Domestic Science O level. It's the kind of thing I wish I'd learned for O level instead of Boyle's Law, the ox-bow lake and the Diet of Worms (1521). 'It's just four plus four plus four,' Mrs H reported from Memory Lane (a pre-metric thoroughfare). 'Four ounces each of self-raising flour, caster sugar and butter – plus two eggs.'

'But why have you got two cake tins out?' I inquired.

'Because it's a *sandwich*,' she replied with eyes rolling heavenwards (a familiar rotation when we're together in the kitchen). 'You put one cake on top of the other.' *The Oxford Companion to Food* says different: 'Usually it is cut

in half and spread with jam/or cream to give a sandwich.'
But the schedule for a Yorkshire produce show, where my
mother's Victoria sponge sandwich was once disparaged
(see page 251), declares: 'To be made in two 8-in sandwich
tins.' It seemed wise not to pursue the great Victoria sponge
sandwich dichotomy at this stage. At least the twin cake
approach spares you the tricky business of latitudinal
bisection. I imagine many a Victoria sponge sandwich has
gone awry during this tricky procedure.

'The first thing we do is lots of preparation.'

'Boo!'

Plonking one of the tins on a length of baking parchment, she drew a circle round the base. 'I'm cutting out two
circles of parchment for the bottom of the cake tins. I know
the tins are non-stick but it's best to be sure. You lightly
grease the inside of the tins with butter and then line the
bottom with baking parchment. The idea is that you can
get them out of the tins. And we don't want it to sink in the
middle. If the centre turns out to be too soggy you make it
into a cake with a hole in the middle like a giant Polo. Then
you cover it in icing sugar and claim it is a great invention.'

The first ingredient was four ounces of butter. I cut a
chunk, which proved to be remarkably accurate. 'Four
point four ounces. That's near enough.'

'Make it four ounces exactly.'

Cussing a bit, I cut off a sliver.

'Four ounces exactly!' I announced. 'Give the man a
cigar!'

'Then four ounces of caster sugar. No! Don't shake the

sugar from the bag on to the scale! Use a spoon.' I then added it to the butter in a large bowl. 'While you're at it, you can weigh out four ounces of self-raising flour.' After weighing this, I started adding it to the butter and sugar. 'Oh no!' said Mrs H dramatically. 'Oh dear! Oh dear! Oh dear! Why did you put the flour in?'

'Because you said four plus four plus four.'

'That's just the weighing. Only a nincompoop would put them all in together.' She began fishing out the flour. 'You mix the butter and the sugar, then add the two beaten eggs and only then mix in the flour.'

When operations resumed, my egg whisking proved inadequate. 'You want a good amalgamation. You've still got great gloops of white in there. I usually angle the bowl and keep the fork flatter. You know when it's done because it goes much paler like this, with froth on top.' I began to be grateful that I didn't do an O level in Victoria sponge sandwiches. After an eternity of whisking, I achieved an acceptable paleness. I was then allowed to add half a teaspoon of vanilla extract.

'Now we're all prepared,' said Mrs H in a manner borrowed from her old cookery teacher, 'so we can start mixing with the cake mixer. First we'll mix the butter so it goes lighter.' The food mixer did its stuff on the butter. 'It's called "creaming",' said Mrs H.

'Oh really? I never knew butter had any connection with cream,' I said sarcastically, but it had no effect with Mrs H in full didactic flow. 'When it's creamed, we add the sugar. We're trying to enrobe each bit of sugar in fat. Can you see it changing in texture so it becomes all crumbly? You want to make sure every bit of butter is incorporated. Keep the machine going while we add the whisked egg. Do it a teaspoon at a time so it doesn't curdle.'

After the third or fourth spoonful, I rebelled. Two whisked eggs turns out to be a surprisingly large amount of liquid when you're adding it by the teaspoonful. 'This is infinitely tedious. Are you just doing it for my benefit? Would you really be adding it a teaspoon at a time if I weren't here?'

'Of course I would.'

'It'll take forever. I'll use a dessertspoon.'

'Well, if you know best,' she said and stalked off in a dudgeon.

'Oh, all right. But how would you go on if you were mixing by hand instead of having the cake mixer on? Not having three hands you'd have to stop all the time.'

Mrs H dodged this clever hypothetical. 'Take it from me, there's a reason for all this.' After an age, the egg was incorporated. 'NOW IT'S TIME TO ADD THE FLOUR,' bellowed Mrs H. 'Did you notice that I was talking in capitals? We'll sift the flour – we want to get some air into it – and then fold it in by hand. You do this by cutting and turning.' It didn't go down well when I pointed out that the mixture looked lumpy.

'I HAVEN'T FINISHED YET,' capitalised Mrs H.

'Is the sugar properly mixed in? The mixture sounds scratchy.'

'It'll be perfect,' she said and turned off the cake mixer.

'Can you divide the mixture into the two tins?'

I did it and weighed them to prove the accuracy of my division: 12.6oz and 11oz. In a rare dispensation, Mrs H did not demand the sharing-out of the outstanding 1.6oz. 'Now spread the mix in each of the cake tins with a palette knife. Turn the tin so the mix reaches the edge.'

'This is quite satisfying.' But it is rather reckless to express culinary contentment within earshot of Mrs H.

'Don't handle it too much. You're just moving the middle. Try and get it to the edge. We want the cakes to have the same thickness – no domes in the middle. And there's one more thing.'

'What?'

'You've got some cake mix on your nose.'

After twenty minutes in the oven, the kitchen filled with a buttery smell tinged with vanilla. You could put on ounces just by sniffing. 'You can see it rising and developing a golden colour. Just look in through the window – don't open the oven door.'

'I've just opened the oven door!'

'It's like that bit in *Ghostbusters*: "Don't cross the streams, Ray!"'

Since the door was open, Mrs H gently pressed the top of one cake. 'It's springing back a bit. Nearly done.' Five minutes later, the two slightly mottled sponges were extracted from their tins (not the slightest sign of sticking) and deposited on cooling racks. When they had cooled, I was delegated to spread the raspberry jam. For those new to the twin-cake method of making Victoria sponge sandwiches, here is the procedure. You invert cake A and spread jam on its bottom, then you put cake B on top. The spreading uses around two-thirds of a jar of jam. 'I want it to go right up to the edge,' directed Mrs H. 'You've got too much there. It's a bit thin over here.' When the jammy layer finally gained her seal of approval, I installed the second cake and tapped icing sugar through a tea-strainer on top of the sandwich.

'Looks very nice,' I said immodestly.

'It wouldn't win a prize at the village show,' tutted Mrs H. 'The cake is thicker in the middle than at the side.'

Despite this deficiency, the regal sarnie tasted even better than I expected. Maybe a sponge cake with a jam filling is scarcely the pinnacle of the pâtissier's art, but it was sensationally good. Exquisitely light in texture, the sponge was pleasantly infused with vanilla and delivered a delicious tang of concentrated raspberry. Mind you, you need an exceptional raspberry jam to achieve such transcendental results. May I refer you to pages 273–286?

Seed cake

My mother possibly made seed cake, but I don't remember it and it is a fairly memorable cake. Maybe it is a cake for grown-ups. Softish but not too soft, rich but not impossibly so, it is almost custardy on the palate, with the scattering of caraway seeds providing an occasional, surprising hint of liquorice. It is certainly an adult cake in the version on the menu of St John restaurant in Smithfield, where it arrives accompanied by a large glass of Madeira (19 per cent ABV). Since Madeira packs a punch like the old one-two manoeuvre favoured by boxers in the Fifties, most people have this combo as a form of dessert, but Fergus Henderson, the charming gaffer at St John (yes, he's the same chap who did the Whelkathon. Versatile, you see) prefers it for elevenses.

'The Madeira doesn't mean you have to write the day off,' he told me. 'Of course, you can if you want to – but one glass, or possibly two, gives us a quick jolt, a bit like a firework display. You have a giddy moment and feel restored.' He is adamant that only one pinch of caraway seeds is required in each cake. 'It's the Sultana Bran principle. When I was a child, I was always tempted to add more sultanas to the Sultana Bran, which ruined it.'

He noted that the steady maturing of the seed cake brought variety to his morning ritual. 'The point about seed cake is that it is good fresh from the oven when it is buttery and eggy with a crisp crust. But it is also very good when it is a day old. The sugar comes to the fore and the eggs and butter calm down. It is more grown-up.'

But why partner the seed cake with Madeira? 'It is hard to get the cake down without some form of lubrication and a glass of Madeira is a lot faster than a cup of coffee.' This most amiable of restaurateurs admits that his elevenses campaign has yet to take off. 'I hope others feel the urge to murder a bit of seed cake at eleven o'clock, but usually I'm on my own. Still, someone eats the St John seed cake at some stage in the day. It always goes. You only have to try it once for it to become a habit.'

Quite so. After floating home on a Madeira-scented cloud, I egged Mrs H into making a seed cake. We obtained a jar of caraway seeds. Brown and curved, the seeds (actually, they are tiny dried fruit) look like dark, miniature bananas. The smell was distantly familiar. Eventually, it came to me. Caraway is the main flavouring in kummel, the under-regarded digestif. Though the British use it only in cakes, caraway was once a big deal. It was the first spice plant to be cultivated in Europe and the Germans remain very keen. Caraway crops up in sauerkraut, rye bread and Munster cheese. It is also used to mitigate the fire in the North African pepper sauce harissa. In contradiction to Fergus's less-is-more line on caraway, the label on the Schwartz bottle of caraway seeds declares, 'Use quite generously,' but this turned out to be with vegetables.

Making the cake began with a mad whirl of butter, sugar and a teaspoon of caraway seeds in the food mixer. 'Can you see it going nice and light and fluffy?' asked Mrs H. 'Now we have to add five beaten eggs. Five! That'll make it nice and floppy.'

I felt obliged to make a small warning. 'In his recipe, Fergus says, "Add the eggs little by little to prevent curdling."'

'Aha!' said Mrs H. 'You see, you're taking notice when Fergus says it. If I say it you say, "Poo!"'

I managed to keep quiet when she added the beaten eggs with a dessertspoon. 'You're adding them slowly to keep it light and fluffy. If you were to add them all at once it would slop around and curdle. If it starts to curdle you've got to beat like mad.' With five eggs, the cake mix became almost liquid, a sort of suspension. By this stage, Mrs H was back in lecturing mode. 'Now, we add the flour. Note that we've sieved it first and we're adding it very slowly to prevent lumps.' After being thickened by flour, the mixture was transformed into a sort of batter by the addition of milk.

Like Mrs H, Fergus advocates greasing the baking tin with butter and lining the base and side with baking parchment. The cake mix, an unctuous mix of good things, plopped into the cake tin like concrete at a building site. Fergus's recipe called for a '16 x 10 x 8cm loaf tin'. Mrs H's nearest equivalent was a bit smaller, though just big enough to accommodate the mixture.

'Hope it'll be OK,' said Mrs H warily.

Indeed it was, though the mixture rose during cooking and stood proud out of the tin, supported by the paper lining, by maybe a centimetre. After half an hour (Fergus says '45 minutes') at 180°C, the cake was deemed done. A skewer inserted into the heart of the cake came out without particles adhering. It looked a tempting light brown. I thought that a long fissure on the top added character, but Mrs H tutted and said that a judge would take points off. This judge said it tasted terrific. The richness of the interior was complemented by the slight crunch of the crust. The cake sufficed for ten days of elevenses. No Madeira, though. Fergus is made of tougher stuff than his seedy acolyte.

Mrs H's recipe for Christmas cake

Christmas cake is best made two months before 25th December to allow time for weekly 'feeding' with liquor. This recipe is based on a free cookery card from Waitrose. I was drawn to the recipe not only because it contained Drambuie and would help empty one of the bottles clogging my kitchen cupboard, but also because of the inclusion of apricots and prunes and the rather attractive sugar-paste robin on the icing – which I didn't do in the end. You make the cake in two stages. Day one: soaking the fruit in alcohol (deliciously smelly and a bit sticky). Day two: mixing and cooking. When I found we didn't own a cake tin of the size recommended, day one also involved zipping along to the kitchen shop to buy a square cake tin with a loose base.

I had a request for no marzipan or icing, so I decorated the cake with nuts and glacé fruits. This was a jolly good excuse to visit Fortnum & Mason, where an impeccably charming young man on the glacé fruit counter admirably kept his cool while trying to fish out a rather resistant glacé clementine at my request.

When you finally have a slice of the cake, you will need a slice of good cheese to accompany it. (Apparently this is a Yorkshire tradition, so Wensleydale is in order.)

750g vine fruit mix
250g soft apricots, quartered
200g tub of Italian mixed peel
200g Provençal glacé cherries, halved
100g pitted soft prunes, quartered
grated zest and juice of 1 large orange, plus the zest from
    another orange
100ml Drambuie, plus extra to 'feed' the cake
250g unsalted butter, softened
200g dark muscovado sugar
5 medium eggs, beaten
300g plain flour, sifted
200g walnut pieces
in the absence of marzipan and icing, a selection of nuts
    and glacé fruits for decorating, plus some apricot glaze

The first stage of making the cake is dead easy: just weigh
out the dried fruit and put it into a large bowl. (Cut up the
prunes and apricots with kitchen scissors – it is quicker and
less sticky than using a knife). Then stir in the grated orange
zest and juice and the Drambuie. Cover with clingfilm and
leave the fruits to soak overnight. Do have a long lingering
sniff of the fruits and alcohol before you cover them up. It is
a heavenly orangey aroma. (Since I like citrusy things, I
added the zest of another orange without any harm to the
final cake. I think!)

Next day, start with a bit of preparation: preheat the oven
to 150°C/Gas Mark 2. Grease and line the base and sides of
a 20cm square (or 23cm diameter round) cake tin with

baking parchment so it stands 5cm above the top. Also tie a double thickness of baking parchment around the outside of the tin. This will help prevent the cake from drying out during cooking. (You may need to ask nicely to borrow someone's finger for knot-tying purposes.)

After this you can return to the task of making the cake. In a large bowl, use a hand-held electric whisk to beat together the butter and sugar until it is pale and fluffy. Gradually beat in the beaten egg a little at a time. There is a tendency for the mixture to curdle if you add too much beaten egg at once. If the mixture begins to curdle, add a little more flour. In any case, add a tablespoonful of flour when beating in the last drop of egg.

Add the soaked fruits and walnuts with any remaining liquid from the mix. Stir in the rest of the flour. (This is the arm-aching stage). When thoroughly mixed, spoon the mixture into the cake tin. Use a round-bladed knife to level the top of the mixture. You do not want a domed cake if you plan to ice it.

Stand the tin on a baking tray and bake for 3–4 hours, until cooked through. If the cake starts to get too brown, cover the top with foil.

To check that the cake is cooked, insert a skewer into its centre. If it comes out clean, the cake is done. If there are any smidgens of cake mix glued to the skewer, cook for a while longer but keep an eye on it. Remove the cake from the oven and leave it to cool down completely in the tin.

When the cake is cold, remove the cake from the tin and store with its lining paper, wrapped tightly in foil. Try to keep the cake in a cool place. Don't think you are through with the cake, though. It needs feeding, which you do by unwrapping the foil, making small holes in the cake with a skewer, then drizzling with a couple of tablespoons of Drambuie. Doing this on a weekly basis will help keep the cake moist and adds extra flavour (as well as helping empty the bottle).

As Christmas draws near, decorate the cake. Deviating from the Waitrose recipe I used pecan nuts, glacé kiwi fruit and glacé clementines plus some gold almond dragées. A smearing of apricot glaze fastened them securely to the cake. I also found a bit of ribbon to tie round the side. Then hide in a tin to prevent samples being nibbled before 25th December.

Mrs H's recipe for seed cake

This recipe is taken from *Beyond Nose to Tail* by Fergus
Henderson. Christopher has spent several happy mornings
in the company of Fergus at his St John restaurant nibbling
away at this cake and slugging Madeira for 'elevenses'. Oh,
the hard life of the freelance writer.

260g unsalted butter, softened
260g caster sugar
1 teaspoon caraway seeds
5 large eggs, lightly beaten
120g self-raising flour
150ml full-fat milk

Grease a 16 x 10 x 8cm loaf tin with butter. Line the base
and sides with non-stick baking parchment.

Cream the butter, sugar and caraway seeds together with
a hand-held or stand mixer until they are white and fluffy.
Gradually mix in the beaten eggs, adding them little by little
to prevent curdling. Sift the flour and fold it carefully into
the cake mix with a metal spoon until fully incorporated.
Lastly, add the milk and gently stir in.

Transfer the mixture to the prepared tin and bake in an
oven preheated to 180°C/ Gas Mark 4 for 45 minutes, or
until it is golden brown and a skewer inserted into the
centre comes out clean. (Our cake reached this stage in 30
minutes.) Leave it to cool a little in the tin before turning it
on to a cooling rack. Serve with a glass of Madeira.

Mrs H's recipe for Victoria sponge sandwich

'Four, four, four and two eggs' was the mantra learned from my schooldays, referring of course to ounces. However, since metrification I have had to learn '113g,113g,113g and two eggs' which is a bit of a whatnot to remember. The problem has been solved by doubling the recipe and using larger tins. I can do 225's.

225g butter, softened, plus a liitle extra for greasing
225g caster sugar
4 large eggs
225g self-raising flour, sifted
vanilla extract
raspberry jam for the filling, preferably homemade
icing sugar for dusting

Preheat the oven to 180°C/Gas Mark 4.

Since this recipe involves making two sponge cakes, you'll need two 17.5–20cm cake tins. Grease the cake tins with a little bit of butter and line the bottom of each one with a circle of non-stick baking parchment.

In a large bowl, cream together the butter and sugar until pale and creamy, using an electric hand-held whisk, stand mixer or by hand with a wooden spoon. Beat well to get lots of air into the mixture.

Beat in the eggs one at a time, adding a tablespoon of flour if the mixture curdles. Add a drop of vanilla extract to the beaten egg if you like to enhance the flavour. Fold in the sifted flour using a large metal spoon. Be careful not to over-mix it.

Pour the mixture equally between the two cake tins and level off the top with a spatula. Make a slight dip in the centre with the tip of the spatula if you don't want your cake to be pointed in the middle. Place the tins in the oven and bake for about 20 minutes, or until the cakes spring back when pressed gently with a finger and are pale gold in colour.

Remove the sponge cakes from the oven and take them out of the tins after about 5–10 minutes. Place them on a wire cooling rack, remove the greaseproof paper and leave to cool completely (about half an hour).

Spread raspberry jam on one of the sponges, then sandwich together with the other one. Dust with icing sugar (I use a small sieve) and serve.

JUDICIAL MATTERS

HAVING MANAGED TO AVOID any position of responsibility whatsoever for five decades, it came as something of a surprise when I was made a judge. Sadly, no one called me 'M'lud', though my adjudication was required on matters as significant and onerous as in any court of law. I was co-opted as a judge at the annual show in the North Yorkshire village of Thornton-le-Dale. Country shows are taken very seriously in these parts. As Harry Pearson, an aficionado who wrote a book on such events, remarked, 'The baking section is ruled over by a set of principles so rigid and arcane they make Japanese etiquette look laissez-faire.'

If anything, this is something of an understatement. My mother refused to have anything to do with the produce show in her village following the ruthless verdict on her entry in 'Class 61 One Victoria Sandwich (Raspberry Jam Filling)'. She came second even though hers was the only entry. At the same event, Mrs H suffered annual agonies over 'Class 69 One Shortcake, 6–6.5inch diameter'. The air turned blue as she alternately applied rolling pin and ruler. Her shortcake always expanded by a fatal fraction of an inch and was condemned to ignominious failure.

I was not asked to adjudicate on such demanding matters. After writing about the Thornton-le-Dale show in my column (I was particularly taken with an equine act called the Four Horsemen of the Apocalypse: 'Let's have a great round of applause for Pestilence!'), I was invited to judge 'Class 166 Best Matching Pair of Pigs'. Despite having a great fondness for pigs, I was slightly lacking in technical expertise. This deficiency was remedied by a brief lesson in porcine pulchritude: 'Look out for a good under-line and an even number of teats.' With the assistance of Mrs H, I carefully assessed the two pairs that had been entered. The laurels went to a charming duo of Gloucester Old Spots.

In subsequent years, I was called on to assay scarecrows, fruit liqueurs and children's crafts (a poisoned chalice second only to the bonny baby competition that survives at Rosedale Show near Whitby). Though I continued to accept the judge's badge (the free pen and cold collation lunch contribute to the allure of the post) at Thornton-le-Dale, I missed the Saddlebacks, Great Whites and Berkshires. I like pigs very much. I empathise with their obsession with food and sleep. I admire their cussedness and belligerence. I enjoy the way that pig shows often teeter on the edge of anarchy, with disputing parties having to be separated by their minders (the pig boards used for this purpose often bear the logos of major banking organisations). And, yes, I very much like eating pork.

This aptitude came in handy when I was called back to adjudicate on pigs, albeit post-mortem. Our tasting of 'Class 90 Homemade Pork Sausage' and 'Class 91 Homemade Pork Sausage (Flavoured)' was unexpectedly demanding. The man in charge of the grill mixed up the thirty-odd entries so we were obliged to have a second cook-off. My appreciation of the Four Horsemen of the Apocalypse, especially Famine, was slightly marred by having sixty nibbles of sausage inside me.

The following year, I was gratified that the show organisers had adopted my proposal for an exciting new category, which appeared in the show schedule as 'Class 93 Homemade Pork Pie (max 4in diam.) Tin baked. Hot water crust' and 'Class 94 Homemade Pork Pie (1lb weight approx.) Hand raised. Hot water crust'. Better still, I was asked to judge the porkies.

At Mrs H's urging, we arrived at the show ground in plenty of time. This was just as well. Discovering the location of the six pork pies that had been entered involved a good deal of shuttling between the Produce Tent, the Show Secretary's Tent and the Judges' Lunch Tent, where the tasting was to take place. 'Get a move on,' urged Mrs H in a manner unbefitting the dignity of my office. 'And stop complaining. At least we'll work up a good appetite for the tasting.' An hour's circumnavigation of the show site produced five pies. The sixth had disappeared, presumably to the final resting place of all good pork pies.

As we started our appraisal, a deluge descended. 'Looks like it's set in,' said a fellow judge with grim relish, a condiment much favoured in Yorkshire. Mrs H cut wedges out of the entries, a task that demanded a fair bit of elbow work. 'I feel a bit like King Arthur,' she said, heaving her knife from the heart of a pie. Though the entries shared the attributes of admirably crunchy pastry, nice even walls and tasty jelly, the nature of the meat revealed that only two makers were responsible for all five pies. One favoured lovely chunks of grey pork, the other preferred a fine mince, richly seasoned. Numerous slices were required for me to make my decision. Both approaches had merit and, anyway, I hadn't had any breakfast. By the time I had reached my judgement, the rain had stopped.

'Can I have a bit more?' I requested.

'No, you can't,' said my assistant. 'You don't want to get a prize for being the greediest judge.'

When the flap of anonymity was removed from the entry slips, I discovered that the chunky pies were made by a Mrs Rooke, while the fine-grind pies were the work of Martin, the show chairman (which possibly explains the ready acceptance of my proposal). The two first prizes of £5 were divided between the two entrants. After the success of this introductory bout, the show anticipates an avalanche of homemade pork pies in future years. Possibly, I will be judging fifty rather than five pork pies. Since we in the judiciary are expected to have a profound knowledge of our specialist fields, it became evident that I had to remedy an omission. Though I had devoted a lifetime to eating pork pies, the time had come to make one.

13

Telling porkies

AT ITS BEST, a pork pie is a deeply satisfying combination of tastes and textures. In a Melton Mowbray pie, which should be hand-raised with bulging sides, the pork is uncured, so the cooked meat looks light grey, like a pork chop. It is no coincidence, incidentally, that this Leicestershire town produces both Britain's most characterful cheese (Stilton) and Britain's best pork pies. The whey from the milk went to feed the pigs. In the nineteenth century, pork pies became a favourite snack for the many hunts in the area. Melton Mowbray pies have become my preference, though I'm not averse to a pie containing pink or cured pork.

They're mostly like this in Yorkshire and particularly good when warm. The phrase 'particularly good' doesn't do justice to the pork pies of B. W. Glaves, the butcher in the village of Brompton-by-Sawdon, near Scarborough. When they come hot from the oven, I know of no food more mouth-watering. They are the quintessence of juicy, seasoned porkiness. There are two drawbacks to this mid-morning snack: 1) A juicy dribble always leaks out after your first bite. Despite the safety warning given by Glaves's staff, I customarily spend the rest of the day sporting a huge greasy blotch on my shirt or sweater; 2) It is such a very sustaining snack that you tend to pick at your lunch.

If the pork is the most important element of a pork pie, the crust doesn't come far behind. This should be crisp on the outside and delicately yielding on the inside. A vegetarian friend of mine (admittedly not a very belligerent vegetarian) found this aspect of the pork pie so tempting that she was prone to take a nibble. Then another nibble and another. Before long, she was past the point of no return and polished off the whole crust, leaving just the meat. Her partner used to complain about the distressing spectacle he encountered when peering into the fridge. Instead of the pork pie he was looking forward to, there was something that resembled 'a bald baby's head'.

It may come as a surprise, but there is a third part to a pork pie, almost as significant as the other two. Some recipes don't mention the jelly until the end (Hugh Fearnley-Whittingstall: 'It's a bit like filling a car with petrol …'), but actually it is the bit that you make first. Unless you're Delia. In a bizarre omission, the pork pie recipe on Delia Online doesn't mention jelly at all. Obviously, she didn't grow up eating pork pies. (It comes as no surprise to learn she hails from Woking.) Jelly-making is pretty simple once you've found a butcher who will sell you a pig's trotter or pork knuckle. It's just a long, long simmer with carrot, onion and spices to produce stock, which is then boiled to make a reduction that will set as translucent porky jelly.

When the jelly is done, you can tackle the meat. A survey of pork pie recipes revealed that Jane Grigson, Delia Smith and Hugh Fearnley-Whittingstall recommended a mixture of around four parts shoulder pork to one part green bacon, which Grigson says, 'improves the flavour'. The recipe is therefore midway between the Melton Mowbray pie and the cured pork pie. Grigson maintains the meat should be 'one part fat to two parts lean'. This might be slightly overdoing it. Mark Hix recommends 20–30 per cent fat. Anyway, plenty is required. Like hamburgers, pork pie is not diet food. Where we went wrong was using belly pork in our first joint effort. This was my fault, I admit it. Instead of buying shoulder pork from the butcher, I had a moment of mental aberration and bought belly pork. This can be sensational – some of the most memorable mouthfuls I've ever had were belly pork – but it's not right for a pork pie. There's too much skin (you don't have crackling in a pork pie) and too much connective tissue. (The same white stringy stuff that caused trouble when we were making hamburgers. You may recall that its tensile strength can be half that of aluminium.) It has to be removed so you can chop up the meat. The grisly task fell to me. 'You bought it. You can deal with it,' said Mrs H.

After an hour spent cutting out connective tissue and skin (which both went into the jelly stock), I'd reduced 615g of belly pork to 480g of acceptable pork that had to be cut into cubes for the pie. Even with shoulder, which spares you the task of removing connective tissue, the pork should be chopped up by hand. Delia Smith says you can use 'a processor with the pulse button – you need a chopped rather than a minced effect', but Mrs H was scathing. 'I've tried it and I don't like it. No matter how briefly you pulse, it turns out like sausage meat, too homogenous and compact.'

She demanded a fine cut of both pork and bacon. 'Quarter-inch cubes.' The template she had in mind was the close-textured pork pie made by Mrs Bullivant, a producer who has a farm outside York and sells her pies at farmers' markets in the area. I like her pies as well. Unusually for Yorkshire, her pork is uncured. Inside tremendously tasty pastry, which Mrs H describes as 'the real McCoy', the meat is close-packed, medium-sized chunks. But when I attempted to imitate her chunk-size, my output was deemed too large. 'Here comes the Food Police,' Mrs H declared, pointing out a long strip of bacon that required further attention. When the meat passed this stringent quality control, she seasoned it with fresh sage, allspice and mace. 'I'm being generous with the salt and pepper. As with pâté, you always put in a bit more than you think is necessary.'

'How much?'

'Delia just says "salt and pepper". I'm putting in a tea-spoon of salt.'

Both Smith and Grigson also add anchovy sauce. According to the latter, this is used 'in the Melton Mowbray area'. Though I love Alan Davidson's *Oxford Companion to*

Food above all other food books, I'm baffled by his explanation that the pie-makers of the town added anchovy essence 'not only for its flavour but because it was thought to give the meat an attractive pink colour, while pies from other districts were brownish or greyish. In modern pies, which are always pink, the colour is achieved by the use of chemicals.' The only explanation that springs to mind is that Davidson wrote the entry before Melton Mowbray pies enjoyed their recent resurgence. The town's manufacturers may have used anchovy sauce (they tend to be a bit cagey about revealing their seasonings), though it is not mentioned in any of the recipes in *The History of the Melton Mowbray Pork Pie* by Trevor Hickman. We ended up putting in the half-teaspoonful recommended by Smith and Grigson.

Having prepared the meat, it was time to tackle the hot water pastry. Though always rather impressed whenever I heard the name, I hadn't much idea of what it was.

'Weigh out 450 grams of flour!' said Mrs H.

'There you are, 445 grams.'

'Then we need a bit more. Now sift the flour.'

'Oops.'

'Try to get it all in the bowl.'

The hot water part of hot water pastry proved to be rather more thrilling than I expected. The water isn't just hot but boiling and it contains molten lard. It might have been poured on the riff-raff of Paris by Quasimodo from the bell-tower of Notre-Dame. You start by heating a rectangular block of lard in a pan of cold water. As this white island disappears, a puddle of molten lard spreads on the surface of the water. Eventually the lard resembles the remnant of a bar of soap, before vanishing entirely. When the lard and water mixture achieves a white boil, the bubbling emulsion is mixed with the flour.

'You add the flour in a series of trickles,' said Mrs H. 'Trickle, stir. Trickle, stir. Trickle, stir.'

The result was a mess of beige lumps.

'You want to amalgamate the bits and knead it,' she directed.

'Ow!'

'That'll be the boiling fat. It's quite warm.'

Being made of sterner stuff, Mrs H gathered the pastry together and rolled it into a ball. Now came the demanding task of making a leakproof jacket for the pork pie. In Melton Mowbray, they form the crust round a circular wooden block or dolly. It is like a shoe last, but for a pie. Since even our outlandish collection of gadgetry lacked such an item, we used a non-stick pie mould.

'We need to line the mould while the pastry is warm,' urged Mrs H. She quickly rolled out the pastry. With some difficulty she lined the mould.

'It's very keen on falling down, isn't it,' I pointed out.

'It's probably too thin.'

'There's loads of pastry left over.'

'So what about the lid?' said Mrs H with a touch of exasperation. 'How many pork pies have you seen without a lid?' Well, you can get novelty pies topped with cran-berries, onions or even gooseberries, but I thought it wise not to make this point. Mrs H rolled the remaining pastry into a rough circle.

We filled the pastry case with chopped, seasoned pork and put on the lid. Mrs H sealed the joint between lid and walls by pushing her thumb repeatedly round the rim of the mould. For the first time our effort began to look like a pie.

'Make a hole in the top so we can fill the pie with jelly,' said Mrs H. 'I bet you'd forgotten that.'

But it turned out that a hole in the lid was not required. I returned from an outing expecting to see an immaculate cooked pork pie. Instead I was greeted by one of the ruins that Cromwell knocked about a bit. A great chunk of pastry was missing from one side of the pie. 'We made the pastry too thin,' wailed Mrs H. 'It might have been all right if I hadn't dropped it when taking it out of the oven. I should have used oven gloves instead of a tea towel. The mould fell over and the juice leaked out and stuck the pastry to the wall of the mould and I'm fed up with the whole bloody thing.'

The pie smelled very nice though. A lovely cloud of sage and cooked pork hung in the air, so we decided to eat the pie warm. It was very tasty, perhaps a bit too tasty. A very savoury pie. We each had a slice, then another slice, then another and that was the end of the ruined castle. Though we polished it off with gusto, certain reservations remained.

'A bit too salty,' tutted Mrs H. 'I don't think you need salt and bacon and anchovy sauce.'

'I think the bacon was wrong. The pie was neither one thing nor another.'

'It was grey, though.'

'Should we have another go?'

'I think I've had enough of pork pies for the time being.'

When our enthusiasm returned, not to mention our appetites, we resumed the task. For our second effort, we went for pork shoulder, which was much easier than belly. I followed my inclinations and chopped the joint into somewhat larger cubes (between a quarter and half an inch across). No bacon, no anchovy, just salt and pepper and spices. As a pork pie purist, I decided that we should also ditch the herbs. Butchers don't usually bother with them. We had some jelly left over from the first pie. All that remained was the problematic pastry. This time we incorporated milk with the water and lard. Boiling these together produced an interesting lava-lamp effect, with stalagmites of milky water rising into the molten fat before forming a white foam.

The major difference with our second effort was that we did not roll the pastry. This decision was taken after lengthy consideration of pie architecture and crust viability. Rolled pastry produces a thin crust that is liable to leak at the jelly stage. Moreover, Melton Mowbray pies have thick walls.

After cutting off a quarter of the pastry for the lid, I used my hands to form the hot-water pastry into a rough circle about twenty centimetres in diameter. I eased this into the mould so the centre of the circle dipped into the hole. Then came the tricky task of pushing the pastry to the bottom of the mould, so it filled snugly into the joint between the base and the wall. 'Try not to make a hole in the bottom,' said Mrs H.

'I've just made a hole in the bottom.'

After repairing the fissure (it's a good idea to reserve some pastry for patching purposes), I massaged the crust up the wall of the mould. 'Use two fingers and work quickly,' said Mrs H. I fought back the impulse to flourish two fingers in her direction. The difficulty of this task was compounded by the tendency of the pastry to spring back. After some deft fingerwork, the pastry reached the rim of the mould. 'No holes ... I think,' said Mrs H. We then filled the pastry with chopped pork. The lid, which I also formed with my hands, then went on top. Well, where else would it go?

When Mrs H suggested decorating our creation, I finally discovered my métier. Hitherto, I have always regarded myself as lacking in any manual talent whatsoever, but somewhat late in life I discovered that I have an innate ability for making tree leaves in pastry. I would have made them in autumnal profusion, but Mrs H said four were enough.

When the pie came out of the oven, we poured in the warm jelly (yes, I remembered the hole) and continued to top up every so often for a few hours. 'Hurray! No cracks,' yelled Mrs H. We let this pie cool before eating. The first slice was a nervous moment, but it came out clean as a whistle. Mrs H expressed satisfaction at the pastry. 'Not too lardy and not too thick. It's not as crisp as a professional pork pie but their crusts can be very greasy.' I liked the meat, a close-packed matrix of chunks set in jelly. 'A pork pie that tastes of pork,' I said, reaching for the chutney. I also discovered that it went extraordinarily well with Tiptree's medlar jelly. A significant part of the pleasure of a pork pie is discovering what goes well with it.

After all this endeavour, would I bother making pork pies at home when rather good ones are available from Glaves the butcher or Mrs Bullivant's market stall? Well, yes, once or twice a year if I felt the urge. 'If I have one criticism, it's that the chunks of pork are still too big,' said Mrs H. 'Now Mrs Bullivant's pies …' But I was too busy chomping.

Mrs H's recipe for pork pie

One day we will make a hand-raised pork pie. But until then, we remain at the wimp's stage and use a non-stick, loose-bottomed, 11cm pork pie tin. (John Lewis and Lakeland sell them.) I have also hired an oval-shaped game pie tin from our local kitchen shop for our Christmas pie. (Even I cannot bring myself to spend £78.50 on one.) This is our favourite variation, but those who feel so inclined can add a tablespoon of chopped fresh sage and a finely chopped rasher of green back bacon to the pork filling. A note on pig's trotters: OK, the animal may have been squelching around in the soil – but when you buy trotters at the butcher, they are just as clean as the rest of the pig. Your main problem might be getting hold of them. Once we had to join a waiting list for the trotters as our local butcher had an order for a dozen and only bought in one pig a week. 'A pig has only four trotters, love – you'll have to wait.'

Jelly
600ml water
1 pig's trotter (or a pork knuckle)
1 bay leaf
6 peppercorns

Pork filling
600g pork shoulder
a rasher of green back bacon or 2 slices of pancetta
   (optional)
½ teaspoon freshly grated nutmeg
½ teaspoon ground mace
½ teaspoon ground allspice
1 tablespoon chopped fresh sage (optional)
2 teaspoons anchovy essence or 1–2 fresh salted anchovies,
   finely chopped (optional)
salt and black pepper

Hot water crust pastry
50ml warm water
50ml whole milk
150g lard
450g plain flour
salt and black pepper
1 fresh egg yolk, beaten, for glazing the pie

First make the jelly. Bring the water, trotter, bay leaf and peppercorns to the boil, cover the pan with a lid, then simmer until the meat is quite soft and leaving the bone – around 3 hours. Strain the liquid into a basin (I use a muslin square lining a sieve to catch all the little bits), discarding the debris. Leave the liquid to cool, then remove any fat from the top. You should have a flavoursome, slightly cloudy jelly.

Cut the shoulder of pork (and bacon, if using) into small pieces, discarding any connective tissue and gristle. Mix the meat well with the spices (and chopped sage and anchovy essence, if you like). Season well with a pinch of salt and a good grind of black pepper and keep chilled.

To make the pastry, boil the water, milk and lard together until the lard has melted. Pour the boiling liquid on to the flour in a bowl and mix in with a table knife. Remember that it will be quite hot. The pastry should soon come together – when it does, turn it out on to the work surface and knead it a little.

Cut off a quarter of the pastry to make the lid and set aside. Form the rest of the pastry into a ball, pop it into the pork pie tin and begin to work it across the base and evenly up the sides of the tin. (Forming your index and middle finger into a paddle shape helps – rather like an upside-down scout salute). Leave the top of the pastry to overhang the side. Pack the pork filling in loosely, but right to the top of the tin.

Pat the remaining pastry into a circle the same thickness as the pastry sides. And, after brushing the rim of the pastry with beaten egg, pop the lid on the top. Crimp the edges of the pastry together and trim the excess pastry away with a knife. Make a small hole in the centre of the pastry lid. Use the surplus pastry to make leaf shapes or whatever you want. Fix the decoration with a dab of egg glaze and give the whole pie a final brush with the egg.

Bake the pie in the oven at 200°C/Gas Mark 6 for 30 minutes, then reduce the heat to 190°C/Gas Mark 5 for a further hour, or until the pastry is golden brown and the meat is cooked. (Test with a skewer – if it comes out clean with clear juices, the meat is cooked.) When fully cooked, remove the pie from the oven and leave it to cool down a bit before removing it from the tin.

When the pie has cooled completely, turn your attention to the jelly. Reheat it so it returns to liquid and either using a jug with a small lip or a basting syringe, pour the jelly through the hole on the top of the pie. You may need to have several goes to fully fill the pie. Leave the jelly to set before eating.

Tip: a baker told me that should your pastry crust have developed any cracks during baking, use bits of leftover pastry as a temporary bung while you pour in the jelly. Remove when the jelly has set.

Mrs H's recipe for game pie

A game pie is made in a similar way to a pork pie, using a hot water crust pastry and substituting pheasant, partridge, wild boar, venison, etc. for the pork shoulder. The meat is cut into strips and layered with seasonings. I like to add grated zest of an orange. The jelly is flavour-boosted with a celery stalk, carrot and white wine or dry white vermouth. If using whole birds, use the carcasses to make stock.

CASH INTO NOSH

DESPITE A YORKSHIRE TENDENCY towards economy on
my side and a southern propensity for dispersing the stuff
on Mrs H's, money is something that we rarely argue about,
at least when it is spent on food. Is any expenditure more
worthwhile than the purchase of pleasurable nutrients?
Admittedly, our priorities are somewhat different. Few
weeks go by without me buying one or two dozen oysters.
Mrs H has a weakness for vegetables – particularly English
asparagus, which she buys by the armful during the season,
artichokes (both kinds), aubergines, red peppers and the
fancier kinds of tomatoes – that can push our greengrocery
bill to surprising heights.

We both find it hard – impossible is a more accurate
word – to economise on comestibles. Aside from braising
cuts and offal, cheap meat is rarely a good idea, still less
cheap (meaning elderly) fish. The only bargain that I punt
on in a big way is cheese. Reduced price cheese has two
advantages: it is cheaper and it is well matured. I buy it by
the kilo. One big chunk of something splendid – Appleby
Cheshire, Montgomery Cheddar or Wensleydale sheep's

milk cheese – makes a much more tempting and impressive cheeseboard than a flotilla of itsy-bitsy wedges.

Curiously, we spend more on food in North Yorkshire than in London, where it is generally more expensive. Crabs, sea trout and salmon (a fiver each if you happen to catch them being landed from the boat) demand to be snapped up. During the game season, when plucked pheasant and partridge are sold in our patch of Yorkshire at £5 per brace, we tend to invest so heavily that it often comes as a slight surprise to the seller that we are not running a restaurant. Sometimes, the northern cornucopia is so tempting that I wish we were, though the first twinge of backache when I'm preparing a meal instantly extinguishes this pipedream.

The odd thing is that when I experience a rare and evanescent urge to be thrifty, the result often ends up being hugely expensive. An example of this occurred prior to our annual summer break in the north. On the brink of departure from Hirst HQ, we gathered vital food supplies from our local Turkish shop. This is not because food is in short supply in North Yorkshire. The reverse is true. However, Turkish supermarkets are a bit of a rarity in the Filey area. I was particularly keen to lay in a large stock of pitta bread. Yes, I know you can get it pretty much anywhere, but the version made by Sofra Bakery of Tottenham is particularly good. It is light, tasty and marbled with carbonised striations. After being sprinkled with water, the pittas puff up on the barbecue like miniature dirigibles. You half expect them to take off and whirl round your head, emitting puffs of steam. At the time of purchase, these edible Zeppelins had another advantage, particularly for the Turkophile Yorkshireman. At £1 for four packets of six, they worked out at 4.16p per pitta.

Or, at least, they should have. While musing in the shop over Mrs H's reaction if I were to buy a hubble-bubble, an assistant started shouting at me. 'Sir, sir, your car! A parking warden!' Dumping my pile of pittas, I dashed. At first, it looked as if I was in the nick of time. The warden was issuing a ticket to another poor blighter. But I'd forgotten that they hunt in packs in South London. A hidden colleague had already stuck the dread notice on my windscreen. Five minutes on a single yellow set me back £50, thus pushing the cost per pitta to an astronomic £2.12.

When we reached our northern base, the world's most expensive pitta breads were utilised in a number of appropriate snacks. We used them for dipping into home-made hummus. They were also filled with the Levantine cold omelette dish known as *eggah* for lunch on the beach. About halfway through my expensive hoard, I felt the urge to switch to the Yorkshire leavened equivalent, which are called breadcakes. These are circular in form, about twelve centimetres in diameter and four centimetres high. More flying saucers than airships, they were a staple of my childhood. Overcoming the hesitation of the outsider, Mrs H has become a convert of sorts. 'A bit like a squashed roll,' she says. At 25p a time, they are considerably more expensive than pitta bread, but this price is not subject to sudden inflation since parking wardens are an easily spotted rarity in our village.

After lunching on breadcakes with a culturally appropriate filling for North Yorkshire (ham and English mustard, roast beef and horseradish) for a couple of days, I returned to the pitta bread. But when I opened the two remaining packs, I experienced an anguish almost as severe as that inflicted by the parking warden. The first pitta was mottled with an archipelago of green and yellow patches of mould. I morosely flipped through the rest like a medieval monk peering into the Book of Lamentations. Each vellum page bore the same unappetising illumination. This second calamity upped the price to £4.25 per pitta. Not good news for a Yorkshireman, though Mrs H pointed out that she paid for both the pitta bread and the fine. 'I don't know what you're moaning about. It cost you, as you would say, "Nowt".'

Despite this reassurance, I have resigned myself to penury due to our outgoings on food. Though I feel boundless admiration and even kinship for certain chefs and food producers, the direction of cash flow delineates the oceanic gulf dividing professional from amateur. They charge. We cough up. Only once have I ever come close (or so I thought) to gaining financial reward for anything I have cooked. In a moment of wild optimism, I saw my raspberry jam as seed capital.

14

Getting the raspberry

IT IS COMMONLY THOUGHT that people engage in jam-making to enjoy the fruits of the sun in colder months, but there is another, less romantic reason why sticky-pawed preservers can be found hovering over steaming pans on the hottest days of the year. The competitive instinct infects this bucolic pastime. As with marmalade, all jam-makers believe their product to be nonpareil. Moreover, they are eager to prove their superiority in that ruthless gladiatorial arena known as the country produce show. Though a placid sort of fellow, I am by no means immune to the lure of the contest. This explains why an entry from C. Hirst was present among the regiment of raspberry jams entered in the 88th Annual Show of Thornton-le-Dale, North Yorkshire. I was in it for the honour, though the prize money (£5, £3, £1) would come in handy. I little realised that this impulse would involve me still being embroiled in competitive conserves twelve months later. You can get stuck with jam.

My rash participation came about when I was alone in Yorkshire. Since Mrs H had been called to London, I made my first-ever batch of raspberry jam under my own steam.

The fruit came from Mr and Mrs Hunter's farm in our village. At their peak in late July and early August, the pick-your-own beds resemble a medieval image of summer bounty. The canes are dotted with fruit in glowing profusion. No pud is better than fresh raspberries 'preferably with sugar and Jersey cream', as Jane Grigson pointed out in her *Fruit Book*, but there is a limit to the amount you can consume. Having reached, possibly surpassed, that point, I felt the urge to try my hand at jam.

You can pick a kilo of fruit in fifteen minutes and that's the hardest bit about making raspberry jam (or so it seemed). According to the formula I obtained from Mrs Hunter, who sells an exemplary version from her farm shop, you gently simmer equal parts raspberries and granulated sugar until the latter has fully dissolved (there must not be the slightest sugary rasp when you stir your spoon). Then you crank up the heat to produce a rolling boil for twenty minutes. At this point, you turn off the heat and pot in sterilised jars. As Mrs Hunter says, 'Raspberry jam cooks itself.'

Nevertheless, I felt that, due to an innate mastery of the art, my very first attempt resulted in a transcendentally excellent example. Set but not excessively so, it was a radiant joy to eye and palate alike. A kilo of raspberries produced around seven jars. It was so easy and the results were so good that I repeated the exercise. Then I did it again. I had thoughts of going into commercial jam-making and even imagined how the label might bear a handsome likeness of the manufacturer along the lines of Newman's Own. Only the reappearance of Mrs H ('Good grief! How are we going to get through all this?') prevented me from jammifying the whole of Mrs Hunter's crop.

I was sure that my raspberry jam would romp home to victory at Thornton-le-Dale, despite the daunting field of eighteen entries. 'Class 5 One Jar Raspberry Jam' is the Grand National of the produce section. When judging was over, I headed confidently for the phalanx of scarlet jars. You may picture my dumbstruck disbelief when I spotted my entry among the also-rans. My jam got the raspberry. As a greenhorn pitting myself against the toughest competition in the world of conserves – Yorkshirewomen who had been making jam before they managed to tie a pinny at the back by themselves – I should scarcely have expected to be among the place money, but the sting was undeniable. It only served me right for the many times I had breezily assessed the efforts of others at Thornton-le-Dale show. 'Judge not lest ye be judged.' Matthew vii.1.

Despite the judicial thumbs-down, I enjoyed my preserve very much. The great plus of raspberry jam is the bite of acid in the fruit that lifts its flavour above others (blackcurrant jam is an equal thrill for the palate). My production run saw me happily through the following year. Jam and bread is my secret vice, a reviving nibble to be consumed when nobody is looking. It's a fairly regular secret vice since I manage to get through twenty-odd jars in the course of a year.

Though primarily a way of preserving fruit for the rest of the year, there is another reason why jam came into being. Because fresh fruit was traditionally regarded with grave suspicion (strawberries were associated with melancholia), simmering with honey and, later, sugar was a way of making it healthy. There is a darker irony about this confection. The British love affair with jam – and, indeed, the word itself – dates from the eighteenth century, when cheap sugar became available from the slave plantations of the West Indies. It was only with the introduction of beet sugar in the nineteenth century, which played a part in the abolition of slavery, that jam became morally acceptable.

Twelve months on from my debacle at Thornton-le-Dale, I decided that radical steps were required. If my previous rendition did not match the stratospheric standards of North Yorkshire jam judges, it was necessary to try a new approach. This time, Mrs H was on hand and we agreed to try the raspberry jam recipe in *Preserves: River Cottage Handbook No.2* by Pam Corbin, formerly a professional jam-maker. It was consoling to learn that even this *maîtresse de confiture* came unstuck in the competitive arena. Ms Corbin describes the 'dismal result' when she entered a pot of strawberry jam in the Uplyme and Lyme Regis Horticultural Show. The strawberry recipe she includes in the book is the result of intense efforts to remedy this catastrophe. (Her secret for 'a wonderful, intense strawberry taste' is the addition of lemon juice.)

Curiously, the book's recipe for raspberry jam comes not from this expert, but from Hugh Fearnley-Whittingstall, the founder/proprietor of River Cottage. It is entitled 'Hugh's prize-winning raspberry fridge jam', though no details are given of the provenance of his triumph. 'Hugh F-W,' writes Ms Corbin, 'thinks the secret of success is to pick the raspberries on a hot, dry day, aiming for a good mixture of ripe and almost-ripe fruit, then to make the jam immediately – to capture the full flavour of the berries.' Well, yes, I did all that (you don't feel much urge to pick on a cold, wet day), but it's not the full story of HFW's innovatory method. The recipe that took the victor's laurels calls for 1.5 kilos of raspberries combined with the staggeringly low quantity of 750g of sugar. HFW uses jam sugar, which includes added pectin. (As you may recall from my adventures with marmalade, pectin is a kind of fruity cement. It helps jams to set, especially when using fruit like apricots and strawberries that are low in natural pectin.) HFW says you should mash half the fruit in a preserving pan with a potato masher, then add the remaining un-mashed fruit plus jam sugar. Stir over a low heat until the sugar is dissolved, then 'bring to a rolling boil for exactly five minutes'. It smelled sensational during this brief bub-bling. The result was a brilliant red, considerably lighter than my effort of the previous year. This was a good sign. Someone told me that judges tends to favour light-coloured raspberry jam. I was just about to start potting when Mrs H appeared in the kitchen. 'Have you checked the wrinkle point?' she asked.

'The recipe doesn't say anything here about checking the wrinkle point,' I replied acidly.

'If I were you, I'd do the wrinkle test.' I'd previously en-countered this infallible analysis when making marmalade.

I deposited a dollop of 'Hugh's prize-winning raspberry fridge jam' on a chilled plate, waited a few moments and prodded. There was not the slightest sign of a wrinkle. It was more of a trickle. Grasping at straws, I hoped the jam would magically thicken after being left overnight in the fridge. In the morning, Mrs W picked up the jar and tilted it. The contents *swirled*. 'That won't win anything in a competition,' she sniffed. I can't remember feeling more disappointed since my defeat at Thornton-le-Dale.

On closer inspection, Pam Corbin's recipe suggested that we should have expected nothing else. 'This light, soft jam is fantastic in cakes or sherry trifles or stirred into creamy rice puddings.' There was nothing about it being 'fantastic' on a bit of bread and butter. The omission was ominous. Obviously, Ms Corbin was not going to rubbish the seigneur of River Cottage, but she seemed to be giving the reader a powerful hint. Reading between the lines, it became clear that HFW's 'prize-winning jam' wasn't jam as such, but a jam-related liquid intended to be used in other dishes.

So where on earth did it win a prize? I decided to apply my investigative skills to the puzzle. I recalled that in HFW's *River Cottage Cookbook* (2001), there is a photo of a certificate from the 1998 Beaminster Summer Show where he scooped third prize for 'Six Different Vegetables'. I therefore tapped 'Beaminster', 'raspberry' and 'Fearnley-Whittingstall' into Google. This produced the River Cottage blog, where HFW preened about his raspberry jam: 'A light boiling produces a loose, almost pourable jam with a fresh, tangy flavour. This version took first prize at the Beaminster summer show, so I must have done something right.'

I gasped. How could it be 'almost pourable' and still be a jam? HFW had actually made something that was more of a sauce or coulis. It certainly would not have won anything in a Women's Institute competition. When I came across a copy of the WI's show guide, entitled 'On with the Show', I instantly turned to the judging instructions on jam. These include the stern specification: 'Consistency jellified, not runny or sticky, no loose liquid or syrup.' The words 'not runny' do not support HFW's cocky, 'I must have done something right.'

Still, his oozy formulation won first prize among the jams at Beaminster, so why not North Yorkshire? I entered a pot made from HFW's dubious recipe in the annual show of the Hunmanby & District Garden Produce Association, which takes place a week before the far larger Thornton-le-Dale event. Giving the judge a bit of a nudge, Mrs H labelled it 'Raspberry Fridge Jam'. Of course, it came nowhere. On reflection, it seems to me that there are two possible reasons for HFW's perplexing success at Beaminster. Either the judges in the West Country are culinary revolutionaries eager to accept avant-garde experimentation in jam-making or they had got some inkling of the celebrity status of the maker. I'm not saying one way or another, but HFW's triumph seems jammy to me.

With three days to go before the 89th Thornton-le-Dale Annual Show, it was time to call on a higher power. I set

Mrs H to work on the HFW jam. 'If it shows no sign of setting, your best bet is to bung in a bottle of Certo,' she said. Mrs H is an ardent believer in this liquid pectin. The label declares: 'Jams made with Certo require less boiling and maintain the full flavour and colour of the fruit.' This proved to be true. When Mrs H produced a jar of the Certo-enriched Fearnley-Whittingstall jam, it looked fantastic. It was the crimson of fresh raspberries, not the maroon of raspberry jam. It also tasted fantastic. Unfortunately, it remained jam of the 'almost pourable' sort.

Once again, we hoped that it would stiffen overnight. Once again, we were disappointed. It did not do any setting whatsoever. Certo made not a scrap of difference. To be fair to Certo, the label does not claim that 'Jams made with Certo require less sugar'. It was time to call on an even higher authority than Mrs H. (They do exist, you know.) Harold McGee's exploration of culinary science *On Food and Cooking* explained the problem. Pectin, he says, is extracted from vegetable cell walls by boiling. 'The long, string-like pectin molecules bind a liquid into a solid by bonding to each other and forming a meshwork that traps the liquid in its interstices. Some fruits, including grapes and most berries, are rich enough in pectin to produce excellent gels on their own.' This explains why recipes for raspberry jam usually require granulated sugar rather than jam sugar, which is pectin enriched.

So why didn't the HFW jam with added pectin do any setting? The answer, according to McGee, is connected with 'the negative electrical charge of pectin molecules'.

'Like poles repel' is one of the very few things I remember from five years of studying physics. Acid in fruit reduces the electrical charge. This should help the pectin to bond. Unfortunately, pectin, which likes to stick to anything but itself, still tends to bond with water molecules. The solution to this quandary is sugar. McGee explains: 'If sugar is added, its highly water-attracting molecules take enough water out of circulation to allow the pectin molecules to reach one another.' In short, you need sugar to make jam. That's why HFW's 'prize-winning jam' isn't jam. 'To thicken a preserve with pectin,' McGee concludes, 'we need acid and sugar: the two substances that fruits specialise in storing. Sounds like a cinch … But as anyone who has tried knows, it's anything but a cinch.' Quite.

We picked punnet after punnet at Mrs Hunter's farm and Mrs H worked furiously to produce a set jam with the fresh flavour of HFW's syrup. I'd say that she worked uncomplainingly but this would not be the truth. As with the marmalade, she complained noisily and at great length. 'Why the hell am I making more jam when we've already got a kitchenful of the stuff?' she inquired. When I pointed out the imminence of the 89th Thornton-le-Dale Annual Show, she used language about the 89th Thornton-le-Dale Annual Show that would be unusual in a food book written by anyone but Anthony Bourdain.

Contrary to my tendency to engage in industrial-scale production, she prefers the small run, maybe four jars at a time. Propelled by irritation at HFW's crowing, she dramatically upped the quantity of both jam sugar and

Certo. The result had not the slightest suggestion of liquidity. Though pleasing in taste, it had the resolute set of brawn. More a jam for slicing than spreading, it was the reverse of HFW's slurry. When I pointed out the minor blemish that it required a bulldozer for spreading, an impressive blast of steam eddied from Mrs H's ears. After cooling sufficiently for operating purposes, this heroine tackled the impossible task of making a set version of HFW jam without a radical increase in the sugar content. It was the jammy equivalent of squaring the circle. On her fifth attempt, she triumphed by slightly increasing the amount of sugar (for 750g of raspberries, she added 400g of jam sugar instead of the suggested 375) and continuing the rolling boil for ten minutes rather than five. The jam had the bright colour and fresh tang of the HFW jam, but passed the wrinkle test with flying colours. When it had cooled, I tried the equally significant test of spreading it on a slice of bread and butter, where it stayed happily in place instead of squirming off and trickling to the floor.

With renewed confidence, we took Mrs H's low-sugar jam to the Produce Tent of the Thornton-le-Dale show. This time, Class 5 contained twenty-two entries. From a discreet distance, we observed a white-coated judge closely scrutinise each jar before tasting a tiny sample. The narrow spatula she used for the purpose was carefully washed in a pot of water before being dipped in the next jar. It was all reassuringly professional, though her intake was molecular compared to my in-depth assessment of pork pies at the same event.

When the barrier came down and the Produce Tent was opened to the public, we casually sauntered towards the phalanx of competing jars. Trying not to look over-eager, we first viewed the neighbouring classes of torpedo-sized marrows, scones like small castles and carrots as long as rapiers. Eventually, we reached Class 5. Prize certificates leaned against three of the jars. I'd like to say that our three weeks' labour, which involved the production of twenty-five jars of raspberry jam, was crowned by glory. But it wasn't. Once again our striving produced zilch. And the same went for Hugh Fearnley-Whittingstall's 'prize-winning jam', which we also entered. This was less of a surprise. He might have done 'something right' in Beaminster, but it wasn't right for Thornton-le-Dale.

At the fag end of August, I decided to test the patience of Mrs H to destruction by making yet another batch of raspberry jam. The reason for this last gasp was a recipe that I came across in Thane Prince's book *Jams & Chutneys*. Displaying the typical modesty of the preserve-maker, it is entitled 'Best-ever Raspberry Jam'. Involving the traditional sugar-to-fruit ratio of 1:1, it requires boiling for a mere 'five to seven minutes'. Mrs Hunter had closed her PYO operation for the season, but she made a special concession for her most obsessively dedicated customer. By this stage, the raspberry canes were parched, brown and blowsy but a few extraordinarily large fruit remained. Fighting off the insects, which have an equal fondness for raspberries, we managed to find a kilo of fruit.

When I put the berries into our preserving pan, Mrs H

pointed out that Thane Prince's recipe required just one pound of raspberries and one pound of granulated sugar. The result would, of course, be two pounds of jam. 'You can't make two pounds of jam if you've just picked a kilo of fruit. It's stark impossible,' I said, heaving a kilo of sugar into the pan.

'You won't get a great load like this to set in seven minutes,' said Mrs H irritatingly. 'I tell you that for free.'

And she was right again, drat it. When I did the wrinkle test after seven minutes' boiling, the jam trickled down the chilled plate. I gave it another four minutes, but the jam still showed no sign of congealment. After a further four minutes – making fifteen minutes in all – it finally displayed sluggishness. As it turned out, my 'great load' only produced three and a half jars. It looked pretty much the same light-red colour as the jam pictured in Thane Prince's book and had exactly the consistency she recommends ('a bit runny'), but the moment of truth had yet to come. It was to be appraised by a judge every bit as discriminating as any at Thornton-le-Dale.

'It's nice and glossy with an excellent set,' said Mrs H. 'Considering it was made from "back-end" fruit, it has a good raspberry taste.'

'Would you say it was supremely excellent?'

'No, but it's quite good jam.' It was only later that I realised I was pretty much back where I started with Mrs Hunter's recipe. See what I mean about getting stuck with jam?

Mrs H's recipe for raspberry jam

We are lucky to have Mr and Mrs Hunter's farm near us in Yorkshire. I've borrowed this recipe from Mrs Hunter. As well as producing tasty eggs, they grow pick-your-own soft fruit, so it means that you can have a happy peaceful time among the canes before the sugary part of making jam. This is the recipe for a jam that sets! It is really easy to make, having only equal quantities of fruit and sugar. It works fine with small batches. You can do as little as two 450g jars. Should you wish to make more, alter the weight of the ingredients as required.

450g freshly picked raspberries
450g granulated sugar

As with all preserves, make sure that your jars are scrupulously washed and dried. Remember to place them in a low oven (80°C) well before you need to pot the jam.

Place the raspberries and sugar in a preserving pan or large saucepan. Stir the fruit gently over a low heat until the sugar has completely dissolved.

Bring the jam to boiling point and boil rapidly for 15–20 minutes, or until a setting point is reached. To test place a small amount on a pre-cooled plate and, after 1–2 minutes, push the surface of your sample with your finger. If the jam wrinkles, it can be potted on. If it fails to pass the 'wrinkle test', boil for another 5 minutes and test again.

Leave the jam to stand for 15 minutes in order to

distribute the fruit evenly, then pour into the warm jars. Fill to the top and allow to cool for another 10 minutes, then place a waxed paper disc on top of the jam. This makes a seal and prevents too much shrinkage. When the jam is completely cool, cover with a screwtop lid. I prefer to use new lids as they have a better seal than recycled ones. If you are aiming for a more traditional look, or want to enter the jam in a competition, cover with a cellophane disc affixed with a rubber band. If you are feeling creative, you could top the jam-pot with a fabric or paper cover. The best-dressed pots last year wore brown paper tied with some brown string and one of those nicely written luggage labels. I'm sorry to say that ours were stored *au naturel* (no label at all) in the cardboard boxes from Lakeland that the pots came in.

RECIPE FOR DISASTER

IN MY EXPERIENCE – and I've got quite a bit in this dept
– a recipe becomes a trial by ordeal because you screw it up
in some way. The reason may be that you measure the
cream inaccurately, you set fire to the pizza or you forget
you're in charge of some baking bread ('I wondered where
the smell was coming from'). Sometimes, however, a recipe
goes right and it is still an unmitigated horror to do. Here
follow examples of both screw-up and intentional torture.

The former occurred when I attempted *sepia con pochas*
(cuttlefish with white beans), from Elisabeth Luard's *The
Food of Spain & Portugal*. It seemed an appropriate dish to
welcome Mrs H back from a work trip to the Costa del Sol.
Another reason for having a bash at this concoction is that
I just happened to have a cuttlefish in the freezer (which
gives you some idea of the contents of the cold store at Hirst
HQ), while in our overflowing store cupboard there was a
packet of dried giant butter beans that I'd purchased at the
Central Market in Athens.

Here are three things you might not know about butter
beans: 1) They originated in tropical America but are

mainly consumed in Greece and Spain; 2) According to *The Cook's Encyclopaedia* by Tom Stobart, they are 'one of the best flavoured of all beans'; 3) They gave the name to the American Forties comedy duo Butterbeans & Susie, best known for a salacious ditty entitled 'I Want a Hot Dog for My Roll'.

After soaking these prodigious legumes for twenty-four hours, I simmered them in white wine and water with gently fried garlic and chopped cuttlefish, as directed by Elisabeth Luard: 'Sprinkle in the oregano, season, put the lid on and leave to cook gently for 20 minutes or so, until the cuttlefish is tender.' After twenty minutes or so, the cuttlefish was tender, but the beans gave cause for concern. They seemed completely unaffected by their braise. Moreover, they produced a daunting rattle in the pan. I fished one out with a spoon and had an experimental nibble. A bullet. Another twenty minutes' simmer produced not the slightest emollience. The beans' granite intransigence remained after a further forty minutes on the hob. In a desperate attempt to induce edibility, I pulled the skin from each bean and gave them another simmer. After an hour, they were marginally chewable but more like biscuits than beans. Having wasted a good chunk of the day on Mrs H's treat, I fed beans and shrivelled cuttlefish into the ever-accepting mouth of the bin.

So what went wrong with the dish that Elisabeth Luard promised was 'unusual but delicious'? A hint appeared in a recipe for prawn salad with haricot beans by Simon Hopkinson: 'Make sure the sell-by date on the dried beans is well advanced, assuring that they are relatively newly dried.' Unfortunately, the traders in Athens market do not put a sell-by date on their produce, but it struck me that I had not been to Athens for three years. My beans were not exactly newly dried.

So what did I do for Mrs H's meal? I still made *sepia con pochas*, but with a bottle of ready-cooked Spanish butter beans from the supermarket and a second frozen cuttlefish (which gives an even better idea of the contents of the Hirst HQ cold store). Mrs H said it was better than anything she had eaten in Andalucia. Over supper, we discussed our varying Spanish experiences. Mrs H told me about Marbella, while I spoke of beans.

For an example of a recipe that goes right and is still excruciating, I refer you to the eight pages of directions for Black Forest gateau in Heston Blumenthal's *In Search of Perfection*. It is a dish that no one in their right mind would want to attempt. I think that can justifiably be said about the twelve-hour grind that it requires. I wonder if anyone else has made Heston's little cake? He obviously thinks his bizarre confection is practicable. Why else would he have included it in two of his books? In case anyone feels tempted by the account in the following chapter, I should point out that it is a complete nightmare. For once, this cliché is spot on. Occasionally, I still dream that I am peering into a cardboard box while wielding a chocolate-filled paint spray gun.

15

Death by chocolate

THE HEART SINKS at the words 'Black Forest gateau', especially if you don't particularly like chocolate. I'm not so desperate about the stuff and Mrs H is even less keen, despite the assiduous efforts of chocolate companies to market their products as a surefire turn-on for females. So why did we make this retro favourite? The answer is that a newspaper asked me to do so.

Along with fish and chips, bangers and mash and spag bol, BFG is one of the dishes that Blumenthal tackled in his book *In Search of Perfection*. His efforts to attain 'the essential character' of these staples involved seeking out the best possible ingredients and applying the outré cooking techniques for which he is famous. Personally, I would sooner have gone for his turbot in batter aerated by soda siphon, but the commissioning editor demanded BFG, which happens to be the most complicated recipe in the book. Obviously, Blumenthal regards his own version as a triumph. It is the only one of the sixteen dishes in *In Search of Perfection* and the sequel volume *Further Adventures in Search of Perfection* that made it into his monumental *Big*

Fat Duck Cookbook (£100). Here the culinary adventurer explains his fondness for this antique confection, 'I like the culinary underdogs ... Black Forest gateau seems to be a dessert that no one remembers with affection.' This certainly proved to be the case at Hirst HQ.

Blumenthal's BFG consists of six different layers. Going from the bottom up they are: 1) Madeleine biscuit base covered in cocoa 'wood-effect'; 2) Aerated chocolate; 3) Flourless chocolate sponge; 4) Gelatinised kirsch cream; 5) Chocolate ganache (flavoured fresh cream); 6) Chocolate mousse. Oh, and cherries come into it somewhere. The whole construction is sprayed with chocolate from a paint spray gun. 'To assemble a whole cake in one day would undeniably be a fair amount of work,' Blumenthal warns. 'Better to think of this as architecture and spread out the building tasks. Prepare the chocolate sponge up to a month in advance ...' If you are foolhardy enough to want to make Heston's confection it is advisable to follow this leisurely schedule. Unfortunately, in the nutty, hell-for-leather way of newspapers, I had just two days to construct this Teutonic masterpiece. It did not help my mood that I was coming down with flu.

The first day was taken up with assembling a curious variety of equipment and ingredients. With the assistance of Mrs H, I managed to track down a pressurised whipping-cream whipper (a kind of soda siphon with attitude). Made in Austria, the Kisag whipper cost £42.29, plus £24.27 for a box of fifty nitrous oxide charges. Almost seventy quid may seem a little on the high side to make one pud, but

I consoled myself with the thought that I would be able to use the Kisag whipper for the foams that play an important role in Blumenthal's molecular gastronomy. Curiously, this never came to pass. Put us down as gastronomic stick-in-the-muds, but a supper of froth has never appealed.

We found our next bit of culinary kit in Homebase. The paint spray gun cost £31.99. 'Will it take molten chocolate?' Mrs H asked an assistant.

'Dunno,' came the reply. 'Most people use emulsion.' However, the store could not oblige with a 'wood-effect painting tool', possibly since no one in their right mind has desired wood-effect walls since 1973. Unfortunately, the car battery decided to pack in immediately after we made our purchase. Waiting in Homebase car park for the AA and wishing I had a Lemsip, my qualms intensified. 'What the hell are we doing?' I asked Mrs H.

'The whole thing is bonkers,' she replied. 'But we might as well carry on. We've got the whipper thing now.' Restored to mobility, we zoomed to our neighbourhood kitchen shop for the thermal probe Mrs H had seen earlier that day (you need one to ensure milk heats to exactly 75°C during the kirsch cream stage), but someone had gazumped us. Cursing the culinary obsession of the suburban middle classes, I settled for a super-sized thermometer. We bought three tins that almost conformed to Blumenthal's specification of 'a 5cm deep, 9 x 19cm loaf tin'. We needed three tins because Blumenthal's ingredients are sufficient to make three cakes. (Each stage of what follows was actually done three times but I'll spare you the repetition.) We also acquired a piping bag and nozzles, a melon baller, a non-stick silicone baking sheet and several vacuum-seal storage bags with one-way air valves. By this stage, the equipment bill topped £150. Fortunately, we already possessed the rest of the kit required for this dish: a large Tupperware-style food box, a vacuum cleaner, an atomiser (optional) and a cardboard box.

Blumenthal is equally particular about ingredients. Without these, you are not going to get the full HB-approved experience. Though we had no trouble getting the eighteen eggs, 515ml whipping cream, six plump vanilla pods, 250ml whole milk and two sheets of leaf gelatine, other items were more elusive. We couldn't find Amadei Toscano chocolate, so we settled for Valrhona chocolate sold by the Chocolate Society in Pimlico. Blumenthal specifies '50ml top quality kirsch (e.g. Franz Fies)', and gives an account of his visit to the Franz Fies production plant in the Black Forest. 'I got a real hit of complex, intense cherry smell,' he enthused. 'It was something I definitely wanted to capture in my Black Forest gateau.' After all this, it was slightly irksome to discover that Franz Fies kirsch was not available in Britain. I settled for Lesgrevil kirsch from Waitrose. Similarly, 'top quality sour cherries in syrup (e.g. Amarena Fabbri)' proved a bit thin on the ground in south London. Mrs H came up with morello cherries in syrup from our local Lidl. What could be more Teutonic? Moreover, the label declared them to be 'Premium Quality'.

With a giant plate forming a halo round his egg-like

cranium, Blumenthal is transformed into a culinary saint on the cover of *In Search of Perfection*. Eight hours into making his BFG, I realised he is a devil. He has taken a straightforward recipe, presumably made for centuries by the honest folk of the Black Forest, and endowed it with every fiendish complexity he could devise. He admits it himself, more or less: 'Here it is – a Black Forest gateau composed of six delicious layers ... Lots of layers mean lots of different cooking techniques.' Let me translate Heston's jolly encouragement: every square centimetre of this insanely complex confection involves hours of irritating, finicky, pointless and wholly preposterous labour. Still, it could have been worse. In *The Big Fat Duck Cookbook*, he reveals the research behind his BFG: 'At one point, every inch of the work surface in the development kitchen was covered with miniature versions of classical pastries – jacondes, financiers, dacquoises, génoises, ganaches, parfaits, madeleines, mousses – and the prospect of trying out every combination was daunting.'

Excluding illustrations, the recipe in *In Search of Perfection* runs to eight pages. We peered at the fifty-two stages in a state of shock. Despite this deluge of instruction, we were puzzled by ambiguities. When it came to combining the various strata that constitute the heart of the gateau, there was no explanation of a mysterious white layer that appeared in a photograph of the BFG during construction. Not only was this one of the strata, but it also formed a sort of stucco on the sides. Because it was white, we deduced that it was the gelatinised kirsch cream. The recipe directed us: 'Manoeuvre it on top of the chocolate sponge using a palette knife or fish slice.' But what the hell should we use to put the white sides in place? A brickie's trowel?

Deciding to cross this bridge when we came to it, we made Blumenthal's madeleine biscuit base, the flourless chocolate sponge and the gelatinised kirsch cream, a white jelly that had to chill in the freezer for an hour. To be absolutely honest, Mrs H made them while I had a lie-down. Rising Lazarus-style from my bed, I tackled the 'wood-effect' on the Madeleine biscuit base. Good God! Was I really making a dish that included such decorative frippery? Despite lacking a wood-effect painting tool, I used a spatula to smear the paste of cocoa and water on to the Madeleine biscuit base. The result was a wood-effect veneer whose verisimilitude would have deceived the most experienced Black Forest axeman.

Buoyed by this success, I moved on to the most dramatic element of the entire enterprise – the aerated chocolate. This is where the Kisag cream whipper came into play. After pouring 500g of molten Valrhona milk chocolate into the stainless steel flask, I screwed the top on and charged the device with three cartridges of nitrous oxide. I gave the warm cylinder a vigorous shake, directed its nozzle into a large plastic food box and depressed the stainless steel lever. The hot chocolate erupted into the box (and beyond). It was a highly satisfactory moment, though it cost £66.56 for a two-second spurt.

But there was no time to admire my handiwork. The

next step was to fix the top on the plastic box, put it in one of the vacuum-seal storage bags and evacuate the air from the bag using the (scrupulously cleaned) nozzle of our vacuum cleaner, which I applied to the one-way valve in the bag. You may wonder how I got the air out of the closed plastic box inside the bag? Simple. I followed Blumenthal's ruthless demand for 'a 2.6-litre hard plastic container with a lid (into which you have bored a small hole using a cork-screw)'.

'But it's my best box!' complained Mrs H. Similar expos-tulations must have been heard from the partners of great inventors throughout the ages. Though the air was sucked out of the bag and, presumably, the box inside, the effect did not conform to Blumenthal's description: 'The choco-late should rise and be riddled with small bubbles.' Despite applying our carefully disinfected vacuum cleaner to the valve several times, the chocolate did not rise. It just sat there. Hoping for the best, I shoved the bag in the fridge. The next job was to make the ganache (a chocolate-flavoured cream stiffened with gelatine) and put it into a piping bag. While that was also cooling in the fridge, we started assembling the BFG. I remembered Heston's in-junction: 'Think of this as architecture.' The first job was to line a loaf tin with clingfilm, which is easier said than done. Then you have to spread apricot glaze on the cling-film at the bottom of the pan, which is even more easier said than done. 'You're going up the sides,' yelped Mrs H.

The next job was to trim the madeleine to fit the base of the loaf tin. Using the madeleine as a template, I cut a rectangle out of the aerated chocolate. (This turned out to be quite a success. It was crunchy and granular with a fair amount of bubbles, but not so many as to make people think we'd just used Aero.) After placing the rectangle of aerated chocolate on the madeleine base, I topped these strata with two lines of chilled ganache. Around the ganache, I placed three rows of Lidl cherries with the delicacy of a Fabergé craftsman. On top of this went chocolate sponge soaked in cherry syrup and kirsch. Finally, I cut out a rectangle of gelatinised kirsch cream and, with some difficulty, managed to place it on top of Blumenthal's Folly, a process akin to nailing jelly to a wall. But that was easy compared to fixing the kirsch cream to the sides of the BFG, a task I delegated to Mrs H.

The basic construction of the pud had taken the best part of a day. Back aching, temper frayed, awash with Lemsip, I totted up how much longer it would take, according to Blumenthal's instructions. Another three hours! My spirits plummeted. Dante's demons could not have devised a more ingenious torment, though this is not Heston's view. 'Do it right and it becomes something wonderful,' he trills like Mary Poppins. 'Food should be fun.' This glib encouragement echoed in my flu-fogged brain as we ploughed on with the futile, fiddly, irksome, brain-numbing complexity.

After being chilled in the freezer, the structure was 'topped off' with chocolate mousse. Once this was set, I used a melon baller to scoop recesses for the final decoration of eight cherries. Then the cake went back into the freezer for an hour. After this, the moment had arrived for the cardboard box. You need the cardboard box as a shield when using the paint sprayer on the BFG. Loaded with a mixture of molten chocolate and groundnut oil (ugh! – you don't want to know the secrets of the professional kitchen), the spraying provided a rare moment of excitement in ten hours of slog. However, this highlight was undermined by the American photographer who was recording our efforts for the newspaper. 'I'm so sorry for you guys,' he said. 'You've been working your asses off all day and it looks like shit. It's funny really.' I could have strangled him, but there was some truth in his observation. The cake was shiny and brown and far from appetising.

Like a mystifying religious rite, Blumenthal's recipe goes on and on. The cake had to go back into the freezer for another twenty minutes. When it came out, the BFG had gained a more appealing matt finish. Blumenthal claims it is 'reminiscent of the close-cropped moss you find on forest boulders'. At this point, I should have bored holes in the top of the BFG and filled them with cherry syrup. But, frankly, I couldn't be arsed. The worm had turned. Similarly, I refused to slit the vanilla pods to form 'decorative stalks' for the embellishing cherries. 'It's a bit tricky,' admitted Mrs H, as she performed this delicate finishing touch. 'I don't think our vanilla pods are plump enough.'

The result of our efforts was three small, rectangular cakes. I placed six cherries (with vanilla 'stalks') into the six little recesses on top of each cake and, as instructed by the young master of the Fat Duck, sprayed kirsch around the room with the atomiser. 'It will magically bring a little of the Black Forest to the dinner table,' claims Blumenthal. Inexplicably, the magic failed to materialise. The final cost of the cakes was in the vicinity of £250. When the photographer had taken a few snaps, we cut into one. It was pretty good – especially if you like chocolate – but very rich. A sliver was sufficient. On the following day, I wrote the feature for the newspaper and went to bed for a week. Eventually, I felt up to having another slice, but the cherries on the remaining Black Forest gateaux had grown a coat of green mould. I chucked them in the bin.

THE FOOD OF LOVE

IF YOU ASK ME, our relationship would have worked just as well if we had both been indifferent about what we ate, though such a state of affairs is hard to imagine. Admittedly, our love of food brought numerous advantages. It gave us something to discuss on car journeys and ensured we had something – often rather a lot – to eat at mealtimes. But, as Mrs H discovered, there was an unexpected drawback to being married to a food writer. On two occasions, I requested her assistance in researching aphrodisiacs. I should explain that this was solely because I had to write articles about them. For some reason, they are a topic of considerable appeal to editors.

There was no problem with asparagus, which Mrs H adores when steamed and served dressed with olive oil and a sprinkle of grated Parmesan ('Yum!'), though its supposed erotic effects do not live up to its erect appearance. Actually, it can have the reverse effect. In P. G. Wodehouse's *Code of the Woosters*, Gussie Fink-Nottle describes the spectacle of his arch enemy Roderick Spode scoffing asparagus: 'Revolting. It alters one's whole conception of man as nature's last word.' Mrs H was also smitten by white truffles, whose eroticism is extolled by Elisabeth Luard in her book *Truffles*: 'Not to put too fine a point on it, the truffle reeks of sex.' We had the good luck to consume these stratospherically priced fungi in some quantity when invited to the truffle town of Moncalvo in Piedmont. 'Earthy and heavenly at the same time,' said Mrs H. We even splashed out 100 euros on a small truffle to bring home, but its thrilling effects went for nought back at Hirst HQ, when Mrs H succumbed to cold, rapidly followed by myself. By the time the colds had gone, so had the potency of the truffle.

Though chickpeas are a male aphrodisiac – according to the *Karma Sutra*, 'If eaten every morning, you will be able to enjoy a hundred women' – my hummus went down very well with Mrs H. 'I think any girl would be impressed if a man made hummus for her. Well, this one would.' Another vegetable with unexpected properties is the onion. In *The Perfumed Garden*, we are informed that when a certain Abu el Heiloukh ate onions 'his member remained erect for thirty uninterrupted days'. Though this is slightly excessive to requirements, my French onion soup has generally gone down well with Mrs H (except when it was made in the small hours).

Other aphrodisiacs were less effective. My rendition of squid sautéd with garlic and chilli, as recommended in *Erotic Cuisine: A Natural History of Aphrodisiac Cookery* by Marilyn Ekdahl Ravicz, did not produce the required effect. I unwisely augmented the recipe with several homegrown chillies of previously untested potency. A Niagara of sweat and a beetroot-red face is not what women generally seek in a bedmate.

Though we were unable to try the sparrows' brains, skink or simmered crane recommended in *Venus in the Kitchen* by Norman Douglas, we were able to get hold of lamb testicles at a Turkish supermarket. The butcher will remove the membrane, but after that you're on your own. With a slight shiver, I sliced the testes in half and followed Douglas's recipe, which, ironically enough, came from the kitchen of a sixteenth-century pontiff. Gently fry in butter with a pinch of saffron. Add a squeeze of lemon before serving. The mousse-like result was less than appetising. Though I doubt if Douglas tried out this dish, Mrs H bravely had a go. 'A bit pale and granular. Doesn't taste of much.' Mrs H's technique with ovine dangly bits was more successful. Once they had been cut into strips and coated with breadcrumbs, they were very tasty. 'But not seductive,' insisted Mrs H. 'Especially when you know how much cholesterol they contain.'

It was high time to spice things up. Black pepper has long been regarded as conducive to a grind. In the ever-encouraging *Karma Sutra*, gents are informed that a pepper and honey anointment on their organ will 'utterly devastate your lady'. Quite. Instead, I procured the Moroccan mixture of spices known as ras-el-hanout (it rather oddly means 'top of the shop') that contains twenty or more spices. According to Paula Wolfert's book *Moroccan Cuisine*, 'The aphrodisiacs (Spanish fly, ash berries, monk's pepper) that appear in most formulae appear to be the reason why the mere mention of this mixture will put a gleam in a Moroccan cook's eye.' Fortunately, the sample I obtained did not contain the telltale blue fragments of the notorious Spanish fly or cantharides. I say fortunately because, contrary to its reputation, Spanish fly is not an aphrodisiac but a potent irritant and poison. The lethal dose is 0.03 grams. A lamb casserole made with a user-friendly version of ras-el-hanout proved to be excellent. 'Unctuous with gentle spices,' said Mrs H, 'but not noticeably sexy.'

Recalling the wise words of Ogden Nash ('Candy is dandy but liquor is quicker'), I mixed Mrs H a cocktail intended to jump-start the engine of love. Two shots of the hazelnut liqueur Fra Angelico, one shot of fresh lemon juice. Shake with ice cubes and serve over crushed ice in a squat glass. Garnish with fresh lemon.

'Mmm,' said Mrs H. 'Can I have another? What's it called?'

'Knicker Dropper Glory.'

'How common.'

At the end of our researches, there was a consensus among participants that the view of aphrodisiacs in *The Oxford Companion to Food* was pretty much spot-on: 'Virtually non-existent ... pathetically feeble ... on a par with finding a crock of gold at the end of a rainbow.' Nevertheless, we have consumed the most esteemed of all aphrodisiacs on a weekly basis for over two decades. For a food that helps to sustain an intimate relationship, may I point you in the direction of the oyster?

16

Shucking revelations

THOUGH MRS H HAS REFUSED to join in several of my gastronomic enthusiasms – she dislikes trifle and is utterly implacable in her opposition to Yorkshire curd tart – I am delighted in my success at pleading the cause of a comestible that many find impossible to contemplate. My favourite of all foods is a cool, fresh oyster. I say 'a' but really I mean 'some', preferably a dozen or so.

When I first met her, Mrs H shared the common British distrust of oysters. 'No, I'd never eaten one before meeting you. Come to think of it, I'd hardly had any fish except for fish fingers.' Though agreeing with Jonathan Swift's view, 'Twas a brave man who first ate an oyster,' Mrs H has overcome her aversion. She tucks in when I open a dozen at home or when I order them in a restaurant. But does she agree that they are the best of all foods?

'I'm not as passionate about them as you are,' she admits warily. 'They're pretty good for you. Not fattening and full of zinc and vitamins, but they're a bit expensive. Really, I only eat them because you eat them – and you eat them all the time. They are quite a companionable thing to eat and it's rather pleasurable watching you eat them with lots of lip-smacking and yum-yumming.' (This may not be a view shared by everyone.) 'But I don't have your homing instinct for oysters – the way that you say, 'Oh, I must have some!' Your little face droops when you can't find any in Waitrose. I will join you, but I usually stop at four if they're alive.'

'You had six yesterday.'

'That's because you cooked them with bacon and dill. I like them that way v. much.'

Yes, I do have them alive, or raw, to put it a little more acceptably, though that swirl of delicate beige flesh lying on the half-shell should certainly be alive. As Mark Kurlansky points out in *The Big Oyster*, 'If the oyster is opened carefully, the diner is eating an animal with a working brain, a stomach, intestines, liver and a still-beating heart.' At their best, the taste is incomparable. It is re-freshing, satisfying without being filling, sublimely mari-time. Mrs H says, 'They taste of the smell of the sea.' This is a more succinct version of Eleanor Clark's rhapsodic evocation in *The Oysters of Locmariaquer*, best of all oyster books. Describing the native oysters of Brittany, she wrote, 'Music or the colour of the sea are easier to describe ... You are eating the sea, that's it, only the sensation of a gulp of sea water has been wafted out of it by some sorcery, and are on the verge of remembering you don't know what, mer-maids or the sudden smell of kelp on the ebb tide or a poem you read once, something connected with the flavour of life itself.' You don't get that with a hamburger.

But raw oysters are not for everyone. Even some shellfish

professionals are not fond. In his book *Edible Seashore*, maritime forager John Wright declares: 'There is nothing wrong with raw ones – for anyone who enjoys sticking their head in a bucket of sea water and taking a deep breath they are a delight.' Like Mrs H, he prefers his oysters to have experienced a touch of heat: 'If there is any fish that tastes better I would be pleased to hear of it ... Cooked oysters are superb.'

In the early days of our relationship, the only time Mrs H and I ate oysters was when we were abroad. A French friend taught Mrs H how to open them with a penknife, so it became her job. 'I remember my jeans getting all wet,' she recalled romantically. 'I opened them on my lap and they leaked all over me.' Recognising that Mrs H's altruism would not last for ever, I took over shucking duties. I go in from the oyster's hinge with a long-bladed oyster knife. You hear a small pop as the bivalve's tight seal, held shut with a force of around 30 lbs, gives way.

When my oyster fever was at its zenith, I lugged the poor girl around the world in pursuit of them. To Brittany, where we ate huge natives known as *fer de cheval* at Cancale and excellent *Belons* at their place of production on the River Belon. To the Bay of Arcachon, a great bite out of the French Atlantic coast where you chew oysters in crumbling shacks. To the Grand Central Oyster Bar in New York, a glorious subterranean temple to the bivalve. To the Davy Byrnes pub in Dublin, where the oysters are great, though Leopold Bloom was not tempted ('Unsightly like a clot of phlegm ... Devil to open them too'). Even to a village called Oyster in Virginia, where no shellfish were available for purchase but the dazzling white roads around the old canning sheds were made of their shells.

On solitary trips to Europe, I would return laden with oysters. I remember bringing them as hand luggage from Amsterdam and watching the overhead locker (not above my seat, of course) for signs of dripping. In pre-Eurostar days, oysters once made me miss the last train to England from Paris. After staying with friends, I made my way to the Gare du Nord, where my main priority was to buy a couple of dozen from one of the restaurants opposite the station. As a result, I was running late, but a quick glance at the departures board told me that I still had plenty of time. When I got to the platform, my train was strangely absent. Puzzled, I returned to the departures board. It was only after looking at it for several minutes that I realised I was actually looking at arrivals. My dash to the right platform made me almost as damp as the oysters. I arrived in time to see the red light at the back of the train disappearing towards Calais. Inexplicably, the greeting back at the apartment of my Parisian friends was a few degrees cooler than when I first arrived. *Non, merci*, they did not desire any *huîtres*.

In Britain, we used to trundle down to Whitstable for oysters. Once I was so desperate to get at them that I managed to prang the car on the central barrier of the M2. It was a relief when oysters steadily became more available in Britain. I and (to a lesser extent) Mrs H tucked in with gusto. The ones we eat 99.9 per cent of the time are long-shelled Pacific oysters, also known as rock oysters or gigas, which, if introduced as youngsters, will happily grow in our waters. Some oyster lovers have shown reluctance to take this interloper to their bosoms and stick to natives. Writing in 1959, Eleanor Clark dismissed Pacific oysters as 'a coarse species ... fast-growing and mostly used in canning'. In 2008, the Irish chef Richard Corrigan continued this disparagement. 'I'm very much an oyster snob ...The native is just perfection. It has to be polished and loved and served on a bed of seaweed or ice, whereas I look at a rock oyster and I think, "Cook you. You're for the deep-fat fryer."'

Yes, the native is rich, sweet and immeasurably satisfying, but they are an expensive rarity (slow to grow and susceptible to disease). Pacific oysters are great for eating at home and cost around one-third the price. Whatever oyster snobs say, a Pacific oyster can be a sensational mouthful when eaten with a squeeze of lemon. Mrs H likes them when they are milky with spat – the French term is *laiteuse* – and, to a lesser extent, so do I, though this self-made sauce is not to everyone's taste. Mrs H is more concerned with size. 'I don't like them if they're too large, like those from Colonel Mustard in Norfolk.' This is true (apart from the name). His oysters were so big that I broke two knives opening them.

Native oysters need no more than a drop of lemon juice (if that) and their preparation is complete. The Pacific oyster stands up to more robust saucing. When embarking on a dozen, I tend to start with lemon, then move on to

Tabasco or Worcestershire sauce, but only one or two drops. Mrs H has tried to wean me off such pungent amendments. But I maintain that, taken in moderation, these condiments work well with the working man's oyster. We both agree that mignonette, the mixture of red wine vinegar and fine chopped shallots often offered with oysters in restaurants, is overwhelming.

In America, a favourite accompaniment for oysters is a compound of tomato ketchup and horseradish. This is because most American oysters are disappointingly bland. There are notable exceptions, such as the tiny Malpeques from Prince Edward Island and Wellfleets from Cape Cod, but the celebrated Bluepoints of New York have only slightly more flavour than Evian. Drenched in tomato ketchup and horseradish and accompanied by the little crackers known as Saltines, they are rather good. Bluepoints are warm water oysters (New York is on the same latitude as Madrid) and grow rapidly without the same saline throughput of their slower-growing cousins in colder waters. The further south you go, the more apparent is this blandness in American oysters. Though I love the Acme Oyster Bar on Iberville Street in New Orleans, where fresh-opened bivalves are slid over to diners across a great marble slab (Dickens would have felt at home here), its oysters from the Mississippi Delta have even less flavour than Bluepoints. Perhaps it is no coincidence that Tabasco is made nearby.

Mrs H's fondness for oysters came to fruition when I started cooking them. Though the raw oyster gets my vote, there is something wonderful about cooked oysters. No other dish offers the same silkiness of texture and depth of flavour. I would cook oysters more frequently if I didn't like raw ones so much.

In Britain, one of the best-known oyster recipes is tagliatelle of oysters and caviar, as served by Marco Pierre White in the late Eighties at Harvey's, the restaurant in Wandsworth that made his name. 'This dish succeeds in every way,' White modestly states in his book *White Heat*. 'It's not enough for a dish to have a great flavour. It's only when the taste of a dish equals its visual appeal that you know you're on to a success. This is one of few dishes I know that actually does that. It's very rare.' When I had this legendary item at Harvey's, an occasion enlivened by the testy chef chasing a photographer down the street, it proved to be pretty and undeniably toothsome, but sadly insubstantial. It consisted of three Pacific oyster shells each containing a few strands of tagliatelle topped by a lightly poached oyster, a small quantity of beurre blanc sauce and a few grains of caviar. It was more of an *amuse-bouche* than a starter. To dull my hunger pangs, I found myself eating the small mounds of mashed potato on which the half-shells were mounted.

The oyster dishes I prefer are much simpler and cooked on the half-shell. They look great and provide their own little bowls when grilled at medium heat or baked. The former is the most natural approach for me, but I've found that cooking the oysters on a tray in the oven for six to eight minutes at 200°C/Gas Mark 6 allows them to firm up without drying out, which sometimes occurs when grilling. The liquor should be drained from the oyster shells before cooking. You can strain it for use in stocks and soups or add it to Bloody Mary, but I usually drink it there and then with a splat of Worcester sauce. 'Are you having a meal before the meal?' inquires Mrs H, whose bat ears can detect a surreptitious slurping from the kitchen. Unlike her limited intake of raw oysters, Mrs H demands equal shares of the cooked ones, particularly the bacon and dill version.

'I suppose it proves what they say,' I said.

'What do they say?'

'About oysters being the food of love.'

'Well, yes.'

'Do you think I should put that in the book?'

'Of course.'

Cooking oysters

Two dozen Pacific oysters at 55p each might not be the cheapest of meals, but no one would worry if a restaurant charged £13 for a starter for four. Once you've mastered the opening of oysters, all these snacks are easy to do. After opening, you might want to free the oyster by cutting the adductor muscle that fastens it to the deep shell and flip it over, though this is not obligatory. How many oysters you cook is up to you, but all should be served with plentiful rounds of baguette. According to Mrs H, these dishes taste 'luxurious, delicious and extraordinary'. A chef could build his reputation on less.

Oysters with bacon and dill

This version delivers the greatest pleasure to Mrs H. It involves putting a fingernail-sized lump of butter on top of each oyster before they go into the oven for 7 minutes at 200°C/Gas Mark 6. When the warm oysters emerge, sprinkle a small quantity of chopped cooked bacon into each one (one back rasher should suffice for three or four oysters) and some chopped dill on top of that. The combination sends Mrs H into paroxysms of ecstasy, although this might be due more to the bacon than the oyster.

Tapas of oysters in hot tomato sauce

Mrs H is also very fond of oysters cooked in a peppery tomato sauce. This should be prepared beforehand. In a small bowl, combine a minced garlic clove, ¼ teaspoon cayenne pepper, 20ml red wine vinegar, 10ml water, a pinch of salt and sufficient tomato purée to thicken up the sauce. After allowing the sauce to meld for 20 minutes, put a teaspoonful on top of each oyster in the half shell. Bake for 7 minutes at 200°C/Gas Mark 6. The result is warm oysters enrobed in hot, spicy tomato – more a soft crust than a sauce.

Oysters baked with shallot and butter

In her fine book *The Art of Simple Food*, Alice Waters of Chez Panisse says that cooked oysters work well with a mixture of chopped shallot, butter, freshly ground black pepper, parsley and grated lemon zest and juice. Place a spoonful of the mixture on to each oyster in the half-shell and bake for 7 minutes at 200°C/Gas Mark 6. The result delivered a pleasing vegetable crunch. 'Oh, I like that – a good discovery,' said Mrs H. 'A bit like eating salad with oysters. It's fresh and green and very lemony.'

Oysters with anchovy butter

This comes from the Grand Central Oyster Bar in New York. For half a dozen oysters gently heat 50g butter with three finely chopped anchovy fillets, ½ teaspoon finely chopped parsley and the juice from ¼ lemon. Put a teaspoon of melted anchovy butter on to each oyster on the half-shell and bake for 7 minutes at 200°C/Gas Mark 6. 'Pretty amazing,' said Mrs H. 'The saltiness of the anchovy somehow wraps itself round the oyster.'

Oysters with Parmesan

Mrs H isn't so keen on this, but I think the combination works well. Open a dozen oysters and pour off the liquor. Free the oysters and flip over in the half shell. Dollop a teaspoon of crème fraîche into each oyster and top with a layer of grated Parmesan. Place side by side on the rack of the grill so they don't fall over and grill for 2 minutes, until the Parmesan forms a crust.

BIBLIOGRAPHY

Adrià, Ferran, *A Day elBulli* (Phaidon, 2008)

Albala, Ken, *Pancake: A Global History* (Reaktion, 2008)

Allen, Darina, *Irish Traditional Cookery* (Kyle Cathie, 2004)

Amandonico, Nikko, *La Pizza* (Mitchell Beazley, 2005)

Ayto, John, *An A-Z of Food & Drink* (Oxford, 2002)

Beeton, Isabella, *Mrs Beeton's Book of Household Management*, first published 1861 (Southover, 1998)

Blumenthal, Heston, *In Search of Perfection* (Bloomsbury, 2006)

——, *Further Adventures in Search of Perfection* (Bloomsbury, 2007)

——, *Big Fat Duck Cook Book* (Bloomsbury, 2008)

Brears, Peter, *Cooking & Dining in Medieval England* (Prospect, 2008)

Buzzi, Aldo, *The Perfect Egg* (Bloomsbury, 2006)

Carluccio, Antonio, *A Passion for Mushrooms* (Pavillion, 1990)

Clark, Eleanor, *The Oysters of Locmariaquer*, first published 1964 (HarperCollins, 1992)

Conran, Terence, and Prescott, Peter, *Eat London* (Conran Octopus, 2007)

Corbin, Pam, *Preserves: River Cottage Handbook No.2* (Bloomsbury, 2008)

Corrigan, Richard, *The Clatter of Forks and Spoons* (Fourth Estate, 2008)

Davidson, Alan, *North Atlantic Seafood*, first published 1979 (Prospect, 2002)

——, *Mediterranean Seafood*, first published 1972 (Prospect, 2002)

——, *The Oxford Companion to Food* (Oxford, 1999)

Del Conte, Anna, *Amaretto, Apple Cake and Artichokes* (Vintage, 2006)

Dods, Margaret, *The Cook and Housewife's Manual* (Margaret Dods, 1826)

Douglas, Norman, *Venus in the Kitchen*, first published 1952 (Bloomsbury, 2002)

Doust, Clifford, *Rhubarb: The Wondrous Drug* (Princeton, 1992)

Ducasse, Alain, *Culinary Encyclopaedia* (Alain Ducasse, 2005)

Edge, John T., *Hamburgers & Fries: An American Story* (Putnam, 2005)

Fearnley-Whittingstall, Hugh, *The River Cottage Meat Book* (Hodder, 2002)

——, *River Cottage Cookbook* (HarperCollins, 2001)

Garnweidner, Edmund, *Mushrooms and Toadstools of Great Britain & Europe* (Collins, 1994)

Glasse, Hannah, *The Art of Cookery Made Plain and Easy*,

first published 1747 (Prospect Books, 2004)

Good Housekeeping Cookery Book (Ebury, 1998)

Graham, Peter, *Classic Cheese Cookery*, first published 1988 (Grub Street, 2003)

Grigson, Geoffrey, *The Englishman's Flora*, first published 1955 (Helicon, 1996)

——, *Dictionary of English Plant Names* (Allen Lane, 1974)

Grigson, Jane, *Jane Grigson's Fruit Book*, first published 1982 (Penguin, 1984)

——, *English Food*, first published 1974 (Penguin, 1998)

——, *Charcuterie*, first published 1967 (Penguin, 1970)

Grossman Chotzinoff, Anne, and Thomas Grossman, Lisa, *Lobscouse & Spotted Dog* (WW Norton & Co, 1998)

Hart, Carolyn, *Cooks' Books* (Simon & Schuster, 2005)

Hartley, Dorothy, *Food in England*, first published 1954 (Little, Brown, 1996)

Hazan, Marcella, *Marcella Cucina* (Macmillan, 1997)

Henderson, Fergus, and Gellatly, Justin Piers, *Beyond Nose to Tail* (Bloomsbury, 2007)

Hickman, Trevor, *History of the Melton Mowbray Pork Pie* (History Press, 2005)

Hix, Mark, *British Regional Food* (Quadrille, 2006)

Kenney-Herbert, Col. Arthur Robert ('Wyvern'), *Culinary Jottings for Madras*, first published 1878 (Prospect, 2007)

Kurlansky, Mark, *The Big Oyster* (Vintage, 2007)

Lane Fox, Robin, 'Search for the True Rhubarb' (*Financial Times*, 2 March 2007)

Larousse Gastronomique (Hamlyn, 2001)

Lawson, Nigella, *Nigella's Express* (Chatto & Windus, 2007)

Leigh, Rowley, *No Place like Home* (Fourth Estate, 2006)

Locatelli, Giorgio, *Made in Italy* (Fourth Estate, 2006)

Loubet, Edouard, *A Chef in Provence* (Hachette, 2004)

Luard, Elisabeth, *The Food of Spain & Portugal* (Kyle Cathie, 2004)

——, *Truffles* (Frances Lincoln, 2006)

Mabey, Richard, *Food for Free*, first published 1972 (Collins, 2007)

Marinetti, Filippo, *Futurist Cookbook*, first published 1932 (Trefoil, 1989)

McGee, Harold, *On Food & Cooking* (Hodder, 2004)

Michael, Pamela, *Edible Wild Plants & Herbs* (Grub Street, 2007)

Michelson, Patricia, *The Cheese Room* (Penguin, 2005)

Motz, George, *Hamburger America* (Running Press, 2008)

Olney, Richard, *Simple French Food*, first published 1974 (Grub Street, 2003)

Phillips, Roger, *Mushrooms* (Macmillan, 2006)

Poilâne, Lionel, *Favourite Savoury Tartines* (Grancher, 2001)

Prince, Thane, *Jams & Preserves* (Dorling Kindersley, 2008)

Prior, Mary, *Rhubarbaria* (Prospect, 2008)

Ravicz Ekdahl, Marilyn, *Erotic Cuisine: A Natural History of Aphrodisiac Cookery* (Xlibris Corporation, 2001)

Rhodes, Gary, *The Complete Cookery Year* (BBC, 2004)

Riley, Gillian, *The Oxford Companion to Italian Food* (Oxford, 2008)

Robuchon, Joel, *The Complete Robuchon* (Grub Street, 2008)

Rodgers, Judy, *The Zuni Café Cookbook* (Norton, 2002)

Roux, Michel, *Eggs* (Quadrille, 2005)

Roux, Michel Jr, *A Life in the Kitchen* (Weidenfeld, 2009)

The Silver Spoon (Phaidon, 2005)

Shaida, Margaret, *The Legendary Cuisine of Persia*, first published 1992 (Grub Street, 2000)

Stein, Rick, *English Seafood Cookery* (Penguin, 1988)

——, *Fruits of the Sea* (BBC, 1997)

Steingarten, Jeffrey, 'On a Roll' (US *Vogue*, October 2007)

——, *It Must've Been Something I Ate* (Review, 2002)

Stobart, Tom, *The Cook's Encyclopaedia*, first published 1980 (Grub Street, 1998)

Stocks, Christopher, *Forgotten Fruits* (Windmill, 2009)

Toklas, Alice B.,*The Alice B.Toklas Cookbook*, first published 1954 (Serif, 2004)

Vitt, Sandi, and Hickman, Michael, *Rhubarb: More Than Just Pies* (University of Alberta Press, 2000)

Waters, Alice, *The Art of Simple Food* (Michael Joseph, 2008)

White, Pierre Marco, *White Heat* (Pyramid, 1990)

Whiteman, Kate, *Brittany Gastronomique* (Conran Octopus, 1996)

Wilson, C. Anne, *The Book of Marmalade* (Prospect, 1999)

Wolfert, Paula, *Moroccan Cuisine* (Grub Street, 2004)

Wrangham, Richard, *Catching Fire: How Cooking Made Us Human* (Profile, 2009)

Wright, John, *Edible Seashore: River Cottage Handbook No.5* (Bloomsbury, 2009)

ACKNOWLEDGEMENTS

It is commonplace for Fourth Estate authors to rain hosannas upon Louise Haines, but they have never more deserved than for the book you are currently holding. For patience, guidance and encouragement, she is a nonpareil. Elizabeth Woabank handled the editorial process with acuity, good humour and kindness. Becky Morrison produced a delightful cover design. I am grateful to Annie Lee for her painless copy editing. I also wish to thank Rachel Smyth, Michelle Kane, Elspeth Dougall and many others at Fourth Estate.

I owe much to newspaper and magazine editors who supported my passion for food by commissioning articles on the topic. They include Michael Watts, Sarah Spankie, Allan Jenkins, Victoria Summerley, Christian Broughton, Simon O'Hagan, Charlotte Ross, Caroline Stacey, Louisa Saunders, Isabel Lloyd, Laurence Earle, Madeleine Lim and Carolyn Hart.

Friends who have encouraged and helped me in the writing of this book include Dominic and Rose Prince, Tim Williams, Emma Hagestadt, John Walsh, Fergus

Henderson, Malcolm Southward, Eileen Cooper, Giorgio and Rachel Alessio, Nick Hargrave and Jeremy Lee. I am particularly indebted to Carolyn Cavele and Mark Hix.

But above all, my thanks go to Alison Hirst. Apart from cleaning up after me, checking my copy, correcting my solecisms and contributing recipes, she spent the best part of two years consuming odd food, often uncomplainingly. Her marriage vows may have included 'for better, for worse', but there was nothing about eating whelks.